Audubon

NORTH AMERICAN
BIRDFEEDER GUIDE

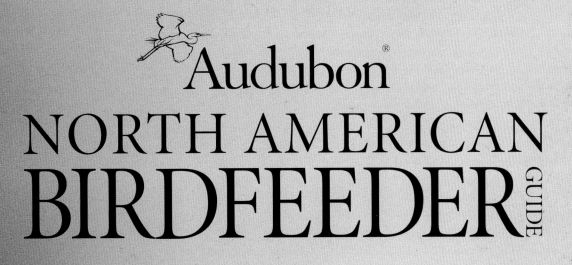

Audubon®
NORTH AMERICAN
BIRDFEEDER GUIDE

Robert Burton
and Stephen W. Kress

DK PUBLISHING

LONDON, NEW YORK, MUNICH,
MELBOURNE, AND DELHI

Senior Editor Angeles Gavira
Senior Art Editor Ina Stradins
Production Kevin Ward
Publishing Manager Liz Wheeler
Managing Editor Sarah Larter
Managing Art Editor Philip Ormerod
Publishing Director Jonathan Metcalf
Art Director Bryn Walls
Editorial Assistants Lizzie Munsey, Erin Richards

Produced for Dorling Kindersley by Studio Cactus,

studio cactus Ⓒ

13 Southgate St., Winchester, Hants SO23 9DZ

Project Editors Sue Gordon,
Irene Lyford, Clare Wallis
Project Art Editors Dawn Terrey,
Laura Watson, Sharon Rudd
Editorial Assistant Lorna Hankin
Picture Researcher Will Jones

Published by Dorling Kindersley Ltd.
in association with the National Audubon Society

First American Edition, 2005
Published in the United States by
DK Publishing
375 Hudson Street
New York, New York 10014
10 9 8 7 6 5 4 3 2 1 10 9 8 7 6 5 4 3 2 1
176567—January 2010

This revised edition published in the United States in
2010 by DK Publishing.

Text copyright © 2005, 2010 Robert Burton
and Stephen W. Kress

A catalog record for this book is available
from the Library of Congress
ISBN 978-0-7566-5883-0

Reproduced by Colourscan, Singapore
Printed and bound in Singapore by Star Standard

Discover more at
www.dk.com

Contents

Foreword

Bird-feeding has become our number one form of interaction with wildlife. By some estimates, more than half the households in North America put out food for wild birds at least occasionally. Such popularity is easy to understand. As I write this, a beautiful goldfinch is just a few feet away from me at the feeder outside my window, glowing with bright color and with the alert intensity of a wild creature. That same intensity is what captured my imagination years ago, as a very young boy staring in amazement at the sparrows and grackles that came to my offerings of breadcrumbs, launching my lifelong fascination with birds. This same intensity is accessible to anyone. For a few dollars' worth of bird seed, we can have an instant connection to nature.

Wild birds may be quick to take advantage of artificial feeding, but most of the time they don't *need* it. Only during exceptionally harsh weather do our feeders make a big difference in their survival. So, in general terms, who benefits most from our bird-feeding? We do. Our feeders bring endless entertainment right to our windows. Entertainment, and education, too. A simple feeder can be a springboard to a greater understanding of the natural world, leading us to start caring for birds and nature in more profound ways. If we start paying attention to our backyards as bird habitats, planting and managing these areas with nature in mind, we can provide major benefits for wildlife.

To help us do just that, this book brings us insights from two top authorities. Robert Burton is a well-known naturalist and a prolific writer, with particular expertise in the familiar wildlife of cities and suburbs. Stephen Kress is a remarkable ornithologist who restores seabirds to remote island wildernesses, but who also thoroughly understands the islands of habitat that we can create in even the smallest gardens. Here, these experts show us how the birdfeeders outside our windows can give us a unique window into the larger world of nature.

Kenn Kaufman

Kenn Kaufman
Naturalist and writer

7

Introduction

OF THE APPROXIMATELY 700 NORTH AMERICAN BIRD SPECIES, about 100 are regular backyard visitors. Observing, studying, and caring for these birds is a fascinating pastime and a significant industry. About one-fifth of all adults in the United States take time to watch birds, according to a recent study of the US Fish and Wildlife Service and the US Census Bureau. This same study found that about 20 million people travel at least a mile, one or more times each year, specifically to watch birds.

A migratory flock *of White-crowned Sparrows finds shelter in a backyard redbud during spring migration. Backyard habitat can provide food and cover, offering shelter from weather and predators.*

Birds for all

Watching bird behavior is an immediate introduction to natural history for anyone, whatever their age. Even pocket-sized city gardens can attract a few species, and nearby parks provide many opportunities for both birds and birdwatchers. Suburban and country gardens can support highly diverse communities of birds as long as there are opportunities for roosting and nesting. Many species are finding it difficult to nest in agricultural areas because of the practice of planting vast monocultures of single species crops that offer little shelter from predators

Backyard birds include *surprising visitors such as the Yellow Warbler (right) and old friends like robins (below). Watching, studying, and understanding the behavior of common species throughout the year is every bit as rewarding as the occasional glimpse of a rarity.*

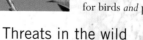

and weather. When birds lose habitat, they usually vacate the area and may have trouble finding nesting places elsewhere.

Whatever the size of your garden, providing food, water, and shelter will tempt more species to visit. Some bird species thrive near human habitation, feeding and nesting in backyards. Others, which may be common in the countryside, rarely come near houses, or only enter the largest properties with mature trees and shrubs. During migration, many others pass overhead. The predictability of welcoming familiar returning residents and the prospect of discovering unexpected visitors makes the backyard the best of all bird observatories. And by adding feeders, nest boxes, and birdbaths, and planting bird-friendly plants, your backyard can serve as a bird sanctuary that will provide wildlife interest throughout the year. Your backyard can serve as a model that will inspire neighbors to do the same on their properties. This book is dedicated to the belief that birds can help to save the world by encouraging us to take actions close to home that create healthy habitats for birds *and* people.

Threats in the wild

Explaining the decline of a species is never easy because a combination of factors is usually involved. Some blame declining populations of songbirds to predators such as hawks and crows, but losses to predators are usually associated with changes in both the size and quality of habitat. Development and certain agricultural practices can prove devastating to birds. Likewise, new buildings and roads have caused hundreds of square miles of countryside to be effectively lost to birds.

Throughout North America and most parts of the world, wild birds are in trouble. A recent review of the "State of the Birds" by the National Audubon Society found that habitat

PAST PRACTICES

Historical documents show that people have fed and cared for wild birds for centuries. The poet Geoffrey Chaucer wrote of the "tame ruddock" (the ancient name for the European Robin), which suggests that it was already a British garden favorite in the 14th century. Burgeoning interest in wildlife and bird conservation in North America in the mid-20th century gave birdfeeding an environmental perspective, and today its importance to monitoring wild bird populations is acknowledged.

By the 19th century, *putting out crumbs for pigeons and other birds became an accepted pastime.*

Gadeners who plant *bird-friendly gardens will be rewarded by color and song from many backyard birds, in return for food, nesting places, and shelter.* loss is the primary factor leading to the decline of most species. The report points out that many grassland birds are rapidly declining in number, mainly as a result of intense agricultural practices. No fewer than 85 percent of 27 grassland species with reliable trend information are declining. For example, Eastern Meadowlark, Bobolink, and Short-eared Owl have declined by more than 50 percent during the last 40 years.

Shrubland birds are also in trouble. In the East, shrub habitat is changing into young forest. For example, Northern Bobwhite and Painted Buntings have declined by more than half. In the West, overgrazing, mineral development, and invasive, non-native plants degrade shrub habitats like sagebrush. Population declines are now documented for 50 of 78 shrubland species with reliable population data. Many woodland birds are also declining because their habitat is at risk of unsustainable logging, plantation forestry, overgrazing by deer or livestock, new tree diseases, invasive species, conversion to agriculture, too-frequent or too-scarce fire, resource extraction, urbanization, and fragmentation by roads and utility lines. Similar habitat loss also affects wetland birds such as rails, herons and coastal shorebirds. For more details about declining North American birds visit the "Watch List" and "State of the Birds" posted on www.audubon.org.

Changes in agricultural *practices have profoundly affected bird numbers. Traditional farms with hedgerows and woodlots are now a rare sight, while today's intensively farmed fields (left) produce barren monocultures.*

places, water, and cover during extreme weather can provide wild birds with a life-saving sanctuary.

The move to backyards

The intensification of agriculture has replaced a varied farmed landscape of fields, hedges, and rough corners with dense monocultures of crops, depriving birds of habitats. Hedgerow shrubs, such as hawthorn, sumac, and cherries are increasingly lost as small farms are converted to large, industrial farms. Too often, pesticides and herbicides have

Backyard successes

Against this backdrop of sobering news, it is important to realize that backyards offer an opportunity to help many species that are in trouble. Relatively few species nest in backyards, but most landbirds use backyard habitats during migration. This is especially true for shrubland and woodland species. Backyard habitats are becoming increasingly important as the quality and quantity of natural habitats change. Yet backyards are too often unfriendly places for wild birds, especially where they consist largely of close-cut lawn that is treated with herbicides and insecticides. In contrast, backyards that offer native food-producing plants, nesting

Backyards that leave *some rough areas can provide useful habitat for ground-nesting species such as warblers.*

Garden flowers can produce useful food for wild birds such as the American Goldfinch (far left). Native trees such as black cherry produce prolific amounts of nutritious food at just the right season to attract Gray Catbirds (left).

shelter for a range of species, varying in size from wrens to hawks. Native plants are the best choice for creating bird habitats as these plants have a long history of benefiting native birds and they are usually better adapted to survive local climates than exotics.

Food, shelter, and water

Providing food for birds in feeders may bring instant gratification, but relatively few species eat typical feeder fare of seeds and suet, and this benefit lasts only as long as feeders are full. In contrast, planting a wildlife garden with native plants can provide food, cover, and nesting places to benefit many species for decades. Like birdfeeders, commercial nest boxes and birdbaths placed in choice habitat can attract a greater variety of backyard birds. Likewise, water is a vital requirement that brings a greater variety of species into view. Bird gardeners that create patches of bird-friendly habitat in their backyard can feel satisfaction that backyard by backyard, they are part of a movement of people making a difference for wild birds.

removed the invertebrates and weeds on which many birds depend for food. In Britain, 60 years ago, a square meter of ordinary ground contained an average of 2,000 seeds, many of them vital weed seeds, but now an average square meter has just 200 seeds. Such reduction in numbers can have a devastating effect on sparrows, juncos, and other ground-feeding birds that require high seed densities to survive, especially in winter when seed is the main food.

More efficient harvesting methods have depleted the amount of grain left on the ground for birds during the tough winter months. A particularly significant change to farming practices has been the move from spring-sown to autumn-sown cereal crops, resulting in the disappearance of stubble, which was once an important source of winter food.

With all these changes in the countryside, it is no surprise that backyard sanctuaries are becoming more important for food and a safe refuge, especially during winter months.

Helping backyard birds

Most backyards are rather poor habitats for birds when compared to meadows, shrubland, and woodland because most gardeners are too tidy. Highly manicured landscapes with clean undergrowth lack the necessary layers and shelter that birds require for feeding and nesting. Over-pruned properties also offer little protection from predators and weather. With time and planning, however, it is possible to transform almost any garden into a haven for birds. This involves planting and landscaping in ways that provide natural sources of food for different birds throughout the year, while still providing suitable cover for roosting and nesting (see pages 34–37). A mixture of trees, shrubs, lawn, and herbaceous beds, for example, recreates a forest wood-land edge habitat and provides opportunities for food and

NEW HABITATS

Each year more than two million acres of open land in the United States is converted to urban and suburban communities where the dominant vegetation is close-cropped lawn dotted with a few exotic trees and shrubs. In these new habitats, approximately 50 percent of all households treat their yards with lawn and garden pesticides that may be lethal to birds. These habitats could provide safe nesting sanctuaries.

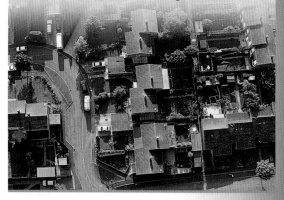

Eastern Bluebirds *now face a hopeful future. Once considered at risk due to scarce nesting cavities, populations of all three North American bluebirds are now flourishing where they find maintained "trails" of bluebird houses and managed meadows.*

Bohemian Waxwings *nest in remote Canadian forests. Their well-being cannot be assured, however, because vast areas of their nesting habitat are now lumbered.*

13

What birds need

Success in attracting birds depends on how well you can provide for their basic needs. Even if your garden does not contain a natural wealth of food, or large, mature trees, you can copy these features in the garden by providing food, birdfeeders, and nest boxes.

Rose-breasted Grosbeak

The basics

MOST WILD ANIMALS ARE DEPENDENT on four major factors in their habitat: food, cover, water, and space. Even in the smallest rooftop garden, it is possible to provide birds with food and water, and the average suburban garden can meet all of the needs of many bird species. Knowing what birds require from their habitat can help us boost the number of species that visit, and help birds survive.

Water is a necessary *feature of most bird habitats. Common Grackles visit birdbaths for drinking and bathing.*

New habitats

Until the 1800s, most of North America was covered in forest. Our ancestors converted much of the woodland to farmland, but now agricultural lands are reverting to forest, especially in eastern states and provinces. Habitats seldom stay the same for long. Meadows change to shrublands, but this is only a temporary habitat that changes to forest. Fire, hurricanes, insect outbreaks, and other dynamic natural events ensure that change always takes place.

Now there is a new change and a new habitat— suburbia. Suburbia is where most of us live, and for many, suburban gardens are where we have our closest contact with nature. The largely forested landscape of our ancestors has become a blend of different habitats, most of which appear in microcosm— a clump of trees here, a grassy clearing there, and perhaps a few isolated shrubs. Some forest residents such as robins and chickadees have readily adapted to this new habitat, while others will use it with modest improvements.

Food and drink

The easiest way to attract birds into the garden is to provide nutritious, energy-rich foods in the winter months. Food gives birds the energy to stay alive, and the colder the weather, the more they need. Small species lose heat quicker than larger ones, and so have to feed more frequently. A chickadee, for example, spends most of each winter day searching for food from dawn

Like most other thrushes, *American Robins were once mainly forest birds. Unlike their relatives, robins now readily nest in backyards and parks with mature trees.*

to dusk in order to survive the long winter night. Likewise, a Bohemian Waxwing may eat over 600 cotoneaster berries in a single day—twice its own body weight.

Ample food in the summer is also important and birds' diet can change dramatically when parents are rearing young. The diet shift of House Sparrows is typical. In winter, the diet of adults contains only about three percent insects and other animal matter, but in summer the growing brood with their high requirement for protein receives a diet containing 68 percent animal matter. Water, too, is essential for birds, both for drinking and bathing. Although birds can obtain much of their water needs from rainwater and dew pecked from grass, adding a water feature such as a garden pool or birdbath will certainly help to increase the variety of your backyard birds and other wildlife.

Safe places

All birds need cover from predators and protection from the elements, especially in the breeding season. Trees, shrubs, and hedgerows provide natural cover. Native shrubs (especially those with thorns) provide the best places for nesting, and a mix of conifers and deciduous plantings provides summer cover as well as protection from winter storms. Outbuildings such as barns and garden sheds can meet the special needs of certain

There are many clever *feeder designs for providing food throughout the year. Some designs (left) provide sustained supplies by storing grain in a hopper. Other feeders (above) exclude squirrels and rats by protecting the feeder within a cage.*

species. For example, by leaving open a barn or shed window, Barn Swallows may nest in the rafters. Likewise, phoebes and Cliff Swallows may discover a secure place to raise their young under the eaves. This chapter contains a wealth of ideas to help you transform your garden into a rich bird habitat that will provide year-round pleasure, while helping birds survive in our rapidly changing world.

Specially made birdfeeders can be used throughout the year. Some designs allow birds to take only the correct size food, so there is no danger to the adults or young. Others are enclosed in cages (see above) to protect the food from rats and squirrels.

Night and day

The amount of time a bird can spend feeding is limited by daylight, which varies greatly with the seasons, especially at northern latitudes. In winter, a bird may have just eight hours or less to feed; it converts its food to fat, and burns the fat reserves to survive the following hours of darkness. Small birds such as chickadees cannot store enough fat to last through more than one night.

SPACE REQUIREMENTS
During the nesting season, birds require territories that may span several acres in size—usually more than a backyard. In winter, space is also needed because many species continue to defend territories. Birds also require specific physical features within their habitats such as singing-posts and perches. Habitat layers are vital for all birds, which use them for feeding and nesting.

Hanging birdfeeders

MANY SEED-EATING BIRDS FIND their winter food at the end of slender branches and twigs. For example, the catkins of birch and alder are packed with tiny, nutritious seeds. Many small, agile species such as goldfinches and chickadees are well adapted to feed from this hanging harvest; this may explain why they are so readily lured to hanging birdfeeders. Different feeder designs favor different species—variety is the key to attracting a greater range of backyard birds.

The specialists

The birds most likely to come to hanging birdfeeders are those seed-eating species adapted to living high in trees or shrubs. These species naturally cling to swinging twigs or hang upside down to grab food from under leaves.

Chickadees, titmice, and goldfinches are among the most regular visitors to hanging feeders, but many winter migrants such as Pine Siskins and Common

Lesser Goldfinches *grip and hang from swaying branches to obtain seeds, giving them the balance and perching power needed for utilizing hanging feeders.*

Redpolls also frequent this type of feeder. Some birds have changed their behavior to utilize feeders. Nuthatches, which are often seen clinging head down on tree trunks, have learned to visit garden feeders, as have woodpeckers, especially Downy and Hairy Woodpeckers.

Feeders fitted with perches enable larger species such as grosbeaks to feed alongside the more accomplished smaller acrobats. Fill hanging feeders with sunflower seeds (whole or hulled) and hang mesh baskets with nut mixtures, a favorite of woodpeckers. Tiny nyger seeds (also called niger and thistle) are especially attractive to goldfinches, redpolls, and siskins.

Learning the ropes

In a garden setting, hanging birdfeeders are often a target for larger birds that have observed the flurry of feeding activity and learned to exploit this ready-made food source.

TYPES OF HANGING BIRDFEEDER

This Blue Jay *is eating hulled peanuts. Jays often fill their crop before disgorging the food in a hidden cache.*

Log-style feeders *blend into the garden landscape—House and Purple Finches feed from hanging feeders with sunflower seeds.*

Evening Grosbeaks *feed on oil sunflower seeds from a table feeder mounted on a pole that supports hanging feeders above.*

Woodpeckers use *their long toes and stiff tail to cling onto hanging bags of suet—one of their favorite winter foods.*

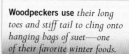

Crows and jays, for example, may dominate such feeders, consuming most of the seed. Likewise, feeders often attract predators such as Cooper's and Sharp-shinned Hawks that may make dashing raids into the garden to snag unsuspecting small birds from hanging feeders.

Pine Siskins feed by hanging from branches of birch or alder to take seeds, and so can easily adapt to feeding on hanging birdfeeders.

Raw beef suet, especially beef kidney suet, is a highly attractive food for woodpeckers, titmice, nuthatches, and chickadees. Birds will eat this high-energy fat all year, but avoid providing it during the heat of summer as it can turn rancid and affect feather waterproofing.

Many species are attracted to beef suet, which can be provided in hanging feeders. Although there are many types of suet blends that use seed, fruit, and nuts, most birds prefer pure suet.

Forest birds, *such as this Hairy Woodpecker, may frequent feeders throughout the year, but they are most likely to visit in the winter. They favor backyards where there are mature trees and shrubs nearby.*

This Chestnut-backed Chickadee *is on a hanging hopper feeder filled with mixed seeds. It will take mostly sunflower seeds.*

House Finches *readily visit hanging tube feeders. Metal feeder ports prevent finches and squirrels from enlarging the holes.*

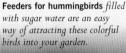

Feeders for hummingbirds *filled with sugar water are an easy way of attracting these colorful birds into your garden.*

This hanging feeder *has multiple feeding ports with offset perches that maximize access for flocking birds such as these goldfinches.*

Specialist birdfeeders

MOST BIRDFEEDERS are designed to attract the widest possible variety of common species. As gardening for birds has become more popular, feeders have been developed that attract specific birds, particularly more unusual ones, or ones which deter certain birds or predators. A good bird garden—one that attracts an interesting mix of visitors—is likely to contain a variety of feeders designed to hold particular types of food for different birds.

This Rose-breasted Grosbeak *is perched on a feeder equipped with a weight-sensitive perch that excludes squirrels.*

Unwanted visitors

Hanging feeders are an excellent means of delivering food to garden birds because they keep seeds or nuts beyond the reach of mice and rats. Grey Squirrels, however, are harder to exclude because they can climb the thinnest branches, jump gaps of 6ft (2m) or more, and chew their way into all but the most robust feeders. In many cases, they not only eat the food, but destroy feeders.

There are a number of squirrel deterrents available for garden feeders. These include plastic-domed baffles with steep sides that hang over the feeder and wire cages that surround the feeder. The cages allow small birds to enter, while denying entry to squirrels and larger birds such as jays and starlings, which may consume most of the seed. Protective cages must be large and robust enough to stop a squirrel reaching the food with its paws. Take care when

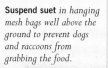

Chipmunks are adept *at gathering up spilled grain, but they may also clean up the seed before birds have a chance for a meal.*

BIRDFEEDERS AND ACCESSORIES

Lightweight brackets *with suction cups are ideal for holding feeders inches from windows, where birds are safer from window crashes.*

Suspend suet *in hanging mesh bags well above the ground to prevent dogs and raccoons from grabbing the food.*

Suspend coconut shells *filled with suet and seed from low branches during winter to provide a high-calorie snack.*

The "squirrel baffle" *over this feeding station has a pivot, and tips to the side when a squirrel attempts to get a foothold.*

Corrosion-proof *poles can elevate a feeder if there are no trees in the garden, or help make the best use of limited space.*

White millet is the preferred feeder food for Painted Buntings, as well as many sparrows and juncos. Metal reinforcements around the feeding ports discourage squirrels from destroying such feeders.

Tube feeders *surrounded by wire mesh help to exclude squirrels and larger birds such as jays and crows. Such feeders favor smaller species that can easily slip through the wire.*

attaching the heavy assembly to a branch—squirrels may gnaw through the supporting rope or wire and carry off the entire feeder.

Increasing the types of foods available in the garden will almost always attract a greater variety of birds. Specialized birdfeeders are designed to hold particular types of food: millet and nyger seed, for example, are smaller than most other bird foods and fall out of conventional feeders. These seeds are best provided in custom feeders with small feeding ports that permit smaller birds to extract the tiny seeds.

Nyger seed *is held in a feeder with small feeding ports. It is a favorite of American Goldfinches and Pine Siskins.*

A feeder guard *made from 2x2in welded wire permits smaller birds the size of cardinals to feed, but not larger species and squirrels.*

Holders for *fat-based bird foods, such as this block of bird pudding, allow the cake to be hung from a branch or pole.*

Suet pudding, *a mix of melted suet and seed, can be rolled into a ball and placed within a cluster of bent twigs tied with twine.*

A Hairy Woodpecker *approaches a hardware cloth feeder holding raw suet. Most birds prefer raw suet over puddings.*

Ground feeders

WHILE MANY COMMON GARDEN birds readily adapt to hanging birdfeeders and bird tables, others are much happier feeding at ground level. A well-planned bird garden should also include the needs of ground-feeding birds as well as those that typically feed in trees and shrubs. In addition to feeders for ground-feeding species, also provide areas of bare soil and composting leaves where ground-feeding birds can scratch for seed, grit, and invertebrates.

GROUND-FEEDER BIRDS

■ Birds likely to visit ground feeders:

- Blackbirds
- Buntings
- Cardinals
- Doves
- Juncos
- Quail
- Sparrows
- Thrashers
- Towhees
- Wild Turkeys

Feeding on the ground

Some birds, such as chickadees and finches, are adept at finding food in the slender branches of trees and shrubs, and they readily adapt to feeding on hanging feeders. Sparrows, cardinals, and towhees will occasionally visit hanging feeders, but they prefer feeding on the ground.

Although ground-feeding birds such as Song Sparrows and juncos are a common sight feeding on spilled food under bird tables and hanging feeders, food on the ground can rot from wet or snowy weather, potentially causing hygiene problems. For these reasons, it is best to provide food on low bird tables or in ground feeders (see page 26) such as hoppers. If squirrels or rats discover ground feeders, protect the grain with wire cages. Many of the larger species that feed

mainly on the ground tend to arrive in flocks, quickly devouring all available food. Supplying the food in hoppers (see below) allows a controlled release of food, ensuring that there is some remaining after the flock has left. This also prevents seed from blowing away in strong winds. Caged hoppers that restrict species by size help to ensure that the smaller, shyer species get their share, and also give protection from predators such as cats and squirrels.

Positioning feeders near windows offers the best views of birds, but such positions may result in collisions due to reflections in the glass. If birds strike windows, move the feeder to within three feet of the glass for safer feeding.

The American Robin *is one of the few birds that feeds on the lawn. Less lawn usually means a greater variety of birds.*

TYPES OF GROUND FEEDER

This plastic hopper *releases food from a lower tray as the birds eat. Prevent damage to the lawn by moving it every few days.*

Plywood hoppers *are simple and inexpensive. This hopper can be easily dismantled for cleaning inside and out.*

Caged hoppers *allow small birds like juncos to feed undisturbed, while larger species such as jays and grackles are excluded.*

Metal hoppers *are sturdy and weather-resistant. The cage prevents large birds and squirrels from feeding.*

SITING FEEDERS

To attract the maximum number of birds to the garden, it is best to provide food in a variety of feeders at different levels. As a general rule, place feeders as close to the house as possible. This not only provides better views, but greatly reduces the tragic loss of birds that die from window collisions. Birds startled from a feeder within three feet of a house will not usually have built up enough momentum for a lethal collision. Put ground feeders and low bird tables on the lawn for those species that cannot normally be encouraged to a bird table or hanging feeder. There is overlap between species and the feeders they use, so the secret is to experiment with different feeders at a variety of levels.

A hanging peanut feeder, *sited close to cover, will attract regular visitors, like White-breasted Nuthatches.*

Positioning a bird table *close to the house provides great views. Purple Finches are frequent visitors.*

The boldest birds, *such as Black-capped Chickadees, visit window feeders, giving wonderful viewing opportunities.*

Caged hopper feeders *are good for open positions, attracting birds such as Dark-eyed Juncos.*

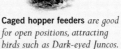

Downy Woodpeckers *prefer vertical feeders such as tube feeders or hanging logs with holes suitable for holding stuffed suet.*

Birds that *do not usually feed on bird tables, such as Mourning Doves, may venture onto a hanging table.*

House Finches *are readily attracted to sunflower seeds offered on a pole-mounted tube feeder. Protect with a baffle cone if squirrels climb the pole.*

Tufted Titmice *are readily attracted to hulled peanuts offered in a hanging feeder consisting of wire mesh.*

Goldfinches *often visit birdfeeders in small flocks, and so make good use of large tubular feeders.*

A well-stocked *bird table close to shrubs and bushes will attract ground-feeding birds, such as the Spotted Towhee.*

Making feeders

ALTHOUGH MANY EXCELLENT commercial feeders are available, it is relatively easy to make your own basic feeders using commonplace materials. The results may be just as successful for attracting a variety of species at considerably less expense, and the rustic look of homemade feeders blends well with the garden setting.

Simple feeders

There are many simple methods of feeding backyard birds that do not involve expensive feeding equipment or complicated construction. For example, a coconut sawn in half with meat removed and drilled with several drainage holes makes a great birdfeeder, or leave the meat in and hang it up. Likewise, threading peanuts (in their shells) on a monofilament line permits titmice and chickadees to cling and peck at one of their favorite foods. Bones from cooked meat suspended on string from trees and bushes will usually be pecked clean by a variety of birds within a few days. Fatty food is very valuable to birds as a winter food.

Suet and peanut-butter recipes

Chickadees, nuthatches, and woodpeckers readily eat raw beef kidney suet. To provide suet, drill holes in a hanging log and pack the cavities tight (see below) or suspend it in mesh bags. Another way of providing suet is to melt it in a stovetop pan and then pour the warm fat into empty, half-coconut shells. Then suspend the shell from a tree or bird table with wire, taking care to keep it out of reach of dogs and raccoons. To make "bird pudding," shred some suet, melt it on a stovetop, and then add millet, hulled sunflower seeds, and nuts. Stuff the mixture into holes drilled in hanging logs. To stretch expensive peanut-butter and attract a greater variety of birds, mix one part peanut-butter with five parts cornmeal. Add shortening to provide additional fat; the flour makes the mixture easier to work.

Home projects

Commercially made bird tables come in all shapes and sizes, and some are very elaborate. Homemade bird tables need not be complex, and can be

To a visiting bird *like this Varied Thrush, it is not the look of a feeder that matters, but the food that it offers and its location.*

a satisfying project to attempt (see opposite). A tray hung from a post or the branches of a tree is all that is required to hold the food and keep it off the ground. Adding a roof helps to keep the food dry and the table cleaner, but is not essential. If even this level of construction is daunting, try simply attaching a small tray to a window sill to display this type of food. Many species will eventually become bold and approach the window.

Seed hoppers keep food dry and stop it from blowing away in the wind. Build a simple hopper by using household materials (see opposite). Small versions can be fixed to trees or posts, while larger hoppers can be placed on the lawn for ground-feeding birds. Fill the hopper with mixed seeds, taking care to cover the jar with a piece of card while fitting it in place so that the contents do not spill.

Hanging half a coconut *makes a simple feeder, but allow it to face downwards so water does not collect in the shell.*

Pileated Woodpeckers *are unusual feeder birds, but they are sometimes lured with beef suet. Males are identified by the extent of red on the head crest and forehead, and red whisker marks.*

MAKING A BIRD TABLE

First construct the tray: fix the side pieces to the base with 1in (25mm) galvanized (rustproof) nails. The side pieces do not butt together—leave gaps at each corner for drainage. To construct the roof, fit a piece of triangular dowel between the long edges of each roof panel so that they butt together neatly. Fix together with wood adhesive. Cut the uprights from ¾x¾in (20x20mm) wood, and angle the top of each by cutting off a ¼in (6mm) wedge. Nail the uprights into the corners of the tray. Attach triangular gables to the uprights, and then, finally, nail the roof to the structure.

Materials

① ½in (12mm) plywood
② ¾in (20mm) wood
③ ¾x¾in (20x20mm) wood
④ ⅜in (9mm) plywood
⑤ ⅜in (9mm) triangular dowel

Gables support the roof and add strength to the structure

Fix hooks to the roof and attach chains to the table from a tree

Completed bird table

The table can be mounted on a pole. This can be driven into the ground or use a free-standing base.

The base *should be wide enough to form a stable support so that the table does not fall over in windy weather.*

MAKING A SEED HOPPER

This homemade hopper uses a 1lb (450g) jam jar, but the sizes of the back panel, base, and sides can be adjusted to fit other jars. Fix the back panel at a right angle to the base with rustproof screws. Attach the sides with nails to form a tray, leaving gaps at each corner for water drainage. Drill two holes in the base to fit the dowels, which steady the jar, and tack the webbing to the back panel to secure the jar. Screw three short screws into the base; the inverted jar rests upon them.

Materials

① 1in (25mm) wood
② ¾in (20mm) wood
③ ½in (12mm) plywood
④ Rustproof screws
⑤ Strip of webbing
⑥ Glass jar
⑦ 3in (80mm) dowel pegs
NOTE: Avoid wood preservative and paint when making bird tables or seed hoppers.

Drill two attachment holes in the back panel before assembly to attach the hopper to a post or tree

Webbing holds the jar firmly in place

Completed seed hopper

Dowel pegs steady the jar

Space the screws evenly around the jar

Side pieces have beveled ends to form a neat corner

Adjust the gap *between the jar rim and the tray by turning the three support screws. This controls the flow of food from the jar.*

Bird tables

NO BIRD GARDEN is complete without a bird table. This traditional feature remains the most efficient feeder for the greatest number of common species, attracting both ground- and tree-feeding birds; not just chickadees and titmice, but Red-winged Blackbird, Cardinal, and Mourning Doves. Bird tables do a simple job—keeping food off the ground and providing a safe place for birds to feed. There are many variations on the basic design.

Black-headed Grosbeaks *and other seed-eating finches are readily attracted to bird tables for sunflower seeds. Grosbeaks prefer these to all other seeds.*

A well-stocked bird table will occasionally reward its keeper with the visit of less common species, such as Rose-breasted Grosbeaks, Scarlet Tanagers, Black-headed Grosbeaks, Summer Tanagers, and Indigo Buntings.

Table features

A well-designed bird table has a number of features that maximize the safety of visiting birds while preventing the loss and spoilage of food. Bird tables should be easy to clean and have good drainage (usually a base of galvanized hardware cloth or stainless steel mesh) to prevent the food from becoming waterlogged. It should have raised edges to prevent food from blowing away in strong winds, and be open in aspect rather than confined, so that feeding birds can spot approaching predators, such as cats and hawks, permitting timely escapes.

A raised table will bring together small birds, such as chickadees, and large species like Red-bellied Woodpeckers. Even pheasants sometimes visit. Aggregations of birds that do not normally feed together may result in behavior called

BIRD TABLE DESIGNS

Table feeders *sometimes hold supplies of seeds within hoppers. These help to keep the seeds dry and require fewer refills.*

This hanging bird table *has a screen floor for drainage. Such feeders are especially practical in wet climates.*

This ground-feeding *table displays food at a suitable height for ground-feeding birds while offering drainage for seeds.*

A roof helps to *protect seeds from the weather. Protect pole-mounted feeders from squirrels with a metal cone under the feeder (see p.40).*

"dominance," where more assertive species drive off others, even those larger than themselves. White-breasted Nuthatches, for example, are notorious for driving other birds away from their favorite feeding sites.

Ideal locations

The classic bird table is mounted on a pole set into the ground, but tables that hang from trees or window sills are just as attractive and effective (unless squirrels are abundant). All types should be set up on lawns away from trees or shrubs that provide cover for cats, and far enough from overhanging branches to deter squirrels from raiding the food. Locate the table within three feet of a good observation window to minimize the risk of birds colliding with windows. It is remarkable how quickly most species become accustomed to feeding in such close proximity.

STYLES TO AVOID

Tables with integral nest boxes (right), may seem a good idea, fulfilling two tasks in one, but in practice birds are very unlikely to nest where so many others feed in their territory. Likewise, also avoid bird tables that are enclosed by solid walls, because birds feel far less secure if they do not have clear sight of their surroundings. Tables should be easy to clean, without cracks and crevices that accumulate seed and excrement.

This table *is made from rot-resistant wood such as cedar. Try to purchase feeders built from sustainable grown woods.*

A multi-tiered *table can hold several different types of food, increasing the number and variety of visiting birds.*

This large feeder *requires a substantial post to support its weight, but this will be difficult to defend from squirrels.*

Choosing bird food

BIRDS TYPICALLY EAT a wide variety of food depending on the season and availability. For example, robins feast on earthworms in early spring, but switch mainly to fruit in fall and winter. Because most birds already have varied diets, they are usually quick to learn about supplemental foods such as suet and sunflower that "magically" appear in backyard bird feeders. These foods can be helpful to birds, especially during extreme weather in late winter and early spring when natural foods are relatively scarce.

Blue Jays readily carry off whole peanuts, often caching them for less abundant times in hollow trees and rain gutters.

Energy to live

Birds have enormous appetites, necessary for providing the energy required to power flight and maintain body temperatures over 100°F, even during frigid winter nights. For example, a Chipping Sparrow will consume about two pounds of weed seeds over the course of a winter and this usually means feeding most of the day. Although research consistently shows that birds visiting feeders also continue eating natural foods, birds that eat supplemental food are likely to spend less time foraging and thus have more time to watch for predators.

Supplemental bird foods once consisted mainly of pure seeds, but as mixtures have gained in popularity, they

Common Grackles *have powerful beaks, capable of cracking acorns, but they also feed on small seeds.*

provide food for a greater range of species. There are more types of seeds available, including mixes that contain dried fruit and "no mess" mixes containing hulled seeds. There are mixes that contain oyster-shell grit, a good source of calcium that birds need to make egg shells, and mixtures specially developed for different types of birds, such as ducks, geese, and swans. There are even "mammal mixes"—blends of corn and nuts to distract squirrels from higher priced foods. Peanuts and other nuts are especially attractive to woodpeckers

---

SUPPLEMENTAL BIRD FOOD

Wild bird foods are available from specialty supply shops, grocery stores, and catalogs. Try a variety of foods in several feeders. It may take a few weeks to attract birds, depending on other available feeders and surrounding habitat. Feeders with nearby shrubs and trees are discovered more quickly than feeders far from cover.

Seed mixes *vary greatly. The most popular mixes contain mainly white millet, cracked corn, and sunflower seeds.*

Generally avoid *low-priced mixes high in grains such as wheat, oats, red millet, and milo. Most birds reject these agricultural grains.*

Nyger seeds *are very attractive to goldfinches, but due to the small size, they must be put in a special feeder or mixed with other foods.*

Peanuts *are rich in oil and protein. Woodpeckers and titmice readily eat them, but they are also a favorite food of starlings.*

Millet seeds *have a high fat content. Placed in ground feeders or on bird tables, they appeal to smaller species, such as finches.*

Raisins and currants *are best offered at a bird table. They may prove attractive to bluebirds and mockingbirds.*

Black sunflower seeds *are the most popular choice for the greatest variety of birds. Hulled seeds reduce the mess under feeders.*

Live mealworms *placed in smooth, steep-sided bowls may attract towhees, catbirds, and robins, especially during nesting season.*

and titmice. Even insect-eating birds such as bluebirds and mockingbirds may come to feeders for mealworms and dried beetle pupae. Young birds in particular benefit from the high-quality protein in live foods such as mealworms.

Although seed mixtures have the allure of attracting many species while reducing the investment and maintenance of multiple feeders, the downside of mixes is that they may result in considerable waste because birds preferring sunflower seeds usually toss less desirable seeds to the ground. Discarded food left on the ground may rot underneath accumulating snow or attract hungry rodents. To reduce the amount of spilled grain under feeders, provide more desirable nuts and sunflower seeds in specially designed feeders dedicated for this purpose.

ANNUAL FEEDING REQUIREMENTS

The types of foods required vary with each season. Some foods help birds to accumulate fat for migration and winter survival, while high-protein foods are necessary for growing new feathers and rearing fast-growing young.

SPECIES	PREFERRED FOOD+
Mourning Dove	Cracked corn, millet, canary seed, black-oil and hulled sunflower seeds
Red-bellied Woodpecker	Suet, bird pudding, striped sunflower seeds, peanut mixes
Downy and Hairy Woodpecker	Suet, bird pudding, peanut-butter mixes*
White-breasted Nuthatch	Suet, sunflower seeds, hulled peanuts, peanut hearts, peanut-butter mixes, bird pudding*
Red-breasted Nuthatch	Black-oil sunflower, bird pudding*
Jays	Striped sunflower seeds, peanuts in shell, mixed seeds, black-oil sunflower seeds, cracked or whole corn, hulled peanuts
Chickadees	Black-oil and striped sunflower seeds, safflower, hulled peanuts, suet, peanut-butter mixes, suet pudding*
Titmice	Black-oil sunflower, peanut-butter mixes, bird pudding, hulled sunflower, safflower, and striped sunflower seeds
Northern Cardinal	Striped, black-oil, and hulled sunflower seeds, mixed seeds, safflower seed
Grosbeaks	Striped, black-oil, and hulled sunflower seeds
Native Sparrows	Millet, cracked corn, hulled sunflower seeds
Juncos	Millet seeds, hulled sunflower seeds, cracked corn
Purple Finch	Black-oil, striped, and hulled sunflower seeds
House Finch	Black-oil, hulled, and striped sunflower seeds, safflower and nyger seeds
Redpolls	Hulled sunflower, nyger, striped, and black-oil sunflower seeds
American Goldfinch	Nyger, canary, black-oil, and hulled sunflower seeds

+Summarized from findings of Project FeederWatch
* See page 24 for peanut-butter mix and suet pudding recipes

PROJECT FEEDERWATCH

Project FeederWatch is a winter-long survey of birds that visits feeders at backyards, nature centers, community areas, and other locales in North America. FeederWatchers periodically count the highest numbers of each species they see at their feeders from November through early April.

FeederWatch helps scientists track broadscale movements of winter bird populations and long-term trends in bird distribution and abundance. Project FeederWatch is operated by the Cornell Laboratory of Ornithology in partnership with the National Audubon Society, Bird Studies Canada, and Canadian Nature Federation.

For more information, contact:

In the US
Project FeederWatch
Cornell Lab of Ornithology
159 Sapsucker Woods Road
Ithaca, NY 14850
Phone: (607) 254-2427
Toll free: (800) 843-2473 (BIRD)
feederwatch@cornell.edu

In Canada
Project FeederWatch
Bird Studies Canada
P.O. Box 160
Port Rowan, ON N0E 1M0
Phone: (519) 586-3531
Toll free: (888) 448-2473 (BIRD)
pfw@bsc-eoc.org

Feeding Hummingbirds

ABOUT 1,600 SPECIES of birds worldwide (20 percent of all living birds) drink nectar, a sweet attractant produced deep within many flowers. Most nectar drinkers live in the tropics where flowers bloom year-round, but at least 53 species of North American birds also have an appetite for sugar and will at least occasionally visit sugar-water feeders.

Hummingbirds are readily attracted to sugar-water offered in a special feeder. The best hummingbird feeders have a red plastic feeder cover to attract the birds. Do not add red food color to your nectar mix.

A sweet tooth

Although hummingbirds are best known for drinking sugar-water, orioles, mockingbirds, grosbeaks, tanagers, and several warblers also readily drink the same sugar solution that attracts hummingbirds. Sugar-water feeders of various sizes, separated in different locations, will help to minimize competition. Many commercial hummingbird feeders are available, but simple homemade feeders are easy to make. A mouse- or hamster-watering bottle (available at most pet stores) makes an excellent oriole feeder.

The best way to attract hummingbirds to your yard is to provide an abundance of orange and red tubular flowers from late spring to early fall (see page 70). Hummingbirds not only feed on flower nectar, but also eat insects and small spiders that they find in flowers. Sugar-water feeders for hummingbirds are useful for holding birds in your yard until flowers bloom or as a lure to entice hummers into better viewing areas. Hummingbirds typically migrate even when feeders are still filled with sugar-water, but it is best to remove the feeders when the first frost arrives to discourage late migrants from lingering. In southern latitudes of the Southeast and Southwest (where hummingbirds normally winter), hummingbirds will continue to visit backyard feeders throughout the winter months.

HOMEMADE ORIOLE FEEDER

To give orioles a secure perch, strap a branch to bottle feeders. Use orange paint or orange plastic flowers to advertise the feeder. Fill the feeder with a mixture of 2 cups water and one-third white sugar. Boil to dissolve sugar. Do not use artificial sweeteners, honey, commercial nectars, or food coloring. Hang feeder from a hook or branch near a window, and clean and replace the mixture regularly, following the guidelines on page 31.

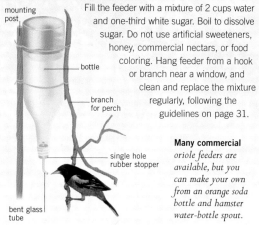

mounting post

bottle

branch for perch

single hole rubber stopper

bent glass tube

Many commercial oriole feeders are available, but you can make your own from an orange soda bottle and hamster water-bottle spout.

Orioles and tanagers may be attracted to fruit placed on a bird table. Oranges secured to a spike are especially attractive.

Housekeeping

The main challenge is to keep hummingbird
feeders clean of fungus that may grow in
fermenting sugar-water. To avoid this problem,
clean feeders every two or three days under
hot running water, thoroughly scrubbing with
a bottlebrush that reaches the entire feeder.
Use a pipe cleaner or smaller brush to clean the
delivery tube and other parts where fungus may
grow. Although honey-water is more nutritious than
granular sugar-water, it ferments faster in the sun
and readily cultures mold that can kill hummingbirds.
Mixtures of water and granular white sugar are the
best food for hummingbirds, as this mixture offers
less risk from fermentation and mold. Avoid mixtures
with more than one part sugar to four parts water, as
these may harm hummingbirds by enlarging their
livers. To prepare a sugar-water solution, mix sugar
and water together in equal (1:1) proportion, then boil
the mixture to retard fermentation and dissolve all
sugar. Then dilute to one part sugar to four parts water
by adding three additional parts of cold water. Store
the unused quantity in a refrigerator.

   Use one part sugar to four parts water when first
attracting hummingbirds, but decrease the proportion
to one part sugar to six parts water after the hummers
learn the location of your feeders. This reduces danger
to the liver and encourages the hummingbirds to feed
more on natural foods.

Male Anna's Hummingbirds
*often guard feeders to keep
away competitors and increase
their use of feeders late in the
day, tanking up on nectar as
they prepare for night.*

Most commercial
*hummingbird feeders have
at least some red plastic
that helps to attract the
birds from a distance. Avoid
adding red food coloring
to sugar-water mixtures.*

Drinking and bathing

WATER IS AN ESSENTIAL INGREDIENT in any bird garden. It will attract
a wide range of species throughout the year, including birds that
feed elsewhere but need fresh water for drinking and bathing. The
simplest way to provide water is in a birdbath, but garden ponds
and pools provide the same facilities, with the added benefit of
giving a home to aquatic animals, including frogs and toads.

A **Black-headed Grosbeak** *soaks itself while
bathing, which helps to keep the feathers in
good order and keeps it cool in hot weather.*

The importance of water

Most small birds, particularly those that feed on seeds,
need to drink (or eat snow) several times daily to replace
fluids lost through respiration and in their droppings. Water
is also essential for bathing, which plays an important role
in feather maintenance: dampening the feathers loosens
the dirt and makes the feathers easier to preen.

Some woodland birds may drink water from droplets
on leaves, but the easiest way to provide water in the
garden is in a birdbath or a pond. A good birdbath is
simple and sturdy, but light enough to clean and refill.

It must have sloping sides with shallow edges. Depth
should range between 1–4in (2.5–10cm) to allow every
species to bathe at its preferred depth. The surface of the
bath should be rough so birds can grip it with their claws,
and it should be large enough to hold sufficient water
to withstand a vigorous bathing session by several birds
at once.

The simplest birdbath is a large plant saucer with
a stone in the middle to serve as a perch, or an inverted
garbage can lid sunk into the ground; custom-made
birdbaths are available from garden centers or wild
bird supply shops. Regardless of design, all birdbaths
should be cleaned weekly with a stiff brush to remove
algae and droppings. This prevents mosquitoes from
breeding and diseases such as salmonella from spreading.

WINTER WATER

Even winter birds like Evening
Grosbeaks will bathe or drink
when they find open water.
In cold conditions, check your
birdbath daily. Break through
the ice so that birds can
bathe and drink, or add
a birdbath heater. Avoid anti-
freeze, as it can poison birds
or damage the waterproofing
of their plumage. Fountains
keep water from freezing.

These **Cedar Waxwings** *are enjoying
bathing in, and drinking from, this
pond. If possible, make a waterfall
or add a fountain to move the water,
keeping it from freezing in winter.*

TYPES OF BIRDBATHS

A stone bath *on a pedestal has a traditional appearance, but it is rather heavy and difficult to move.*

Ceramic baths *may benefit from a thin layer of gravel on the bottom to give birds a surer footing.*

This stone-effect *fiberglass bath is light and easy to move. It has deep and shallow areas, so is suitable for birds of all sizes.*

Shallow metal containers *are fine, but water freezes quickly in cold weather. A floating tennis ball delays ice buildup.*

Safety first

Birds are distracted while bathing, making them vulnerable to predator attack. Locate the bath near bushes or trees, where birds can retreat, perch, and preen. If cats are a threat, place birdbaths on pedestals rather than the ground, and provide thorny shrubs such as raspberries, currants, and roses to provide nearby cover. During periods of drought, birds may try to use water barrels or troughs for drinking, and sadly many drown. If these containers cannot be covered, provide a floating plank of wood or branch on the water surface so that birds can land and drink.

Birds such as this *titmouse are quick to find tiny water sources such as dripping pipes and hoses.*

When bathing, *most garden birds crouch in the water, ruffle their feathers, and flick their wings, which helps spread the water over the body. After bathing, they shake off the water and preen their feathers into position.*

Nest boxes

EVEN IF A GARDEN IS WELL STOCKED with food, birds will leave in the breeding season if they can't find suitable nest sites. For many species, scarce cavities limit nesting populations. To keep cavity-nesting birds such as chickadees, nuthatches, and titmice in your backyard all year around, place good-sized boxes in a suitable nesting habitat. At least 86 species of North American birds use nest boxes.

Purple Martins *once nested in cavities created by woodpeckers and in rock crevices. Now nearly all nest in artificial nest boxes.*

Enclosed and open boxes

Successful use of nest boxes depends mainly on siting the box in proper habitat, and positioning the box at the correct distance above ground. Many garden birds nest in tree cavities. In towns, where old trees are in short supply, bird gardeners can help by providing artificial holes in the form of "enclosed" nest boxes. A typical box is rectangular, upright, with a small hole at the front. Dimensions of the box depend on the nesting species: small boxes attract House Wrens and chickadees, while large boxes can house Barred Owls. Social species, such as Purple Martins, typically nest near each other, but most birds defend larger territories around their nest box.

Nest boxes that are in use *should not be inspected. It is best to watch and enjoy from a distance or to buy a tiny nest box camera. This can be linked up to your television for a front-row view from inside the box.*

"Open-fronted" nest boxes are used by species, such as phoebes, robins, and Barn Swallows, that naturally nest on ledges and partly enclosed spaces. Raw wood boxes are adequate for most species; those made from cedar are especially resistant to rot. It is not necessary to paint or preserve the inside or outside of boxes. Add 3–4in (6–8cm) of wood chips for duck, hawk, owl, and flicker nest boxes, but do not use sawdust as this tends to collect moisture and mold.

Erect boxes in the fall when some pairs are just starting to explore for nesting places. Take great care to avoid distrubing birds when they are first exploring nest boxes. After the nesting

NEST BOXES

Nest box placement *determines which species will use a box. Boxes in forests are likely to attract chickadees and titmice; boxes located at the edge of the forest will attract House Wrens.*

Shelf-nesting birds *such as Barn Swallows often choose inappropriate places for their nests such as lights. Reduce such use by mounting nest platforms (page 154) as alternatives.*

Rustic nest boxes *blend into the landscape, but birds are just as likely to use a wood box. The size of the entrance hole, habitat, and distance above ground are important.*

CHOOSING A NEST BOX

Nest boxes are designed with various hole sizes suited to particular species. This table lists birds that prefer open and enclosed boxes, and the hole dimensions they require.

ENCLOSED NEST BOXES

Bird species	Diameter of hole
Wood Duck	4in (100mm)
Screech-owl	3in (76mm)
Flicker	2½in (76mm)
Titmouse	2¼in (57mm)
House Wren	1¼in (31mm)
Great-crested Flycatcher	1¼in (31mm)
Mountain Bluebird	2in (50mm)
Chickadee	1⅛in (28mm)
Tree/Violet-green Swallow	1½in (37mm)
Bluebird (eastern/western)	1¼in (31mm)

NEST SHELF (4inx4in)

Bird species
American Robin
Barn Swallow
Black Phoebe
Eastern Phoebe
House Finch
Mourning Dove
Say's Phoebe

season, use a paint or ice scraper to clean out nesting material and wasp nests. Leave the boxes in place for winter roosts and check them again in early spring to remove mouse nests. Chemical disinfectants are not necessary.

Do not despair if your nest box is not used in the first year; be patient and wait for birds to discover it in future years. If you put up several boxes it will increase the

White-headed Woodpeckers *and their relatives create most of the natural homes used by cavity-nesting birds such as House Wrens (above left).*

Nest boxes that open *from the front or the side make it easy to remove old bird nests, mouse nests, and wasps that may keep birds from nesting.*

Brown Creepers *wedge their nests in crevices in trees. This specially designed nest box provides a similar nesting place.*

Eastern Screech-owls *typically nest and roost in old woodpecker cavities, but they also use nest boxes intended for Wood Ducks. They prefer boxes with several inches of wood chips.*

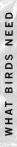

likelihood of at least one box being used, and by introducing a variety of styles there is a good chance that unusual species will begin nesting.

Purple Martins are one of the most sought-after cavity nesting birds, but sometimes they are slow to colonize new houses. To speed up the process, Purple Martin researchers have adapted a technique first used to create tern colonies— the playback of nesting birds calls. Martin houses equipped with speakers broadcasting the "dawn song" of male martins and placement of life-like decoys speeds up colonization of martin houses.

Nest boxes not only encourage garden birds to stay and breed near our homes, but also help species that are declining in their natural habitats (see box opposite). Many specialist boxes are used on nature reserves, but they can also be put up in suitable gardens (see below).

Nest box design and positioning

Natural nest sites for cavity-nesting birds, such as woodpecker holes, usually have excellent drainage, as wood chips rest on absorbent heartwood, creating a snug, insulating cavity. To provide drainage, cut the corners off the floor of the box or drill ⅜in (0.9cm) drainage holes in each corner of the bottom.

Boxes constructed from 1in (2.5cm) thick wood generally have ample insulation to protect birds from excessive summer heat and unseasonably cold weather during the nesting season. Accomplish this by drilling several vent holes near the top of the sides or by dropping the front of the box down from the roof by ¼in (0.6cm).

Some cavity-nesting birds do not build their own nest in boxes, but rely on a layer of wood chips in the bottom to cradle their eggs: Wood Ducks, American Kestrels, Screech-owls, Barred Owls, and flickers will reject artificial nest boxes without 3–4in (7.5–10cm) of wood as this retains water and favors mold.

Place nest boxes for small cavity-nesting birds on mounting poles or fence posts to reduce the chances of predation and to help cleaning. Mount nest boxes for forest species directly to trees at the height recommended on page 39.

In northern states and Canadian provinces, it is best to face bluebird and Tree Swallow nest box entrances toward the east, to warm the box in the morning sunlight.

Nest boxes placed *too close to human housing or barns will likely attract House Sparrows, an introduced European species that aggressively competes with native species such as bluebirds and Tree Swallows.*

Cleaning and maintenance

Annual cleaning (and even cleaning between broods) is helpful in controlling parasitic insects, mites, and lice, although researchers have found no difference in comparing the number of parasitic blowflies in boxes with and without removal of old nests. This may be because there are complex relationships between populations of tiny wasps that inhabit old nests and destroy some of the parasitic blowflies. In general, however, the sheer bulk of old nests and mouse nests is ample reason to remove old nests and scrape boxes clean early in the nesting cycle. Also, building on top of an old nest means eggs and nestlings are closer to the box entrance where they are at greater risk from marauding raccoons.

When cleaning boxes, use a spatula or ice scraper and remove the old nest from the immediate vicinity. Do not use insecticides of any kind in boxes.

Purple Martins *are a colonial species that prefer nesting near each other. This cluster of gourd-shaped nest boxes can provide housing for hundreds of martins.*

NEST BOXES AND SPECIES RECOVERY

Nest boxes have helped bluebirds stage a dramatic comeback. Bluebird populations declined throughout most of North America when natural nesting cavities became scarce due to replacement of wooden fence posts with metal posts. Also, introduced House Sparrows and European Starlings have displaced bluebirds from many locations. To help these native birds, enthusiasts have

established "bluebird trails" that can include hundreds of nest boxes. The boxes must be cleaned and repaired annually, but the results are a great success, showing how people can make a difference.

Three species *of bluebirds have increased in number due to well-tended bluebird nest box trails.*

Making nest boxes

MAKING A NEST BOX REQUIRES little carpentry skill and it's a great family or school project. There is no guarantee that a nest box will attract birds, but careful siting increases the chances of success. Be patient—some boxes are not adopted for several years after installation; others have a succession of residents even within the same nesting season.

In northern latitudes, *position boxes facing east so that they warm during the morning hours.*

Nest box designs

There are two basic designs of nest boxes: enclosed boxes with a small hole for birds such as bluebirds and chickadees, or open nest boxes, favored by robins and phoebes. One of the advantages of building your own nest box is that you can tailor it to the species you want to attract. By modifying the dimensions of the box, size of the entrance hole, and distance above the ground, it is possible to custom build a nest box that appeals to specific species (see page 35). Locating the box in appropriate habitat is essential for successful nesting.

Construct boxes from strong, untreated wood. Pine will last many years, but cedar, cypress, or exterior grade plywood will last much longer. Be sure that the cavity in the box is big enough for a nest and several young; boxes that are too small can lead to overcrowding, poor circulation, and overheating in warm weather. If a box is too large, it requires parents to waste time filling the box with extra nesting material. At the end of each season, remove old nests and scrape the box clean.

HOW TO BUILD A NEST BOX

To make a standard enclosed nest box, cut plywood into the sizes shown here. Saw the back side of the roof that butts onto the back panel at an angle, so that it fits tightly to the back of the box. With 1½in (38mm) galvanized nails, secure the sides of the box to the edges of the base, then attach the front and back panels. Attach the swing-down door panel by nailing from each side to create a pivot point. Screw top of door panel into the block under the roof panel to secure.

Materials

① ¾in (19mm) thick shelving or plywood
② 1½in (38mm) galvanized nails
③ 1½in (38mm) galvanized Phillips head screw
④ Metal hole protector (deters squirrels from enlarging holes)

Attach a block to underside of roof to insert screw (3) into.

6in

6in

8in

①

①

①

③

Removable screw to allow easy door release for cleaning

④

10in

10in

5in

6in

12½in

10in

19½in

①

6in

②

Select an entrance hole appropriate for the bird species you want to attract

Nail used as pivot

Completed enclosed nest box

Before assembly, drill a small attachment hole at the top and bottom of the back panel

An open nest box *is suitable for birds that nest on ledges and shelves, such as robins, phoebes, and Barn Swallows.*

SITING NEST BOXES

Location is the key to successful nest box siting. Bluebirds, for example, prefer open fields and rarely nest in small backyards. Location also helps to reduce competition with House Sparrows as these aggressive birds seldom nest far from human housing. Birds like privacy when nesting, so locate nest boxes where there will be minimal disturbance and where predators, such as cats,

will find it difficult to attack. Installing several boxes increases the chance that one will be used, and they should be spread out around the garden. Avoid locating nest boxes too close to a bird table or feeder because it makes it more difficult for the resident birds to defend a territory around their home.

Flickers *use large enclosed nest boxes with entrance holes 2in (50mm) in diameter. Position 6–30ft (2–10m) above the ground on a wall, snag, or pole.*

Tree and Violet-green Swallows *and bluebirds prefer open habitat. Position boxes in pairs within 9ft (12m) of each other.*

Screech-owls *roost and nest in boxes placed 15ft (3.5m) or more above the ground with a 3in (7½cm) entrance hole. Place several inches of wood chips in the bottom of the box.*

Titmice *use enclosed nest boxes. Position the box in a grove of trees or near forest edge.*

Barn Swallows *and phoebes often build their nests under the eaves of buildings and readily use open nest boxes.*

Chickadees *readily use enclosed nest boxes located just 4ft (1.3m) above the ground. Prevent larger species from using the box by restricting the entrance hole to just 1½in (40mm).*

Nuthatches *use enclosed boxes with entrance holes 1¼in (32mm) in diameter, at least 7ft (2m) from the ground.*

House Wrens *are hole-nesters and readily use enclosed nest boxes. Attach wren boxes to garden fence posts or position in or near shrubby habitat or forest edge.*

Robins *use open nest boxes placed in a sheltered position. Try hiding a box in the foliage of a climbing plant or conifer.*

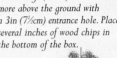

Garden threats

ATTRACTING BIRDS INTO THE BACKYARD may expose them to deadly threats. For example, garden birds may be disturbed or attacked by domestic pets, especially cats, or endangered by home and garden chemicals. In addition, a huge number are killed or injured in collisions with windows. Birds are also threatened by other wildlife that may steal their eggs or take their young. A few simple measures can reduce these risks and maximize the benefits that your garden offers to wildlife.

Garden pesticides kill birds and deplete insect numbers on which many birds depend.

Greatest threat

Collisions with windows are the single greatest threat to garden birds. In the United States alone, an estimated billion wild birds die each year from collisions with plate glass. The temptation to place birdfeeders near large picture windows often leads to the death of birds that are fooled by reflections. Seeing what appears to be trees and open space, birds departing feeders may fly into the glass, especially when spooked by a hawk or other threat. To reduce window collision risk, place feeders within three feet of windows (to minimize momentum), break up reflection by hanging mobiles and other ornaments outside the window, or cover windows with fruit-tree netting. Silhouettes of birds attached to the inside of windows are largely ineffective because they do little to break up reflected scenery.

Many animals are tempted into gardens to eat birds and bird foods. Grey and red squirrels take not only bird seed and nuts, but also nestlings; rats, mink, and raccoons raid nests for eggs; and Cooper's and Sharp-shinned Hawks prey upon birds at feeders.

Predators are quick to make a meal out of a clutch of eggs or a brood of young. Siting nest boxes on isolated posts and planting native thorny shrubs and trees offers protection. Fit posts supporting nest boxes with plastic or metal cones with a 36in (1m) diameter under the box to prevent raccoons and snakes from gaining access. As an alternative to cones, wooden nest hole covers with a depth of 1in (2.5cm) make it difficult for a raccoon to reach into the box (see page 38).

The most dangerous garden visitors are domestic cats. Even sedentary cats may kill birds near the house, especially in spring when young birds are often on the ground. Birds stunned from window collisions are also vulnerable, as are birds feeding and bathing on the ground. Outdoor wire cat enclosures are a safer alternative to bells attached to cat collars, which are unreliable for warning birds.

Large glass windows and doors are a danger; birds see reflected sky and trees, and attempt to fly through. Locate feeders within three feet of windows to reduce momentum as birds depart feeders.

PROTECTING FEEDERS

To discourage squirrels, locate feeders on isolated poles fitted with a cone-shaped baffle at least 20in (50cm) in diameter and locate the feeder far from trees. Where this is impractical, use caged feeders to exclude squirrels and larger birds. Weight-sensitive feeders are also effective against the most determined squirrels. If hawks attack birds at your feeders, suspend feeding until the hawk moves on. In bear country, feed birds only in the winter when bears are hibernating.

Provide whole corn *and peanuts for squirrels at "distraction feeders," reducing competition for high-priced seed at birdfeeders.*

Cat owners can *reduce the killing of backyard birds by keeping their pets indoors, especially during spring, and early morning and evening hours. Indoor cats are also safer from disease, animal bites and car accidents. For more about protecting wild birds from cats, visit:www.abcbirds.org/cats; www.hsus.org*

The bird-friendly garden

Changes in the countryside and in agricultural practices have made gardens a vitally important bird habitat. Maximizing your garden's appeal to birds is about making the most of what you already have, and planting with wildlife in mind.

Painted Bunting

Bird garden basics

GARDENERS WHO REDUCE THE AMOUNT of close-cropped lawn, avoid pesticides, and provide selected native plants will reap the reward of both colorful birds and beautiful plants. Birds are most likely to be attracted to less "managed" areas where they find weed seeds, insects at many levels, cover, and nesting places. However, this does not mean that an untidy yard is a neglected garden. Keep the indoors tidy if you like, but don't straighten up the yard too much!

Avoid the tidy look

Practice sensible, low-intensity cultivation. Do not trim all of your herbaceous plants in the fall as they provide seeds and shelter for insects. Similarly, do not clear away fallen leaf litter and branches in wooded areas. Leaf mulch is habitat for ground beetles, spiders, ants, and earthworms that provide essential food for sparrows, thrashers, and wrens. Young songbirds are especially dependent on such foods.

Both the mature backyard *with taller trees (left) and the younger plantings of the more recent yard (right) have a small patch of lawn surrounded by a variety of trees and shrubs.*

Also, create a brush pile in a corner by stacking fallen tree branches. This provides cover and feeding places for many species, especially during extreme weather.

If you have a large lawn, devise a plan for reducing the size of closely cut grass. Let at least half of your lawn grow into meadow and cut this only once a year in the fall. This gives birds a chance to nest without disturbance. It also gives plants a chance to flower and produce seed that will nourish birds during the fall, winter and spring. In summer, your flower-rich lawn will become alive with insects that help to feed hungry nestlings. If you have a large garden, restrict lawn to the vicinity of your home and even here let it grow several inches high between cuttings. Avoid lawn chemicals as they can kill birds that feed on poisoned foods. About seven million birds die each year in the United States from lawn chemicals.

Lamb's Quarters, *a common annual weed, is an important seed-producing plant for wild birds.*

Native or exotic

Learn to recognize the native plants that already live on your property, and work to protect and enhance them. Native plants have co-evolved with the birds of your region and they are remarkably suited to benefit each other. For example, in the northeast, about 300 species of trees, shrubs, vines, and ground covers depend on birds to distribute their seeds. Some birds are distributors of seed because they usually regurgitate or pass the seed without damaging it. They derive nutrition from the fruit, rather than the seed.

A damp, grassy patch *can be transformed into a flower-rich meadow, attractive for birds, bees, and butterflies. It can be planted with specialist meadow flowers such as the Bee-balm (right).*

Bird-distributed plants entice birds to eat their fruit by meeting the nutritional needs of birds at just the right time of year. For example, Flowering Dog-wood (*Cornus florida*) fruit ripens in the fall just as migrants are building fat reserves in preparation for migration. Flowering Dogwood lures birds by providing fruits that are just the right size for thrush-sized birds to swallow. To attract the attention of birds, ripe flowering dogwood fruits turn screaming red just when the migrants arrive. Likewise, many kinds of hummingbird-pollinated flowers open just when these tiny birds arrive from migration.

In contrast, exotic plants are not co-evolved with the local birds. Therefore, they may not provide the same opportunities for feeding or nesting. Some, however, are good for birds, but, worse, they often become invasive, spreading from backyards to nearby land. Once they are loose on the landscape, they crowd out native plants, and it requires enormous effort to contain and eventually eradicate them.

CHOOSING PLANTS

Selecting plants for your garden calls for research. You must take into account soil type, aspect, and maintenance, as well as a plant's size, appearance, and value to wildlife. The following pages list a handful of species of known value to birds. In general, you should choose old-fashioned, single varieties, because modern, double petal varieties produce little or no nectar. Also, remember that varieties that are susceptible to attack by caterpillars and other insects may be the best choices for planting in bird gardens.

Purple Coneflower *is a native plant, known for its medicinal value. Finches readily eat its seeds, and butterflies relish its nectar.*

Arrowwood is a *native, shrubby vibernum that produces dark blue fruits in fall. These are readily eaten by seasonal migrants.*

Before buying, *check plants for vigorous, balanced growth and healthy leaves. Look at the roots by easing the plant out of the pot if possible, to see if they are overcrowded.*

Soil held firmly around the roots

Well-established root system

Choose a bare-root *tree or shrub with roots spread evenly around the stem. It should have plenty of small "feeder" roots.*

Bare-rooted plants must be planted when dormant

Fibrous "feeder" roots

Arranging plants

Use a survey map or make a sketch of your property as the first step in creating a planting plan. On paper, place the tallest trees at the border of the property. Locate tall conifers on the north side of the property, to provide wind breaks to help insulate your home from winter winds, and tall deciduous trees on the south side to provide summer shade and more light in winter. Create plantings in a tiered effect, stepping increasingly shorter plants toward your home in the following sequence: tall trees, shorter trees, tall shrubs, short shrubs, wildflower meadow, and lawn. Where space permits, plant shrubs in clumps, locating at least three of each species and create property borders of shrubs that include several different species to provide a variety of food, shelter, and nesting opportunities.

Local conditions

The key to maintaining a successful bird garden with minimum effort and expense is to adapt to local conditions. Use bird-friendly plants that are sympathetic to the local soil type, shade, and weather extremes. For example, if you live in the arid southwest, select xerophytes (plants that require minimum water). Or, if you have thin soil near rock outcrops, rather than bringing in soil for deeper-rooted plants or more lawn, plant ground covers such as Creeping Junipers (*Juniperus horizontalis*) and Bearberry (*Arctostaphylos*

LAYERS OF PLANTING

The tiered approach (see left) has several advantages. First, it decreases the amount of high maintenance, close-cropped lawn; secondly, it provides quality bird-attracting habitats that can be seen from the house, and thirdly, it decreases the energy costs of heating and cooling your home by offering shade in the summer and blocking chilling wind in the winter. Landscaping with trees and shrubs also increases the property value of your home.

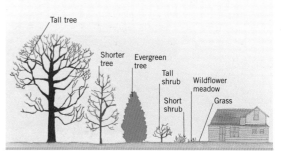

uva-ursi) that provide food for birds. Likewise, if your garden is shady, work with native wild flowers and other shade-adapted plants such as ferns and other groundcovers, encouraging vines like Wild Grape and Virginia Creeper to climb trees.

It is equally important to select plants that are hardy during extreme temperatures. Both severe winters and

PLANTING GUIDE

Your landscaping design should take into effect local climate and fire hazard conditions. For example, coniferous trees are best planted on the north/northwest side to block winter winds. The design opposite, and its recommended plant list, is a sample garden for the Northeast, but the design will work for any suburban backyard. This chapter recommends plants for five regions.

Plant list

1. Sugar Maple (*Acer saccharum*)
2. Serviceberry (*Amelanchier sp.*)
3. Hawthorn (*Crataegus sp.*)
4. Winterberry (*Ilex verticillata*)
5. Spicebush (*Lindera benzoin*)
6. Bayberry (*Myrica pensylvanica*)
7. Trumpet Vine (*Campsis radicans*)
8. Flower garden (*Monarda sp.* and *Echinacea sp.*)
9. Brambles (*Rubus sp.*)
10. Water lilies (*Nymphaea sp.*)
11. Cattails (*Typha sp.*)
12. Gray Dogwood (*Cornus racemosa*)
13. Elderberry (*Sambucus sp.*)
14. Outlined trees to left side: White Pine (*Pinus strobus*)

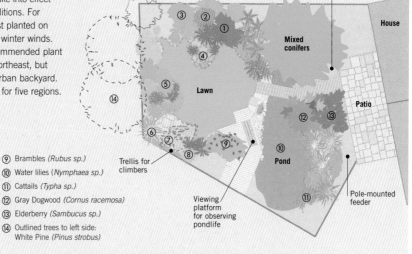

extreme summer temperatures can kill expensive plantings that are inappropriate for your climate. Select plants that survive temperature extremes by paying careful attention to plant hardiness zones. These are included for each of the plants listed on the following pages.

The pages that follow divide North America into five regions of similar plant choices, but even within these regions there is enormous variation. Typically, south-facing hillsides (or the side of your home) are better places to grow more southerly plants as they will receive more hours of daylight than northern slopes on the same hill. The following selections are the most useful plants for backyards and beyond.

If local plant sellers do not already offer your chosen selection, then request advance orders. By creating demand, native plants will become more common in the nursery trade. To learn more about responsible backyard management, visit Audubon At Home: www.audubon.org/bird/at-home/index.html.

The Eastern Bluebird *is one of several species that feed on Common Winterberry* (Ilex verticillata).

CLIMATE

The plant selections that follow are native to North America and recommended for planting in one or more of the following regions: Northeast, Southeast, Prairies and Plains, Mountains and Deserts, and Pacific Coast. There is enormous variation within each region and microclimates may affect the chances of plants surviving. The colored regions represent 11 plant-hardiness zones following the system established by the US National Arboretum, the Agricultural Service, the US Department of Agriculture, and the American Horticultural Society. The zones are based on average annual low temperatures. To help select plants that have the best chance of surviving on your property, locate your home on the chart below to be sure that the plant is hardy for your area.

RANGE OF AVERAGE MINIMUM TEMPERATURES

°F	Zones	°C
Below -50°	1	Below -46°
-50° to -40°	2	-46° to -40°
-40° to -30°	3	-40° to -34°
-30° to -20°	4	-34° to -29°
-20° to -10°	5	-29° to -23°
-10° to 0°	6	-23° to -18°
0° to 10°	7	-18° to -12°
10° to 20°	8	-12° to -7°
20° to 30°	9	-7° to -1°
30° to 40°	10	-1° to 4°
40° to 50°	11	Above 4°

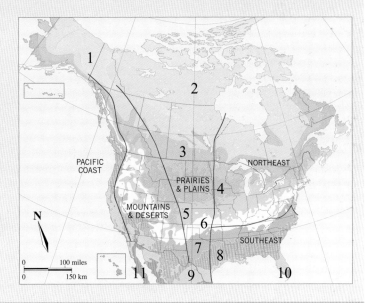

THE BIRD-FRIENDLY GARDEN

Northeast: trees

White Pine
Pinus strobes

Growing to more than 100ft, White Pine is the tallest conifer in the northeast. Its cones contain a wealth of nutritious seed consumed by at least 38 bird species.

HEIGHT 100ft (30m) **SPREAD** 20–25ft (6–7.5m)

CULTIVATION Full sun best. Will tolerate different soils, but prefers well-drained. Zones 4–8.

ALTERNATIVES Jack Pine *(P. banksiana)* is short-lived and slow-growing in a variety of conditions from 1,000–2,700ft (305–823m) elevation.

White Oak
Quercus alba

White Oak may live for 500 years and grow to 100ft with huge spreading branches. A tree for large properties and open fields, at least 28 bird species consume its acorns.

HEIGHT 100ft (30m) **SPREAD** 165ft (50m)

CULTIVATION Prefers sunny spots with rich, deep, well-drained loam, but will grow in a variety of soils. Zones 6–9.

ALTERNATIVES Black Oak *(Q. velutina)* is a fast-growing tree that grows well on sandy and rocky soils.

Eastern Hemlock
Tsuga Canadensis

Chickadees, goldfinches, crossbills, and siskins are especially attracted to its seeds. Roosting and nesting species include the Mourning Dove and Northern Cardinal.

HEIGHT 50–80ft (15–24m) **SPREAD** 30ft (9m)

CULTIVATION Does best in shade. Needs moist, loamy soil and protection from wind. Zones 3–8.

ALTERNATIVES White Spruce *(Picea glauca)* needs some sun, and prefers a moist, well-drained soil. It grows to 60–70ft (18–21m).

Eastern Redcedar
Juniperus virginiana

This small tree or prostrate cultivar provides food for over 30 species, including American Robin, Cedar Waxwing, Eastern Bluebird, and the Yellow-rumped Warbler.

HEIGHT 40–50ft (12–15m)

SPREAD 15–25ft (4.5–7.5m)

CULTIVATION Does best in open, sunny areas with limestone-rich soils, but it will grow in a variety of conditions, including poor, eroded, overgrazed soils. Zones 2–9.

ALTERNATIVE Common Juniper *(J. communis).*

Paper Birch
Betula papyrifera

This decorative spreading tree is an excellent winter food source for at least 12 species, including goldfinches, juncos, chickadees, and Pine Siskins. Paper Birch produces a good seed crop every one or two years.

HEIGHT 50–80ft (15–24m) **SPREAD** 30ft (9m)

CULTIVATION Grows best in sun to half sun. Moist, well-drained soils are ideal. Zones 2–7.

ALTERNATIVES Sweet Birch *(B. lenta)* is more shade-tolerant than Paper Birch. It is adapted to moist, fertile, and rocky soils. Yellow Birch *(B. allegheniensis)* prefers cool, moist, well-drained soils. Both are suitable for zones 4–7.

Black-capped Chickadee

Washington Hawthorn
Craetaegus phaenopyrum

Washington Hawthorns produce a mass of white flowers in spring and orange fruits in fall. At least 18 species feed on the fruit, especially Cedar Waxwings.

HEIGHT 40ft (12m) **SPREAD** 20–25ft (6–7.5m)

CULTIVATION Full sun, tolerates almost any well-drained soil except alkaline. Prune in winter or early spring. Zones 3–8.

ALTERNATIVES Dotted Hawthorn (*C. punctata*) tolerates most acidic to neutral, well-drained soils. Also Fourleaf Hawthorn (*C. flabellata*).

Flowering Dogwood
Cornus florida

A common understory tree of eastern forests, Flowering Dogwood produces an abundant supply of white or pink flowers that mature by fall into high lipid fruit that helps to build the necessary fat deposits for fall migrants. At least 36 species of thrush, woodpeckers, tanagers, and grosbeaks consume the brilliant red fruit. Use Flowering Dogwood as a backyard landscape plant or to enhance borders of forest.

HEIGHT 10–30ft (3–9m) **SPREAD** 25ft (7.5m)

CULTIVATION Suited to moist, well-drained soils, prefers pH of 5–7. Grow in full sun if anthracnose is a problem. Zones 5–9.

ALTERNATIVES Alternate Leaf Dogwood (*C. alternifolia*) is a fast-growing, short-lived species that prefers moist, rich, acidic soils. Red Osier Dogwood (*C. stolonifera*) tolerates sun to partial shade with moist soils.

Rose-breasted Grosbeak

Shadbush Serviceberry
Amelanchier canadensis

Serviceberries are early spring flowering trees and shrubs producing small purple fruits by May and June. At least 26 species eat the fruit including robins and waxwings.

HEIGHT 20–25ft (6–7.5m)

SPREAD 10ft (3m)

CULTIVATION Grows best in sun to partial shade in damp, boggy and swampy soils. Zones 5–7.

ALTERNATIVES Bartram Serviceberry (*A. bartramiana*) prefers sun to part shade in rich peaty soil.

Crabapples
Malus sp.

Many cultivars of crabapple are available, ranging up to 50ft. Select trees that have small, winter-persistent fruits. The fruit is important winter food for many species.

HEIGHT 10–50ft (3–15m) .

SPREAD 10–20ft (3–6m)

CULTIVATION Tolerates a range of well-drained soils in open sunlight. Some can be pruned as hedges. Zones 3–9.

ALTERNATIVES Common Apple (*M. pumila*) prefers sunny sites in clay loam, but grows in any soil.

Red Mulberry
Morus rubra

The juicy red fruit is readily eaten by at least 44 bird species. Plant male and female trees for ample pollination. Avoid planting near sidewalks as the fallen fruit is messy.

HEIGHT 40–70ft (12–21m)

SPREAD 40–50ft (12–15m)

CULTIVATION Enjoys full sun to light shade and prefers deep, rich, moist soil with good drainage. A rapid-growing tree, it should be pruned in winter. Zones 4–8.

ALTERNATIVE None.

Northeast: shrubs

Gray Dogwood
Cornus racemosa

This dense shrub provides excellent cover, nesting places, and food. In the fall at least 16 species, including the Gray Catbird, are known to eat the white berries. This is a good choice for both city and country conditions where it makes an excellent hedge. Slow-growing, it reaches mature height at about 10 years of age.

HEIGHT 10–15ft (3–4.5m)

SPREAD 10–15ft (3–4.5m)

CULTIVATION Grows in full sun to partial shade on a variety of soils from swampy to well-drained ones. Zones 5–7.

ALTERNATIVES Alternate Leaf Dogwood (*C. alternifolia*) is a fast-growing, short-lived shrub that prefers rich, moist, acid soils. Partial shade is preferred. Best in zones 3–7.

Gray Catbird

Winterberry
Ilex verticillata

Brilliant red berries cling to the stems of this deciduous holly in late fall and early winter. They provide food for at least 12 bird species, including Brown Thrashers.

HEIGHT 5–15ft (1.5–4.5m)

SPREAD 15–26ft (4.5–8m)

CULTIVATION Does best in full sun to half sun in slightly acidic, rich, wet soil. Zones 4–8.

ALTERNATIVES Inkberry (*I. glabra*) grows well in sun or shade in dry to moist acidic, sandy, well-drained soils. Need male and female plants for berries.

Common Spicebush
Lindera benzoin

The high fat content of the red fruit makes this a highly attractive food for fall migrants. At least 15 species, especially thrushes, robins, and Gray Catbirds, eat the fruit.

HEIGHT 15ft (4.5m)

SPREAD 8ft (2m)

CULTIVATION Does well in sun or shade. Prefers moist, fertile soil, but tolerates dry ones as well. Difficult to transplant. Zones 5–9.

ALTERNATIVES None.

Northern Bayberry
Myrica pensylvanica

A favorite winter food for at least 25 species, the waxy gray fruits are especially important for Yellow-rumped Warblers, Tree Swallows, and Red-bellied Woodpeckers.

HEIGHT 3–8ft (.9–2.4m)

SPREAD 5–12ft (1.5–3.7m)

CULTIVATION Hardy plant that grows well in swampy and sandy, dry soils in sun to half sun. Zones 2–6.

ALTERNATIVES None.

American Elderberry
Sambucus canadensis

Purple fruits are readily eaten in late summer by at least 23 species. It is a preferred food of the American Robin, Veery, and Rose-breasted Grosbeak.

HEIGHT 3–10ft (.9–3m)

SPREAD 12ft (3.7m)

CULTIVATION Fast-growing, short-lived shrub that prefers moist soils, suckers can be removed to prevent the plant from forming thickets. Zones 4–9.

ALTERNATIVES Red Elder (*S. pubens*).

Northeast: vines & ground cover

Virginia Creeper
Parthenocissus quinquefolia

Brilliant red leaves contrast with the dark purple fruit. Bluebirds, Great-crested Flycatchers, Pileated Woodpeckers, and many other species eat the fruit of this beautiful, native vine. Plant this fast-growing native vine on a sturdy arbor or near large trees, especially at the forest edge where it receives abundant light.

HEIGHT Can climb 30–50ft (9–15m)

SPREAD Depends upon its support.

CULTIVATION Tolerates any conditions and soils from sun to full shade. Will withstand wind and pollution. Zones 4–9.

ALTERNATIVES None.

Eastern
Bluebird

Cowberry
Vaccinium vitis-idaea

The bright red fruits of this vigorous prostrate member of the blueberry family are eaten by White-throated Sparrows and other ground-feeding birds.

HEIGHT Less than 1ft (.3m)

SPREAD Indefinite, spreads by suckers.

CULTIVATION Best for open, partially shaded areas in dry, well-drained soil. Zones 1–6.

ALTERNATIVES Bog Bilberry *(V. uliginosum)* for shallow soils, zones 2–6. Dwarf Blueberry *(V. caespitosum)* for acid, well-drained soils, zones 4–7.

Wintergreen
Gaultheria procumbens

A good choice for shady areas, wintergreen produces red berries eaten by at least eight bird species including Bobwhites and Ring-necked Pheasants.

HEIGHT Less than 1ft (.3m)

SPREAD 3–4ft (.9–12m)

CULTIVATION This slow-growing, trailing plant prefers half sun with cool, moist soil having low to moderate fertility. Zones 4–8.

ALTERNATIVES Creeping Snowberry *(G. hispidula).*

Creeping Juniper
Juniper horizontalis

This mat-forming shrub produces blue-green fruits that are readily eaten by waxwings, American Robins, Swainson's Thrushes, and other ground-feeding birds.

HEIGHT 1–2ft (.3–.6m)

SPREAD 4–8ft (1.2–2.4m)

CULTIVATION Requires full sun and well-drained soil. Best growth is over gravel or shallow soils. Zones 3–9.

ALTERNATIVES Common Juniper *(J. communis).*

Bearberry
Arctostaphylos uva-ursi

This evergreen, low-growing shrub produces pink flowers before abundant red fruit, a favorite food of ground-feeding birds such as Fox Sparrow and Ruffed Grouse.

HEIGHT Less than 1ft (.3m)

SPREAD 2–4ft (.6–1.2m)

CULTIVATION Prefers sun to partial shade in a well-drained, acid soil, but it also thrives in very poor soils. Zones 2–6.

ALTERNATIVES Alpine Bearberry *(A. alpina).*

Southeast: trees

Longleaf Pine
Pinus palustris

A strikingly beautiful tree with very long, graceful needles, Longleaf Pines were once widely distributed on sandy soils near the southeastern coast. Frequently used as a nesting site, the seeds are an important food for cardinals, Brown-headed Nuthatches, and Tufted Titmice.

HEIGHT 100–125ft (30–38m) **SPREAD** 40ft (12m)

CULTIVATION Full sun, variety of soils from sandy to poor, acid ones. Salt-tolerant. Zones 7–10.

ALTERNATIVES Shortleaf Pine (*P. echinata*) is a fast-growing tree that tolerates a range of soils in sun.

Tufted Titmouse

Southern Redcedar
Juniperus silicicola

Many species eat the seeds from the cones of the Southern Redcedar, including Cedar Waxwings, Eastern Bluebirds, Yellow-rumped Warblers, and Northern Flickers.

HEIGHT 50ft (15m) **SPREAD** 25ft (7.6m)

CULTIVATION Grows in wet places, but tolerates different moisture levels. Prefers limestone-rich soils. Full sun. Zones 7–10

ALTERNATIVES Eastern Redcedar (*J. virginiana*) does well in sunny spots where soils are high in limestone but grows in varied conditions. Zones 2–8.

Southern Magnolia
Magnolia grandiflora

The brilliant red fruit of Southern Magnolia has a high fat content and is favored by Red-eyed Vireos, Eastern Towhees, and Red-cockaded Woodpeckers.

HEIGHT 50ft (15m) **SPREAD** 50ft (15m)

CULTIVATION Prefers sun to part shade with wet to moist, acid, well-drained soil. Zones 7–9.

ALTERNATIVES Bigleaf Magnolia (*M. macrophylla*) needs rich, acid, well-drained soil in partial shade. Zones 5–8. Cucumbertree Magnolia (*M. acuminata*) requires a slightly acidic, moist, well-drained soil.

Live Oak
Quercus virginiana

At least 15 species eat the acorns of this tree, including the Northern Bobwhite, Wood Duck, Red-cockaded and Red-headed Woodpecker, and Florida Scrub Jay.

HEIGHT 50ft (15m) **SPREAD** 60–100ft (18–30m)

CULTIVATION Fast-growing tree that does well in a variety of soils, but prefers coastal sandy soils. Tolerates salinity. Zones 7–10.

ALTERNATIVES Swamp Chestnut Oak (*Q. michauxii*). Suitable for zones 6–9, it prefers moist areas.

Blackgum
Nyssa sylvatica

Scarlet leaves mean the purple fruits are ripe and ready for distributors, such as Eastern Bluebirds. Growing to 60ft, mature trees break through the canopy in lowland forests.

HEIGHT 40–60ft (12–18m) **SPREAD** 60ft (18m)

CULTIVATION Suited to sun and partial sun in moist or dry conditions. Prefers pH of 5.5 to 6.5. Zones 5–9.

ALTERNATIVES Ogeechee Tupelo (*N. ogeche*) is a shrub or small tree limited to alluvial soils along rivers and in coastal plains.

River Birch
Betula nigra

Tough, drought-resistant River Birch can adapt to extreme conditions. Its seeds are a favorite food for winter finches, such as the Common Redpoll and Pine Siskin.

HEIGHT 50–80ft (15–25m) **SPREAD** 40–60ft (12–18m)

CULTIVATION Best for moist, acid soils with pH of 6.5 or below, but will tolerate other conditions. Transplants well. Zones 4–9.

ALTERNATIVES Sweet Birch (*B. lenta*) is adapted to moist, fertile, deep soils; also very rocky spots.

Cabbage Palmetto
Sabal palmetto

Cabbage Palmetto is native from North Carolina to Florida, thriving in prairies and often mixed with pines on sandy soils. The clusters of small, black fruits are eaten by a variety of birds, including American Robins.

HEIGHT 80ft (24m)

SPREAD 12–18ft (3.7–5.5m)

CULTIVATION Prefers sun. Tolerates a wide range of soils and moisture levels. Zones 7–10.

ALTERNATIVES Dwarf Palmetto (*S. minor*) grows in sunny areas in various kinds of soils, including sand. Scrub Palmetto (*S. etonia*) is a drought-tolerant plant that grows in full sun in sandy soils.

American Robin

American Holly
Ilex opaca

Slow-growing and long-lived, American Holly can live 200 years. At least 12 bird species, including the Eastern Bluebird and Cedar Waxwing, feed on its bright red fruit.

HEIGHT 40–50ft (12–15m)

SPREAD 20–40ft (6–12m)

CULTIVATION Full and partial shade, it grows in a variety of soils. Zones 6–9.

ALTERNATIVES Large Gallberry (*I. coriacea*).

Sweetgum
Liquidambar styraciflua

At least 21 bird species eat the fruit of this fast-growing deciduous tree. The Bobwhite, Mourning Dove, Northern Cardinal, and Evening Grosbeak are fond of its seeds.

HEIGHT 50–120ft (15–36m) **SPREAD** 40ft (12m)

CULTIVATION Does best in sun to half sun in a moist, slightly acid, well-drained soil. Prune during the winter. This tree is highly disease-resistant, but isn't tolerant of pollution. Zones 6–9.

ALTERNATIVES None.

Sugarberry
Celtis laevigata

Often found in river bottoms, this tree has great potential for backyard landscaping. Fruits ripen in late summer and persist on the trees through winter.

HEIGHT 60–80ft (18–24m) **SPREAD** 40ft (12m)

CULTIVATION Suitable for full sun in dry to moist soil, tolerant of clay. Resistant to Witches' Broom. Zones 7–9.

ALTERNATIVES Dwarf hackberry (*C. tenuifolia*) is a shrub or small tree that thrives in dry, rocky, and gravelly soils, but it does best on rich, moist soil.

Southeast: shrubs

Inkberry
Ilex glabra

The black berries of this adaptable evergreen shrub are eaten by at least 15 species of bird, including Northern Mockingbirds, Hermit Thrushes, Northern Bobwhites, and Wild Turkeys. Plant male and female plants near each other to produce the best crops of fruit. It is very hardy and slow-growing.

HEIGHT 6–10ft (1.8–3m) **SPREAD** 10ft (3m)

CULTIVATION This shrub tolerates shade, but does best in full sun. So long as the soil is slightly acidic, it is adapted to a range of moisture levels. Zones 4–10.

ALTERNATIVES Mountain Holly (*I. montana*) is a tall shrub or small tree that grows on rich, wooded slopes, and mountainsides.

Northern Mockingbird

Beautyberry
Callicarpa americana

Small blue flowers form in the clusters of leaves, followed by lustrous pink fruits that are eaten by at least 12 species, particularly the Northern Bobwhite. The fruit contains about 80 percent water.

HEIGHT 3–6ft (.9–1.8m) **SPREAD** 5ft (1.5m)

CULTIVATION Suitable for sun and partial shades. Grows best in well-drained soils. Very fast-growing. Zones 7–10.

ALTERNATIVES None.

Yaupon Holly
Ilex vomitoria

An ideal choice for a wildlife hedge, Yaupon provides good nest sites and red fruit in fall. Gray Catbird, Brown Thrasher, and N. Mockingbird are especially attracted by it.

HEIGHT 15–25ft (4.5–7.6m)

SPREAD 10–15ft (3–4.6m)

CULTIVATION Open sun is best, but tolerates partial shade. Prefers moist soil. Zones 7–10.

ALTERNATIVES Carolina Holly (*I. ambigua*) likes moist and dry soils.

Wax Myrtle
Myrica cerifera

This adaptable, evergreen shrub thrives in a wide range of soil conditions. The fruit is especially important for the Yellow-rumped Warbler and Tree Swallow.

HEIGHT 40ft (12m)

SPREAD 15ft (4.6m)

CULTIVATION Good for sun and partial shade. Tolerates salt spray and infertile soil, but grows better if it is watered and fertilized. Can be grown as a hedge or as a small tree. Zones 7–9.

ALTERNATIVES None.

Saw Palmetto
Serenoa repens

This native palm requires little maintenance and thrives in poor soils. The blue-black fruit is eaten by many species including N. Mockingbirds and American Robins.

HEIGHT Can grow to 23ft (7m) but usually has a prostrate growth habit, only 6in (.2m) tall.

SPREAD 3–8ft (.9–2.4m)

CULTIVATION Must have an acid, moderately to well-drained soil since it can't tolerate wetness. Prefers sun. Zones 7–10.

ALTERNATIVES Dwarf Palmetto (*Sabal minor*).

Southeast: vines & ground cover

Wild Grape
Vitis spp.

At least 52 bird species are known to eat wild grapes; for 24 they are a preferred food. Many species nest among grapevines.

HEIGHT/SPREAD Most are very large vines, usually grown on supports.

CULTIVATION Most do well in open, sunny areas. Prune in winter to prevent bleeding. Zones 4–11.

ALTERNATIVES None.

Trumpet Honeysuckle
Lonicera sempervirens

The nectar of this fast-growing deciduous vine attracts hummingbirds. Flowers produce scarlet berries eaten by songbirds.

HEIGHT/SPREAD Grows 10–20ft (3–6m) tall or more.

CULTIVATION Adapted to full sun and partial shade. Suited to most pH levels and soil types.

ALTERNATIVES None.

Lowbush Blueberry
Vaccinium angustifium

This spreading deciduous shrub provides food for at least 37 bird species, including Northern Mockingbirds, Gray Catbirds and several species of thrush.

HEIGHT 1–2ft (.3–.6m) **SPREAD** 2ft (.6m)

CULTIVATION Requires full sun, does best in an acid, well-drained soil. Zones 3–8.

ALTERNATIVES Dwarf Blueberry (*V. caespitosum*) is a dense suckering plant that prefers acid, well-drained, granite-based soils, but also grows in drier, infertile ones.

Trumpet Creeper
Campsis radicans

Orange or yellow tube-shaped flowers provide nectar for hummingbirds. This sturdy vine grows up tree trunks to reach the canopy. In backyards, provide a trellis.

HEIGHT 30–40ft (9–12m)

SPREAD Depends upon the support provided for this fast-growing vine.

CULTIVATION Needs full sun, lots of room, and a strong support on which it can climb. Suited to both dry and moist, well-drained soils. Zones 5–9.

ALTERNATIVES None.

Bunchberry
Cornus canadensis

This low-growing dogwood has whorls of oval leaves, large white flowers and clusters of bright red berries. The fruit is eaten by ground-feeding species such as veery. Although it may be difficult to establish, it can spread rapidly by sending out rhizomes.

HEIGHT Less than 1ft (.3m)

SPREAD 2ft (.6m)

CULTIVATION Requires shade and a cool, moist, acid soil. Slow-growing. Zones 2–7.

ALTERNATIVES Wintergreen (*Gaultheria procumbens*) is an evergreen ground cover that is less than 1ft (.3m) tall. Suited to shady areas, it prefers a cool, moist soil.

Dark-eyed Junco

THE BIRD-FRIENDLY GARDEN

Prairies and plains: trees

Ponderosa Pine
Pinus ponderosa

An effective shelter belt in open country, Ponderosa Pines provide cover throughout the year. The tiny, abundant seeds are eaten by many species such as chickadees. Good seed crops occur every two to five years. It adapts to a wide range of soils and elevations and can live for over 150 years.

HEIGHT 150ft (45m) **SPREAD** 61–76ft (20–25m)

CULTIVATION Needs sun to part shade, tolerates many kinds of soil, including dry and deep, well-drained. Drought-tolerant. Zones 5–8.

ALTERNATIVES Red Pine *(P. resinosa)* grows 65–100ft (20–30.5m) tall. It prefers a slightly acid, light sandy loam. Slow-growing.

Chestnut-backed
Chickadee

Black Hills Spruce
Picea glauca var. densata

An extremely hardy native variety of the White Spruce and an excellent choice for the northern plains, providing food and cover for Evening Grosbeak and crossbills.

HEIGHT 70ft (21m) **SPREAD** 10–20ft (3–6m)

CULTIVATION Does well in partial shade to sun. Needs moist soil. More resistant to winter desiccation than Colorado Blue Spruce. Transplants easily. Zones 3–6.

ALTERNATIVES White Spruce *(P. glauca)* prefers full sun, and does well in various kinds of soil.

Bur Oak
Quercus macrocarpa

This member of the White Oak group is native to the prairie states; it may grow to great stature. Many species including woodpeckers, titmice, and jays feed on its acorns.

HEIGHT 70–80ft (21–24m) **SPREAD** 30ft (9m)

CULTIVATION Sun. Tolerant of poor soils, but does best in dry, well-drained ones. Withstands city conditions, wind, and drought. Zones 4–9.

ALTERNATIVES Chinkapin Oak *(Q. muehlenbergii)*

Downy Serviceberry
Amerlanchier arborea

This attractive small tree is great for forest edge and backyards. Nineteen species, such as Scarlet Tanagers and Wood Thrush, will eat the ripe fruit in early summer.

HEIGHT 20–40ft (6–12m) **SPREAD** 30ft (9m)

CULTIVATION Adapted to sun and partial shade. Best in well-drained acid soil, but tolerant of others. Zones 3–7.

ALTERNATIVES Allegheny Serviceberry *(A. laevis)* resembles Downy Serviceberry in appearance and growing requirements. Hardy to zone 4.

Hackberry
Celtis occidentalis

This deciduous tree grows in open pastures and backyards. Its purple fruits are eaten in fall by at least 24 species, including the Northern Flicker and Northern Cardinal.

HEIGHT 30–50ft (9–15m) **SPREAD** 50ft (15m)

CULTIVATION Tolerates a range of soils from sandy, dry rocky ones with almost any pH. Sun to shade. Drought-resistant. Zones 5–9.

ALTERNATIVES Dwarf Hackberry *(C. tenuifolia)* grows on dry, rocky, and gravelly foothills and bluffs.

Green Ash
Fraxinus pennsylvanica

Tolerant of city conditions, Green Ash is an excellent choice for backyards. The seeds are preferred foods for Evening and Pine Grosbeaks, and Purple Finches.

HEIGHT 30–50ft (9–15m) **SPREAD** 70ft (21m)

CULTIVATION Sun to part shade, moist to dry, well-drained soil. Tolerates drought, high pH, and salt. Zones 2–9.

ALTERNATIVES Pumpkin Ash (*F. profunda*) does well in moist and swampy places. Can be twice as tall as Green Ash, has narrow open crown.

Box Elder
Acer negundo

An excellent choice for shelterbelt plantings, Box Elder is a preferred food for Evening Grosbeak. This winter-hardy maple can survive extreme temperatures.

HEIGHT 50–75ft (25-23m) **SPREAD** 50–80ft (15-24m)

CULTIVATION Sun or shade. Prefers moist soil, tolerates poor ones. Fast-growing, but short-lived. Zones 2–10.

ALTERNATIVES Vine Maple (*A. circinatum*) is a dwarf shrub or small tree. Prefers moist places.

Common Chokecherry
Prunus virginiana

This small tree or deciduous shrub has red fruit in summer. Plant as part of a hedgerow or backyard planting. Many species eat the fruit, including bluebirds.

HEIGHT 6–20ft (1.8–6m) **SPREAD** 25ft (7.5m)

CULTIVATION Sun. Does well in a great variety of soils, including sand. Prefers rich, well-drained. Zones 2–8.

ALTERNATIVES Bessey Cherry (*P. besseyi*) occurs in open plains, sandhills, and rocky areas in Zones 3–6.

Slippery Elm
Ulmus rubra

This moderate-size tree grows best in full sun and moist soils. The buds are eaten by many species. The seeds are a favorite food of Purple Finch and American Goldfinch.

HEIGHT 60ft (18m) **SPREAD** 50ft (15m)

CULTIVATION Sun, dry to moist, rich, well-drained soils. Moderately fast-growing. Zones 4–9.

ALTERNATIVES Rock Elm (*U. thomasii*) tolerates poor soil, but does best in deep moist ones.

Cockspur Hawthorn
Crataegus crus-galli

An attractive small tree ideal for backyards and hedgerows that provides both food and nesting places among its long, curved thorns. The tree is covered with white to red flowers in the spring, which mature into a profuse crop of red fruit by fall that often persist into winter. More than 20 bird species, including Cedar Waxwings and Fox Sparrows, eat the fruit.

HEIGHT 20–30ft (6–9m)

SPREAD 30ft (9m)

CULTIVATION Full sun, well-drained soil, but will tolerate most types and pH levels. Zones 5–7.

ALTERNATIVES Fleshy Hawthorn (*C. succulenta*) is often cultivated. Considered one of the best native hawthorns. Has large crops of fruits. Round-leaved Hawthorn (*C. chrysocarpa*) can be a large shrub or small tree. Needs sun and well-drained soil.

Cedar Waxwing

PLANT GUIDE: PRAIRIES AND PLAINS

Prairies and plains: shrubs

Buffaloberry
Shepherdia argentea

This bushy, tree-like shrub has yellow flowers among silvery leaves. At least 12 species feed on the red fruits that appear on female plants. It is a preferred food for American Robins and Sharp-tailed Grouse.

HEIGHT 5–6ft (1.5–1.8m)

SPREAD 12ft (3.7m)

CULTIVATION Part shade to sun. Does best in dry, well-drained soil, tolerates alkaline and salty conditions. Both male and female plants needed for fruit production. Zones 3–7.

ALTERNATIVES Buffaloberry (*S. canadensis*) prefers sun. Tolerates any dry soil, including alkaline ones. Slow to moderate growth rate.

American Robin

Rough-leaved Dogwood
Cornus drummondii

This shrub-form dogwood has white fruit in the fall that is eaten by at least 40 species, including N. Cardinals, Gray Catbirds, American Robins, and Eastern Bluebirds.

HEIGHT 4–8ft (1.2–1.4m)

SPREAD 10–15ft (3–4.5m)

CULTIVATION Sun to partial shade. Prefers deep, rich, well-drained soil. Drought-tolerant. Withstands extreme cold. Fast-growing. Zones 4–9.

ALTERNATIVES Flowering Dogwood (*C. florida*) grows in a variety of soils.

Smooth Sumac
Rhus glabra

Sumac fruit is eaten in the fall and winter by at least 12 species. Plant as a windbreak or informal screen. Sumac thickets provide nest sites for insect-eating birds.

HEIGHT 10–15ft (3–4.5m)

SPREAD 8ft (2.4m)

CULTIVATION Needs full sun. Does best in rich, moist soil, but tolerates poor ones. Male and female flowers on separate plants. Zones 2–8.

ALTERNATIVES Prairie Sumac (*R. lanceolata*). Shrub or small tree suited to dry, rocky soils.

Deciduous Holly
Ilex decidua

Plant deciduous holly (or Possum Haw) in clumps, borders, and hedges to provide adequate pollination as this species has male and female plants. Favored by bluebirds.

HEIGHT 10–20ft (3–6m)

SPREAD 5–10ft (1.8m)

CULTIVATION Sun to half shade. Does well in a variety of soils, including dry to wet, and alkaline. Zones 5–9.

ALTERNATIVES American Holly (*I. opaca*) is an evergreen that grows best on acidic, moist sites.

Fragrant Sumac
Rhus aromatica

This deep-rooted shrub is an excellent choice for windy areas. The red summer fruit is eaten by at least 25 species including Evening Grosbeaks and American Robins.

HEIGHT 4–12ft (1–3.6m)

SPREAD 6–10ft (1.8–3m)

CULTIVATION Best in sunny spots. Tolerates a range of conditions, but prefers a limestone-rich soil. Drought-tolerant. Zones 3–9.

ALTERNATIVES Shining Sumac (*R. copallina*). Full sun, well-drained soil. Good for dry, rocky sites.

Prairies and plains: vines & ground cover

Cowberry
Vaccinium vitis-idea

This creeping member of the blueberry family is good ground cover for sunny, well-drained soils. Ground-feeding birds, like Northern Cardinals, eat the red fruits in fall and winter. In early spring, it produces tiny white to deep pink bell-shaped flowers.

HEIGHT Less than 1ft (.3m)

SPREAD Indefinite, spreads by suckers.

CULTIVATION Best for open, partially shaded areas in dry, well-drained soils. Zones 1–6.

ALTERNATIVES Black Highbush Blueberry (*V. atrococcum*) grows in swamps, low woods, and barrens.

Northern Cardinal

Little Bluestem
Schizachyrium scoparium

This colorful grass grows in clumps that provide excellent habitat for ground-dwelling birds. Sparrows and juncos perch on the stalks to eat the seeds.

HEIGHT 2–3ft (.6–.9m)

SPREAD 2ft (.6m)

CULTIVATION Full sun to light shade, dry to moist, fertile soil. Drought-tolerant. Zones 3–9.

ALTERNATIVES Broomsedge Bluestem (*Andropogon virginicus*) prefers full sun. Grows best in dry, open soil with low fertility. Drought-tolerant.

Purple Coneflower
Echinacea purpurea

This tough prairie perennial is drought-resistant and spreads to form clumps. The mature seeds are readily eaten by sparrows, American Goldfinches, and Pine Siskins.

HEIGHT 1–2ft (.3–.6m)

SPREAD 2–3ft (.6–.9m)

CULTIVATION Full sun is best. Dry infertile soil. Very drought-resistant. Zones 3–7.

ALTERNATIVES Pale Coneflower (*E. pallida*) prefers sun. Tolerates poor, infertile soil. Divide every two years. Short-lived.

Knotweeds
Polygonum spp.

Knotweeds are a diverse group of annual creeping species (*P. aviculare*), erect forms (*P. erectum*) and twining species (such as *P. convolvulus*). They grow in dry or wet habitats and provide supplies of seeds in late summer and fall. At least 39 species eat these seeds, including many kinds of sparrow.

HEIGHT Varies, up to 4ft (1.2m)

SPREAD Varies, to 3ft (.9m)

CULTIVATION Sun is best. A range of soils and moisture levels. Alien species can be invasive. Zones 3–9.

ALTERNATIVES None.

Chipping Sparrow

Mountains and deserts: trees

Colorado Blue Spruce
Picea pungens

This prickly spruce provides excellent cover throughout the year and is usually safe from deer browse. Plant this spruce where there is plenty of space as it may grow 150ft (45m) tall with a trunk 3ft (.9m) in diameter. Pine Grosbeaks, Pine Siskins, crossbills, and chickadees feed on its seeds. Typically, good cone crops occur every two to three years.

HEIGHT 80–150ft (24–45m)

SPREAD 15ft (4.5m)

CULTIVATION Needs full sun to part shade. Prefers deep, rich, well-drained, or gravelly soil. Slow-growing, long-lived. Zones 3–8.

ALTERNATIVES Engelman Spruce (*P. engelmannii*) requires well-drained soils.

Pine Siskin

Mountain Hemlock
Tsuga mertensiana

Excellent for shady backyards, Mountain Hemlock makes a good property screen or hedge. Every 2 to 3 years, it produces cones that provide seeds for chickadees.

HEIGHT 50–90ft (15–27m)

SPREAD 10–20ft (3–6m)

CULTIVATION Adaptable to full sun and shade. Needs cool, deep, moist, well-drained soil. Does best in sheltered locations. Zones 5–8.

ALTERNATIVES Western Hemlock (*T. heterophylla*) does best in deep, well-drained soil. Long-lived.

Rocky Mountain Juniper
Juniperus scopulorum

This drought-resistant tree is an excellent choice for arid habitats. Waxwings and thrashers often nest in the dense, prickly shelter, and many species eat the fruit.

HEIGHT 30–40ft (9–12m)

SPREAD 12ft (3.5m)

CULTIVATION Grows best in sun. Prefers dry, rocky alkaline soils. Drought-tolerant. Similar to Redcedar. Zones 4–7.

ALTERNATIVES Alligator Juniper (*J. deppeana*) does well in sunny spots with dry, rocky, sterile soils.

Mesquite
Prosopis velutina

The thorny branches of this tree or small shrub provide excellent nesting habitat. Mesquite grows best along stream banks and canyons, but this drought-resistant native is also a good choice for extreme, arid habitats. Doves eat the seeds.

HEIGHT 33ft (10m)

SPREAD 15–25ft (4.5–7.5m)

CULTIVATION Grows well in rocky, sandy soils in full sun. Drought-tolerant. Zones 8–10.

ALTERNATIVES Glandular Mesquite (*P. glandulosa*) prefers dry, sunny areas with well-drained soil. May need some supplemental watering when hot.

Mourning Dove

White Alder
Alnus rhombifolia

This fast-growing shade tree readily adapts to backyard habitats, attracting many species such as quail, grouse, and towhees, which feed on its buds and seeds.

HEIGHT 40–100ft (12–30m)

SPREAD 70ft (21m)

CULTIVATION Excellent choice for shady sites with moist soils. Zones 5–8.

ALTERNATIVES Arizona Alder (*A. oblongifolia*) is hardy to zone 7. Sitka alder (*A. sinuate*) and Thinleaf Alder (*A. tenuifolia*) are suited to zone 2.

Coyote Willow
Salix exigua

This small tree or shrub stabilizes stream banks and provides cover for sparrows. It attracts insects, which are eaten by many species of flycatchers, wrens, and kinglets.

HEIGHT 15ft (4.5m)

SPREAD 15ft (4.5m)

CULTIVATION Prefers sunny spots with moist, well-drained soils. Grows to 8,200ft elevation. Zones 2–6.

ALTERNATIVES Arroyo Willow (*S. lasiolepis*) grows from sea level to 7,400 feet elevation. Heart-Leaved Willow (*S. rigida*) grows to 8,000 feet.

Quaking Aspen
Populus tremuloides

This fast-growing tree makes an excellent choice for property borders. Many species feed on the leaf buds, including grosbeaks, orioles, and shrikes.

HEIGHT 40–60ft (12–18m)

SPREAD 30ft (9m)

CULTIVATION Sun to half sun. Adaptable to dry and moist soils as well as poor, rocky ones. Fast-growing. Zones 1–8.

ALTERNATIVE Narrowleaf Cottonwood (*P. angustifolia*) will grow in partial shade to full sun.

Gambel Oak
Quercus gambellii

Depending on growing conditions, this oak varies from tree to low shrub. The annual acorns are a favorite food of Acorn Woodpeckers, and Scaled and Montezuma Quail.

HEIGHT 15–30ft (4.5–9m)

SPREAD 10–12ft (3–3.5m)

CULTIVATION Sunny spot with dry, well-drained soil. Suitable for sand and loam. Slow-growing. Zones 4–7.

ALTERNATIVES Arizona Live Oak (*Q. chrysolepis*). Zones 7–9. Slow-growing evergreen shrub or tree.

Douglas Hawthorn
Crataegus douglasii

Variable in form as a small tree or many-branched shrub, Douglas Hawthorn possesses long, straight thorns, with numerous mosses and lichens present upon the entire bark system. The tree is an excellent choice for nesting birds. It is covered in white flowers in the spring and has dark green, glossy leaves. Spines provide well-protected nesting places. Townsend's Solitaire, Hermit Thrush, Cedar Waxwing, and Pine Grosbeak are among many species that eat its smooth, blackish fruit.

HEIGHT 15–30ft (4.5–9m)

SPREAD 6–9ft (1.8–2.7m)

CULTIVATION Needs full sun. Grows in a variety of situations from deep, moist, fine-textured to dry, well-drained soils. Can also grow on steep, exposed slopes. Zones 3–10.

ALTERNATIVES Cerro Hawthorn (*C. erythropoda*) occurs in woodland margins and abandoned fields. Round-Leaved Hawthorn (*C. chrysocarpa*) is a small tree with large, broad leaves. These prefer full sun, and dry to moist, well-drained soils.

Mountains and deserts: shrubs

Blue Elderberry
Sambucus caerulea

This large, deciduous shrub produces large clusters of blue fruit in late summer that are readily eaten by many species, including Mountain Bluebirds, Black Phoebes, Western Kingbirds, and Black-headed Grosbeaks. An excellent choice for landscaping pond and stream edges.

HEIGHT 30–40ft (9–12m)

SPREAD 15ft (4.5m)

CULTIVATION Does best in sun to partial shade in moist areas. Fast-growing and short-lived. Zones 4–9.

ALTERNATIVES Black Elderberry *(S. melanocarpa)* is suited to moist soils in sunny spots. Suitable for zones 6–8.

Mountain Bluebird

Oregon Grape
Mahonia nervosa

This native shrub's dense foliage provides excellent cover and nesting places for many species. Its berries are eaten by Ruffed and Blue Grouse.

HEIGHT 2ft (.6m) **SPREAD** 3ft (.9m)

CULTIVATION Adapted to sun and full shade in dry, well-drained soils. Lime-free soil is best. Resistant to black stem rust. Zones 5–8.

ALTERNATIVES Creeping Mahonia *(M. repens)* is a 3ft (.9m) tall shrub with a sprawling growth habit. It needs sun or partial shade.

Prickly Pear Cactus
Opuntia phaeacantha

Its prickly shelter offers safe nesting and roosting places. The juicy fruits and seeds are eaten by many species, including Gambel's Quails and Cactus Wrens.

HEIGHT 3ft (.9m) **SPREAD** 5–6ft (1.5–1.8m)

CULTIVATION Requires full sun and free-draining soil. Needs a little water in winter. Zones 9–11.

ALTERNATIVES Pancake Prickly Pear *(O. chlorotica)* can be 3–5ft (.9m–1.5m) tall, and needs very little water. Violet Prickly Pear *(O. violacea)* needs full sun, and almost no supplemental watering.

Flowering Currant
Ribes sanguineum

Red tubular flowers attract hummingbirds in the spring, and flowers develop into black fruit in summer. Eaten by Northern Flickers, Hermit and Swainson's Thrushes.

HEIGHT 6ft (1.8m) **SPREAD** 6ft (1.8m)

CULTIVATION Prefers sunny to partially shaded spots with moist, well-drained soils. Takes adverse conditions, drought-tolerant. Zones 6–8.

ALTERNATIVES Sticky Currant *(R. viscosissimum)* tolerates partial shade and sun. Adapted to rocky areas, it grows in any well-drained soil.

Northern Flicker

Mountains and deserts: vines & ground cover

Honeysuckle
Lonicera periclymemum

Two-inch long yellow flowers are fragrant and attractive to hummingbirds, especially Ruby-throated, Rufous and Anna's Hummingbirds. In the fall, abundant red fruits provide food for many species. It is evergreen in the warmer parts of its range and deciduous further north.

HEIGHT/SPREAD 15–30ft (4.5–9m)

CULTIVATION Fast-growing, untidy vine that needs regular pruning. Is evergreen in warm areas. Zones 4–10.

ALTERNATIVES *L. involucrate* grows on banks of streams and in chalky woods. It is 3–10ft (.9m–3m) tall.

Anna's Hummingbird

California Fuchsia
Epilobium canum

This low-growing shrub produces tubular scarlet or orange flowers that attract hummingbirds. Suitable in western regions on dry hillsides and rock gardens.

HEIGHT 3–4ft (.9–1.2m) **SPREAD** ⅓–1ft (.1–.3m)

CULTIVATION Full sun to part shade. Tolerates a wide range of conditions and soils. Prefers well-drained soil. Zones 8–10.

ALTERNATIVES Hardy Hummingbird Trumpet (*Zauschneria arizonica*) is tolerant of hot, dry summers. Blooms summer to fall. Full sun.

Mexican Manzanita
Arctostaphylos pungens

Arctostaphylos pungens is a low-growing woody shrub with waxy, oval leaves and red bark. It provides cover and food for grouse, quail, towhees, and sparrows.

HEIGHT 1–10ft (.3–3m) **SPREAD** 3–7ft (.1–2m)

CULTIVATION Prefers full sun and dry, well-drained gravelly soils. Zones 7–10.

ALTERNATIVES Green-leaved Manzanita (*Arctostaphylos patula*) grows 1–10ft (.3–3m) tall, and Pinemat manzanita (*A. nevadensis*). Both need full sun with dry, well-drained soils. Zones 7–10.

Mesquite
Prosopis sp.

Mesquite plants are extremely hardy and drought-tolerant; they grow quickly and furnish shade where other trees will not prosper. There are 44 species of North American trees and shrubs that belong to the mesquite genus. The group provides vital cover and food for birds of arid habitats in this region. White-winged Doves eat the seeds, and many species, including the Tufted Titmouse, nest in the shade of the plant's dense, thorny branches and yellow flowers.

HEIGHT 33ft (10m)

SPREAD 15–25ft (4.6–7.6m)

CULTIVATION Grows well in rocky, sandy soils in full sun. Drought-tolerant. Zones 8–10.

ALTERNATIVES Glandular mesquite (*P. glandulosa*) prefers dry, sunny areas with well-drained soil. May need some supplemental watering when hot.

Pacific coast: trees

California Juniper
Juniperus californicus

Well adapted to arid habitats, California Juniper produces blue-green fruit in late summer that can last through the winter, so birds can consume and distribute the seed for longer. At least 10 species eat the fruit, including the N. Mockingbird, Townsend's Solitare, and Varied Thrush.

HEIGHT 10–30ft (3–9m)

SPREAD 10–15ft (3–4.5m)

CULTIVATION Needs full sun and dry soil. Likes sandy and rocky sites. Grows to 10,000ft (3,048m) elevation. Zones 8–9.

ALTERNATIVES Western Juniper *(J. occidentalis)* is well suited to areas with cold winters and dry summers.

Varied Thrush

Shore Pine
Pinus contorta

This popular landscape plant provides shelter, cover, and insects for woodpeckers, chickadees, and titmice. One of the best pines for small gardens and backyards.

HEIGHT 33–100ft (10–30m) **SPREAD** 10–20ft (3–6m)

CULTIVATION Grows in a variety of soils, but does best on deep, well-drained. Slow-growing and long-lived. Either a straight tree or short, shrubby contorted shrub. Zones 3–8.

ALTERNATIVES Jeffrey Pine *(P. jeffreyi)*.

California Live Oak
Quercus agrifolia

Dense foliage and widespread branches provide shelter and food for many western birds. Acorns are especially important for Acorn Woodpeckers and Scrub Jays.

HEIGHT 75ft (23m) **SPREAD** 130ft (39m)

CULTIVATION Prefers dry, well-drained soil. Thrives in a range of soil types. Zones 6–9.

ALTERNATIVES Blue Oak *(Q. douglasii)* and Engelmann Oak *(Q. engelmannii)* grow in gravelly, well-drained soils in low hills and dry slopes. Canyon Live Oak *(Q. chrysolepis)* tolerates more moisture.

Madrone
Arbutus menziesii

Madrone fruits are important for many species in the fall and winter. They are readily consumed by the Band-tailed Pigeon, Wild Turkey, and California Quail.

HEIGHT 20–100ft (6–30m)

SPREAD 50ft (15m)

CULTIVATION Grows best in full sun in rich, dry to moist, well-drained soil. Once established, water infrequently with non-alkaline water. In the open it can have a spreading form. Zones 7–9.

ALTERNATIVES None.

Californian Quail

Mexican Bush Sage
Salvia leucantha

A favorite of wintering Anna's Humming-birds, it can grow up to 7ft (2.1m) tall. It usually produces its pink to purple flower spikes in October and November.

HEIGHT 3–4ft (.9–1.2m) **SPREAD** 3–4ft (.9–1.2m)

CULTIVATION Although mature plants form a shrubby hedge, cut back after flowering to make a striking ground cover. Plant as a perennial in zones 8–10 and as an annual further north.

ALTERNATIVES Mountain Sage *(Salvia regla).*

Pacific Dogwood
Cornus nuttallii

White flower bracts surround inconspicuous flowers that produce bright red fruits in the fall. These are highly attractive to Northern Flickers and Band-tailed Pigeons.

HEIGHT 10–40ft (3–12m) **SPREAD** 25ft (7.6m)

CULTIVATION Adaptable to partial shade in areas with very well-drained, rich, moist soils. Water infrequently during the summer. Zones 7–9.

ALTERNATIVES Brown Dogwood *(C. glabrata)* grows in moist areas and by streams to 5,800ft; Red Osier Dogwood *(C. sericea)* to over 8,000ft.

Saskatoon Serviceberry
Amelanchier alnifolia

This adaptable tree may take the form of a shrub in moist soils. It may also take a tree or prostrate shape. Thrushes, waxwings, and finches readily eat its juicy fruits.

HEIGHT 6–12ft (2.5–3.75m) **SPREAD** 12ft (3.75m)

CULTIVATION Prefers full to partial sun. Tolerates a variety of soils, including hard and dry to rich, moist ones. Zones 4–8.

ALTERNATIVES Roundleaf Serviceberry *(A. sanguinea)* does well in zones 5–8.

Western Cottonwood
Populus fremontii

This large, many-branched tree grows best in full sun. Cedar Waxwings feed on the unopened catkin buds in spring, warblers feed on insects attracted to flowers.

HEIGHT 100ft (30m) **SPREAD** 50ft (15m)

CULTIVATION Prefers sun with dry or moist, well-drained soil. Zones 7–9.

ALTERNATIVES Black Cottonwood *(P. trichocarpa)* does best in deep, moist to wet boggy soils. Quaking Aspen *(P. tremuloides)* grows in moist areas in the mountains, but also does well at low elevations.

Toyon
Heteromeles arbutifolia

Also known as Christmas Berry or California Holly, this evergreen shrub produces abundant crops of orange fruit, which ripen from early fall through winter. Toyon usually grows as a tree, but it sometimes takes on a shrubby growth form. Northern Flickers, American Robins, Northern Mockingbirds, and Cedar Waxwings eat Toyon fruit.

HEIGHT 10–25ft. (3–7.6m)

SPREAD 10–25ft (3–7.6m)

CULTIVATION Grows in sun and part shade in fertile, well-drained soil. Water infrequently but deeply during the first winter after transplanting. Zones 8–10.

ALTERNATIVES None.

Northern Mockingbird

Pacific coast: shrubs

Wax Myrtle
Myrica cerifera

Dense evergreen foliage makes this an excellent choice for providing cover and roosting places. Purplish, waxy fruits develop in July and persist over winter until the following June. The fruits are important to many species, including Yellow-rumped Warblers, Tree Swallows, Western and Mountain Bluebirds, Wren-tits, and towhees.

HEIGHT 40ft (12m) **SPREAD** 15ft (4.6m)

CULTIVATION Suitable for sun and partial shade. Sandy soils are best. It will grow in infertile ones, but does better if it receives supplemental water and fertilizer. Tolerates salt spray. Zones 7–9.

ALTERNATIVES None.

Yellow-rumped Warbler

Sugar Bush
Rhus ovata

Evergreen leaves offer shelter from very arid and salty conditions. At least six bird species eat the red berries. It is a favorite food of the Wren-tit and California Quail.

HEIGHT 10ft (3m) **SPREAD** 10ft (3m)

CULTIVATION Does best in sun to part shade. Thrives in dry, rocky areas. Requires well-drained soil. Very heat- and drought-tolerant. Zones 7–9.

ALTERNATIVES Laurel Sumac (*R. laurina*) is very drought-resistant. Occurs on dry slopes from sea level to 3,300ft (1,000m). Suitable for zones 9–10.

California Grape Holly
Mahonia pinnata

Drought-resistant and evergreen, this is an excellent choice for arid backyards in the south of the Pacific coast region. Many birds including Cedar Waxwings eat the berries.

HEIGHT 6ft (1.8m) **SPREAD** 1–3ft (.3–1m)

CULTIVATION Partial shade is best. Prefers fertile, well-drained soil. Takes drought better than Oregon Grape Holly. Zones 7–10.

ALTERNATIVES Oregon Grape Holly (*M. aquifolium*) is better adapted to cooler, wetter climates in the north Pacific region; good choice for partial shade.

Mexican Elderberry
Sambucus caerulea mexicana

This large evergreen shrub or tree can develop a trunk 18in (46cm) in diameter. It is adapted to arid climates, but still prefers damp habitats such as moist grasslands and stream banks. At least 12 species, including Western Scrub Jays, eat the clusters of blue fruit.

HEIGHT 4–10ft (1.2–3m)

SPREAD 6–13ft (2–4m)

CULTIVATION Full sun. Prefers a deep, loamy, moist soil, but suitable for other well-drained ones. Zones 7–10.

ALTERNATIVES Black Elderberry (*S. melanocarpa*), zones 6–8. Blue Elderberry (*S. caerulea*) prefers pH of 6–7. New Mexican Elderberry (*S. caerulea neomexicana*), zones 7–10. All grow in sun to part shade in moist soils.

Western Scrub Jay

Pacific coast: vines & ground cover

Fuchsia-flowering Gooseberry
Ribes speciosum

This is a low-growing shrub producing drooping, cherry-red flowers attractive to hummingbirds. The prickly branches create excellent cover and nesting habitat. Tube-shaped red flowers mature into red fruit eaten by many species, including White-crowned Sparrow and bluebirds.

HEIGHT 4–6ft (1.2–1.8m) **SPREAD** 3ft (1m)

CULTIVATION Good for sun and partial shade. Tolerates a range of soils from sand to clay. Good for coastal areas. Zones 6–10.

ALTERNATIVES Golden Currant (*R. aureum*). This spineless shrub thrives in sun.

White-crowned Sparrow

Mexican Bush Sage
Salvia leucantha

The arching, graceful spikes of this shrub are attractive to hummingbirds in winter. It is perennial in the southern Pacific zone and planted as a perennial further north.

HEIGHT 3–4ft (.9–1.2m) **SPREAD** 3–4ft (.9–1.2m)

CULTIVATION Grows in sun or light shade in loamy, gravelly, and sandy soil. Tolerates drought. Cut old stems to the ground for a constant supply of blooms from summer to fall. Zones 8–10.

ALTERNATIVES Autumn Sage (*S. greggii*).

Pacific Madrone
Arbutus menziesii

This spreading shrub produces large crops of colorful red or orange fruit in late fall. Eaten by Band-tailed Pigeons, Wild Turkies, and many songbirds.

HEIGHT 15–80ft (4.5–25m) **SPREAD** 50ft (15m)

CULTIVATION Spreads over large areas in full sun; grows more tree-like in part shade. Requires rich soils with deep watering in summer. Zones 7–9.

ALTERNATIVES Bearberry (*Arctostaphylos uva-ursi*): low-growing, requires full sun. Zones 2–6.

Wild Grape
Vitis spp.

There are 65 species of wild grape in North America. Most are twining vines in forest canopy and woodland borders where they thrive in full sun. Vireos and many species use the bark for their nests. At least 52 species, including Cedar Waxwings, eat wild grapes.

HEIGHT/SPREAD 30ft (9m) tall and wide.

CULTIVATION Grows best in a sunny, moist, well-drained site. Zones 7–10.

ALTERNATIVES Canyon grape (*V. arizonica*) grows best in moist, sandy soils. Prefers well-drained sites. This vine is 5–50ft (1.5–15m) long. Suited to zones 7–9.

Cedar Waxwing

Water gardens

WATER FEATURES CAN BE integrated into virtually any garden, whatever its size. Pools are used for drinking, bathing, and feeding. Larger ponds may attract water birds, varying in size from sparrow-sized shorebirds to Great Blue Herons with wingspans of six feet. Muddy pond margins draw in species like Spotted Sandpiper, which bobs along shorelines searching for insects, while Barn Swallows use mud for nesting material.

Mallards frequent *small ponds for feeding and preening (above). In spring, they visit as soon as ice thaws.*

Attracted to water

Add a patch of water of any size and soon aquatic life will colonize. The boundary between land and water, usually sheltered by dense foliage, presents an ideal habitat for invertebrates, amphibians, and birds.

Constructing ponds and pools

There are many ways to build a pond. Where soils permit, larger ponds can be created with a backhoe and a dike, or bentonite clay can help to create a pond in sandy and gravelly soils.

    The simplest way to create a small garden pool is to position a rigid plastic or fiberglass liner into the ground. However, these preformed pools are limited in shape and size and typically lack the shallow slope that short-legged birds prefer for bathing.

    Small backyard pools are best created with a flexible rubber pond liner. First excavate a hole with a gradual sloping shore with a deep end that is at least 2ft (60cm) deep. This depth is usually adequate to keep water from freezing to the bottom, a necessity for fish and most potted plants. Then place an old carpet or carpet liner in the hole to prevent rocks from migrating

Moving water features, *such as waterfalls and fountains, prevent water from freezing in winter.*

PLANNING AND PLANTING

When making a garden pool, create shallow edges on at least part of the circumference and plant with marsh species such as iris, sedges, and marsh marigolds. The edges of the pond should slope away gently so that a bird can wade in up to its belly. If this is not possible (for example, if using a preformed pool), build a platform from bricks or stone that provides a water perch for birds such as this American Goldfinch.

Birds bathe *and drink all year around, but especially require water on extremely hot days (above). Some species, such as this Cliff Swallow, also visit puddles to collect mud to construct nests (left).*

upward and possibly puncturing the liner. Flexible liners allow gradations of shape and depth, which maximize the appeal of the pool for wildlife and facilitate access for drinking and bathing. The gradual slope also permits animals such as rabbits and mice to escape if they fall in by accident. The more varied the slopes and longer the shoreline, the better for wildlife.

Position and stocking

Avoid locating the pool under trees as it will fill with fall leaves, and growing roots could puncture the lining. Instead, plant a low bush nearby to provide cover. Do not automatically place your pond in a wet or damp hollow because such areas may already be important for wildlife. The pond is incomplete without plants, as these provide food and cover. The best time for planting is late spring when the water is beginning to warm. Submerge the plants in plastic baskets or flowerpots and, if necessary, sink the pots with stones until trapped air has dispersed.

Provide enough potted water lilies (*Nymphaea sp.*) to cover at least one third of the surface with floating leaves. These reduce sunlight that favors algae. Also plant submerged plants such as hornwort (*Ceratophyllum demersum*) and waterweed (*Egeria densa*). These provide oxygen and purify the water by absorbing carbon dioxide while providing food for fish.

Use a submerged pump that moves about 275 gallons (1,040 liters) per hour to bring water from the bottom of the pool to an above-ground tub with an overflow spout. Plant the tub with wild iris (*Iris versicolor*) that purifies the water. This biological filter is especially important if there are fish in the pool as their excrement can overload the pool with nitrates that favor rampant algae growth. As water travels back to the pool, it can trickle through a bird bathing pool. Birds avoid gushing waterfalls.

Green Frogs *are usually the first frogs to appear in backyard pools. Their tadpoles provide a ready source of protein for herons.*

Cattails provide nesting habitat *and cover for Marsh Wrens, blackbirds, ducks, and other waterbirds. Ducks eat the roots.*

A new, freshly filled pool is barren at first, but life soon appears in the form of water beetles, dragonflies, and other insects that fly in and settle. Frogs, toads, and newts may discover the pond for themselves. Adding a bucket of water with mud from an established pond can start populations of tiny creatures such as water fleas and snails that feed fish and eat algae.

Fish such as fatheaded minnows and top minnows readily eat mosquitoes. Obtain these or other small minnows from bait shops. These breed in small pools, often attracting herons.

Pools with mature vegetation *take years to develop (below). A garden pool (below right) for birds should offer a circulating trickle that falls into a shallow rock depression where birds can bathe.*

Hummingbird gardens

HUMMINGBIRDS ARE ATTRACTED to backyard gardens, where they find flowers rich with nectar and insects. They also require water and nesting places. Although sugar-water feeders will lure hummingbirds in for close-up views, they require frequent cleaning and refilling. However, many flowers naturally attract hummingbirds by offering sweet nectar. Here are some tips to bring these dazzlers into your backyard.

Create a sketch of your property, indicating the location of buildings, including existing trees, shrubs, and plantings that benefit hummingbirds.

Locate a site for a hummingbird garden that is in a convenient place for viewing.

Plan your garden with vertical dimensions, including walls of buildings. Arrange foundation plantings, containers, trellises, and windowboxes to provide a tiered effect.

Favor native plants. Hummingbirds have evolved to feed on specific plants, and even the timing of blooming may occur to match hummingbird migration patterns. For example, native columbine blooms almost to the day that Ruby-throated Hummingbirds return to breeding areas. In contrast, showy cultivars may have little nectar.

Select plants with tubular flowers (usually red or orange) with flower parts that extend out of the tube—indications that these flowers have evolved to attract hummingbird pollinators. Such plants usually have a good nectar source that attracts insects that are also important hummingbird foods. Plants with sweet smells usually have little nectar.

Plant patches of nectar-producing plants and make selections that offer food from early spring to fall.

Offer water for hummingbirds from misters and dripping devices attached to birdbaths.

Plant hummingbird vines, bushes, and trees as well as flowers, as these provide shelter at night and nesting places.

Avoid insecticides. Hummingbirds are especially vulnerable to garden poisons as their diet includes many insects.

A male Rufous Hummingbird *hovers while feeding at a spike of red-hot poker flowers. Unlike some plants from other parts of the world, this garden favorite does not usually wander from the garden.*

Hummingbirds, *such as this Broad-billed Hummingbird, visit flowers in search of nectar and insects. The frequency of visits to a particular flower depends on the amount of food in the flower and the number of other hummingbirds competing for the food.*

HUMMINGBIRD PLANTS

NORTHEAST
Beebalm (*Monarda didyma*): spreading perennial herb, sun. Zones 4–9.
Cardinal Flower (*Lobelia cardinalis*): perennial herb, sun. Zones 3–9.
Coral Bells (*Heuchera sanguinea*): clump-forming perennial, part sun. Zones 3–8.
Fringed Bleeding Heart (*Dicentra eximia*): clump-forming perennial, part sun. Zones 4–8.
Hummingbird Mint (*Agastache cana*): spreading perennial herb, sun. Zones 5–10.
Red Morning Glory (*Ipomoea coccinea*): vine, sun, annual. Zones 10–11.
Scarlet Runner Bean (*Phaseolus coccineus*): vine, sun, annual. Zones 9–10.
Solomon's Seal (*Polygonatum biflorum*): perennial spreading herb, shade. Zones 3–9.
Trumpet Vine (*Campsis radicans*): perennial vine, sun. Zones 5–9.
Wild Columbine (*Aquilegia canadensis*): perennial herb, part shade. Zones 3–8.

SOUTHEAST
Autumn Sage (*Salvia greggii*): perennial or annual herb, sun. Zones 7–9.
Coral Bean (*Erythrina herbacea*): perennial herb or shrub, part shade. Zone 9.
Coral Honeysuckle (*Lonicera sempervirens*): perennial vine, part shade/sun. Zones 5–9.
Cross-Vine (*Bignonia capreolata*): perennial vine, sun, part shade. Zones 7–9.
Cypress Vine (*Ipomoea quamoclit*): vine, sun, annual. Zones 5–11.
Desert Honeysuckle (*Aniscantus wrightii*): spreading shrub, sun, Zones 8–9.
Firebush (*Hamelia patens*): shrub, full sun. Zone 9.
Firecracker Plant (*Russelia equisetiformis*): upright herb, sun. Zone 9.
Lyre-leaved Sage (*Salvia lyrata*): herb, sun. Zones 7–8.
Texas Olive (*Cordia boissieri*): evergreen tree, full sun, part shade. Zone 9.
Trumpet Honeysuckle (*Lonicera sempervirens*): semievergreen climbing vine, full sun. Zone 4.

WESTERN MOUNTAINS AND DESERTS
Baja Fairy Duster (*Calliandra californica*): shrub, full sun. Zones 9–10.
Chuparosa (*Justicia californica*): shrub, full sun, drought-resistant. Zones 8–10.
Coral Bells (*Heuchera versicolor*): evergreen, clumping perennial, shade. Zones 5–8.
Crimson Monkeyflower (*Mimulus cardinalis*): perennial herb, shade. Zones 6–9.
Ocotillo (*Fouquieria splendens*): thorny shrub, full sun. Zones 8–10.
Red Yucca (*Hesperaloe parviflora*): evergreen perennial, full sun, part shade. Zones 7–10.
Scarlet Bugler (*Penstemon barbatus*): perennial herb, full sun/part shade. Zones 5–8.
Scarlet Gilia (*Ipomopsis aggregata*): biennial herb, full sun. Zones 5–8.
Smooth Bouvardia (*Bouvardia glaberrima*): shrub, part shade. Zones 6–8.
Wolfberry (*Lycium andersonii*): spiny shrub, flowers and berries, sun, part shade. Zones 7–10.

PACIFIC COAST
California Fuchsia (*Epilobium canum*): shrub, drought-resistant, sun. Zones 8–10.
Desert Willow (*Chilopsis linearis*): shrub and tree, full sun. Zones 7–9.
Firebird Penstemon (*Penstemon gloxinioides*): perennial herb, full sun. Zones 8–10.
Flowering Currant (*Ribes sanguineum*): deciduous shrub, full sun/part shade. Zones 6–8.
Island Bush Snapdragon (*Galvezia speciosa*): perennial shrub, sun/part shade. Zones 9–10.
Justica (*Justica spicigera*): perennial shrub, full sun, part shade. Zones 9–10.
Pineapple Sage (*Salvia elegans*): perennial shrub, full sun, part shade. Zones 5–10.
Bush Monkeyflower (*Mimulus aurantiacus*): perennial shrub, sun. Zones 9–10.
Scarlet Monardella (*Madronella macrantha*): deciduous shrub, sun. Zones 8–9.
Twinberry (*Lonicera involucrata*): herbaceous shrubby vine, sun, part shade. Zones 6–9.

Trumpet Vine

Trumpet Honeysuckle

Coral Bells

Flowering Currant

A peanut feeder *made of wire mesh is ideal for the roof terrace or patio. Spilled fragments of nuts are taken by birds that cannot perch on the feeder itself.*

Open-fronted *nest boxes may attract urban species such as robins and Pied Wagtails. A nest box on a trellis will become camouflaged and sheltered when climbing plants grow up around it.*

A birdbath *will always draw birds into a roof-top garden, and can be a very attractive feature in a container garden. Metal containers add visual interest, but ensure they are not too deep for birds to enter.*

Starlings *are seen in and around towns, searching for insects on paved surfaces. They are common on roofs, usually calling before flying off. In winter they gather in large numbers to roost in town centers.*

Nasturtiums *are easy to grow and bring swathes of color to the garden. They produce copious nectar, which attracts a range of insects that are in turn taken by birds.*

Urban roof garden

SPACE IS LIMITED in the city environment, but the pleasure of wildlife gardening need not be denied to anyone who has access to an area of flat roof, or even a balcony. Birds are attracted by the green oasis of vegetation to search for food and a place to nest.

American Goldfinches *often visit rooftop gardens, attracted by sunflowers, cosmos, and Purple Coneflower.*

The diversity and number of birds in a city center are often lower than in the suburbs, and in a roof garden the variety of species depends largely on the abundance of trees in adjacent neighborhood parks or road-sides. However, with careful planting and supplementary feeding, it is possible to make the smallest pocket of garden in to a magnet for nearby birds.

A roof garden compensates for low bird diversity by offering unusual or intimate views of certain species: swallows and swifts can be seen hunting from above; starlings, House Sparrows, House Finches, and Rock Pigeons often nest at close quarters, and nighthawks may pursue insects over city buildings. In summer, hummingbirds may take up residence amid rooftop gardens planted with nectar-producing plantings. Even birds of prey use city habitats, feeding on squirrels, rats, and pigeons.

Migration is the best season for rooftop gardeners as warblers, wrens, and other small migrants may seek shelter in an otherwise inhospitable urban landscape. A water source such as a birdbath, and supplemental feeding of mealworms and seed, can sustain these birds, giving them an oasis during migration.

PLANTING AND MAINTENANCE

Roof-garden plants are exposed to the elements. If they are not sheltered by walls, windbreaks of closely woven mesh may be needed. Always consult a structural engineer before building raised beds on a flat roof. Note: These recommended plants are for eastern North America only.

Plant list

① Trumpet Honeysuckle (*Lonicera sempervirens*)
② Serviceberry (*Amelanchier sp.*)
③ Trumpet Vine (*Campsis radicans*)
④ Purple Coneflower (*Echinacea purpurea*)
⑤ Beebalm (*Monarda didyma*)
⑥ Flowering Crabapple (*Malus sp.*)
⑦ Creeping Juniper (*Juniperus horizontalis*)
⑧ Fragrant Sumac (*Rhus aromatica*)

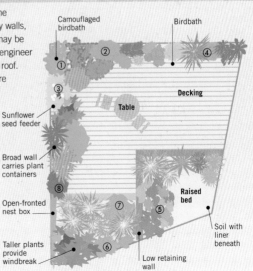

Camouflaged birdbath

Birdbath

Decking

Table

Raised bed

Soil with liner beneath

Sunflower seed feeder

Broad wall carries plant containers

Open-fronted nest box

Taller plants provide windbreak

Low retaining wall

Observing garden birds

Even the smallest of urban gardens attracts a variety of birds. An understanding of what to look for will greatly enhance your enjoyment of these visitors, and knowing what basic equipment to use will help you explore their secret lives.

Cedar Waxwing

How to look

BIRDWATCHING CAN BEGIN AT HOME. While it is exciting to look for birds in wild places, the elements of observation and identification are best learned in the familiar surroundings near home. And because you have some control over your backyard environment, it is possible to conduct simple ecological studies and experiments that will help you understand bird behavior.

Home study

Your house is an ideal, ready-made observation blind. It is easy to watch and identify birds at close range without disturbing them, especially if you position feeders close to windows. Proximity gives you luxuries rarely afforded in the field: the time and opportunity to examine plumage, bill shape, eye color, and other details that would normally be missed in a whir of activity.

Brief observations can be made while you go about your everyday activities, but it is worth putting aside some time for "serious" garden birdwatching. Leave a pair of binoculars by the window, ready to be used when an unexpected bird turns up or something unusual happens,

or leave your telescope permanently trained on a busy birdfeeder. When observing from within your house, try standing further back in the room; wary species, such as crows, hawks, and herons, can be scared off by the slightest movement.

Learning how to identify birds is a goal in itself (see pages 77–78), but even in this limited space, it is possible to see 100 or more species, especially during migration season. To record the details of bird behavior, record behavior throughout the day, and over the year. Investigating birds' private lives and noting changes in activity over time

The backyard *is an ideal place for watching birds at close range, allowing for careful study of plumage and everyday behavior.*

Spotting scopes *permit closeup views of familiar birds. Even the most common birds can provide stunning views when magnified 20 or more times.*

A garden shed *or ice-fishing tent makes a convenient bird blind to allow observation in remote corners of the backyard.*

Ornithologists *use colored bird bands to readily identify individual birds.*

provides a fascinating dimension to birdwatching, and a means of understanding your backyard as a wildlife habitat.

Studying bird behavior is not simply about observing what is happening. Ask yourself—"how" and "why?" You may, for example, see a bird taking food from a feeder for the first time. It could be a blackbird or a towhee (both of which normally feed on the ground) or perhaps a new visitor to the garden such as a nuthatch or woodpecker. Note how it manages the new technique. Does it struggle to cling to the feeder with much flapping of wings, or is it naturally acrobatic—like a chickadee?

Understanding why a bird behaves in a certain way is more difficult. We can only describe behavior and infer functions as carefully as possible. For example, on sunny days robins may spread their wings on the ground, a behavior called "sunbathing" (see page 90). Likewise, crows and jays may sit on ant hills and let the ants swarm over them, a behavior called "anting" (see page 91). Both behaviors probably help to control parasites, or perhaps they just bring pleasure to the birds in ways we can only imagine.

KEEPING A DISTANCE
The basic rule of birdwatching is that the welfare of the birds comes first. Birds cope with everyday disturbances in the garden, but it is tempting to try to get too close to identify a rare species, or move vegetation to peer into a bird's nest. The sitting parent may be driven off, but even if it sits tight, the disturbance may attract predators. It may be necessary to avoid part of the garden until young birds leave the nest.

Identifying individuals
To study behavior over time, it helps to be able to identify individual birds in the garden. They can sometimes be distinguished by details of plumage, anatomy, or chance damage. This way, the dynamics of a group can be examined, as well as breeding behavior of individual birds throughout the year. Professional ornithologists often identify individuals by attaching numbered metal or colored plastic bands to their legs. Handling and banding birds requires a special permit, but you may well find bands on dead or injured birds. If you do, send the number and details to a bird-banding laboratory; you will find details on the band. You will then receive a history of the bird, saying when and where it was ringed.

BIRD DETECTIVES
Diligent birdwatchers habitually examine the ground as well as the skies. Birds leave many traces that reveal something about their habits and their identities. Examining traces helps to build up a natural history of backyard birds.

Feathers *may be molted or lost during an attack. Molted feathers typically show wear on the vane. If lost in an attack, feathers may show damage.*

Footprints *in the snow or on mud reflect a bird's gait, revealing if the bird was walking or hopping. They may also suggest behavior such as feeding.*

A post *covered with droppings is likely a regular perch. It may be used as a song-post or a roost. Train your scope on the post, and wait for a visitor.*

An acorn *or spruce cone lodged in a tree crevice is usually a sign of bird activity. Cones and nuts are wedged before being hammered open by birds.*

Plucking posts *are perches where birds of prey pluck and dismember their catch. They are worth checking regularly for recent activity.*

Birdsong and calls *are important clues to a bird's identity, especially when it is hidden. Use a tape recorder to capture the sounds and assist your memory. A CD recording of common birdsong is a good investment for learning bird songs. DVD / CD-ROM products provide visuals as well.*

Take notes *of what you see and hear as soon as possible. Do not trust your memory. A daily written record, organized by date, is useful, allowing comparative observations at different times and places.*

Making records

To be of value, observations must be recorded. Use a notebook to write down numbers of birds seen, what they were doing, details of plumage, and other identification tips.

Descriptions of a bird's appearance and sound in your own words are invaluable, because they will mean far more to you than the generic descriptions given in bird books. Wherever possible, use annotated sketches to record characteristics (see below). It does not matter if you cannot draw well. Work fast, and try to make several sketches before the bird disappears from view. Remember that the size and shape of the bird and the relative sizes of its body parts can

be as important as colors, but try also to jot down the colors of the legs, bill, and any stripes, especially on the breast, wings, and around the eyes.

A bird's songs and calls are also characteristic, but harder to record than physical attributes. Descriptions in your notebook like "a high-pitched, clear warble" may not mean much on re-reading, but paraphrases like "*tuey*" or "*tsk-tsk-tsk*" may paint a better picture of the sound. Songs and calls are easiest to remember if they fit phrases such

HOW TO SKETCH BIRDS

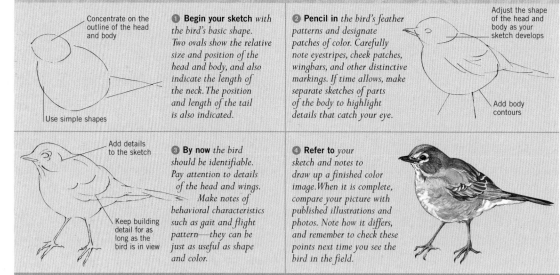

Concentrate on the outline of the head and body

Use simple shapes

1 Begin your sketch *with the bird's basic shape. Two ovals show the relative size and position of the head and body, and also indicate the length of the neck. The position and length of the tail is also indicated.*

2 Pencil in *the bird's feather patterns and designate patches of color. Carefully note eyestripes, cheek patches, wingbars, and other distinctive markings. If time allows, make separate sketches of parts of the body to highlight details that catch your eye.*

Adjust the shape of the head and body as your sketch develops

Add body contours

Add details to the sketch

Keep building detail for as long as the bird is in view

3 By now *the bird should be identifiable. Pay attention to details of the head and wings. Make notes of behavioral characteristics such as gait and flight pattern—they can be just as useful as shape and color.*

4 Refer to *your sketch and notes to draw up a finished color image. When it is complete, compare your picture with published illustrations and photos. Note how it differs, and remember to check these points next time you see the bird in the field.*

as "*teacher-teacher-teacher*" for the Ovenbird or "*peter-peter*" for the Tufted Titmouse. The combination of birdsong with habitat, range, and time of year will help to identify birds by the process of elimination.

Analyzing records

Bird lists are the simplest records. These may be lists of species seen in the yard, state/province, or country. The possibilities are endless. Lists can be interesting in themselves, but are more valuable if you can compare them week by week, because it becomes possible to analyze what is happening on your property or other area of interest. You can answer questions like: do some birds appear at certain times of year? Do robin food preferences change from spring to fall? Did the first Field Sparrow arrive before the departure of the last American Tree Sparrow? Do birds arrive on the same day each year? Is it an early or late spring based on bird arrival times? This could even have the practical benefit of predicting frost dates for gardens.

If you keep a thorough account of the numbers of birds in the garden, you may be able to detect subtle changes in bird populations, for example, the arrival of immigrant sparrows and thrushes that boost the local population. You will also be able to record occurrences of rare migrants that will be of interest to neighbors and perhaps worthy of posting on a rare bird alert website or phone listing.

Some birdwatchers simply keep their observations in the original notebooks, but transcribing notes into a permanent diary allows you to organize and analyze data in more detail. If you are thinking of making ongoing records, an inexpensive database program for your computer is definitely a worthwhile investment.

Species Accounts are a more detailed method for making field records. Using this method, each species has a different section in a loose-leaf notebook. Soon after returning home from a field trip, copy over individual comments about the behavior of a species from your field notes, adding these by date on the same page as other observations for the species. Many birders also keep a daily journal of their observations, organized by date through the year, and this is the place to record locations, the weather, and highlights of particular species. These techniques result in more accurate field records. Data collected by citizen scientists is a vital way of monitoring changes in population status of most North American birds. To learn more, visit www.birdsource.org.

A systematic watch *on a feeder may show that some birds prefer to feed at particular times of the day or feed in flocks. For example, a hundred or more Mountain Bluebirds may flock together during winter.*

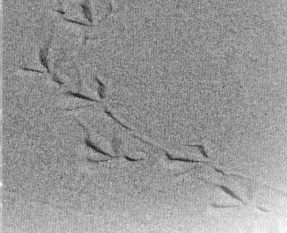

other birds assist the parents. When the eggs have hatched, record the number of visits made by each parent to the nest—which one brings the most food? You could try to correlate breeding success with temperature and rainfall; form your own hypotheses, and use bird records from previous years to test your ideas.

Nest investigations

In late fall, when birds have departed nesting territories, it is possible to examine nests without causing a disturbance. Try to identify the building materials used and look for differences in construction between species. The nest of a robin, for example, is distinguished from that of a phoebe by the mossy exterior added to the phoebe's nest. When nests are vacated, look to see if you can find addled eggs or dead nestlings, piles of berries hoarded by mice, or bumblebee nests. To avoid infection, wear protective gloves and avoid inhaling dust from the nest material.

Ecological experiments

If observing and recording bird activity stimulates your interest in natural history, try devising a few simple methods of observation. When you next see a nuthatch or creeper searching for food in the rough bark of a tree trunk, use a magnifying glass to see if you can find what it was eating.

If a jay is flying off with whole peanuts from a feeder, see if you can find where it is hiding them. And keep a watch on blackbirds, crows, and robins to find out where they roost at night (the position of communal roosts is often revealed by tell-tale accumulations of droppings).

Nesting is perhaps the most interesting and varied behavior to observe and study in the backyard. Try to see if it is the male or female parent that builds the nest and incubates the eggs. Perhaps the duties are split, or maybe

Taking part

Systematic, year-round recording of garden birds becomes even more interesting if it is linked with local or national surveys conducted by wildlife organizations. In North America, the Christmas Bird Count is the longest standing citizen–scientist program. Each year thousands of birders

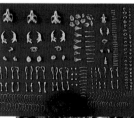

Owl pellets *(below) accumulate under owl perches. Careful dissection of the pellets (left) reveals what the owl has eaten. Skulls of small mammals and birds are easy to identify but there may also be hard parts of insects' bodies.*

Plant life *can give valuable clues about bird activity. If birds perch regularly on a fence, they deposit seeds of their favorite food plants in their droppings. These may germinate to produce a natural and unique hedge or weed patch.*

Counting the birds *visiting your backyard each day will reveal unexpected fluctuations in numbers. For birds that feed in large flocks, such as starlings, a hand counter is a useful tool.*

THE GREAT BACKYARD BIRD COUNT

Every year, during the third week of February, the National Audubon Society and the Cornell Laboratory of Ornithology sponsor the Great Backyard Bird Count. In 2004, counts came in from an incredible 42,509 observers. The count showed that nationwide, Canadian Geese are the most numerous backyard birds, followed by European Starlings, American Goldfinches, and Red-winged Blackbirds. The most widespread backyard birds are Mourning Doves (below), which were recorded by 55 percent of observers, followed by Northern Cardinals, reported from 54 percent of backyards. Because the birds have been counted using the same methods since 1999, it is possible to see changes in their abundance. To learn more about the Great Backyard Bird Count and how you can participate, visit: www.birdsource.org/gbbc.

count birds in a systematic way and contribute their data to the National Audubon Society for analysis. The data are used to identify species with declining populations and devise conservation plans. For information on this and other Audubon citizen–science projects visit: www.audubon.org. The Cornell Laboratory of Ornithology also has many citizen-science programs. To learn about these, visit: www.birds.cornell.edu.

BIRD TIMETABLES

Recording the timing of annual events in a bird's life can reveal unexpected influences on its behavior. For example, global warming can be detected by the earlier arrival of spring migrants and changes in the distributions of birds. Several types of birds that fly north to Michigan during spring now arrive two or three weeks earlier than in 1960. Scientists at the British Trust for Ornithology have found that 20 of 65 species of birds lay their eggs an average of nine days earlier today than in 1971. The earlier nesting appears to result in part because plants are flowering and growing leaves sooner, causing earlier availability of insects.

First seen April 10	First visit to nest site May 2	Collecting nest material May 16	Feeding young June 21	Premigration flocks September 5

April	May	June	July	August	September

Equipment

ALTHOUGH IT IS OFTEN POSSIBLE to get great views of birds with the naked eye, binoculars greatly increase the pleasure of birdwatching, and spotting scopes bring birds even closer. These tools greatly aid behavior watching and provide views of fine anatomical details. It is also possible to take remarkably intimate photographs of garden birds with basic equipment.

Adjusting your *eyepiece settings according to the manufacturer's instructions ensures the crispest image.*

Choosing binoculars

Binoculars are an essential tool, especially for serious birdwatchers. Binoculars come in a bewildering variety of shapes and sizes. Generally, larger models give greater magnification, but magnifying power is not the only factor to bear in mind when choosing a pair. Also consider image brightness, quality, ease of use, and, of course, price. Birdwatching festivals, birding classes, and specialty shops are good places to test equipment in the field before parting with your cash.

Comfort and magnification

The key specifications of a pair of binoculars are given by a pair of numbers etched into the binocular housing, for example, 10x40 or 8x32. The first number is the magnification, indicating how many times larger an object will appear when viewed; the second is the diameter of the objective lens—a measure of brightness as larger diameters provide brighter images. Ranges of 7x35 to 10x50 are

Binoculars for use *in the garden should have a short minimum focus for close-up views of birds and butterflies. Check the closest focus before buying—models vary considerably.*

TYPES OF BINOCULARS

All binoculars use reflective prisms to extend the path of light, while retaining a compact body. There are two basic designs: roof prism (right) and the simpler, and cheaper porro prism (see below). Each design has its advantages.

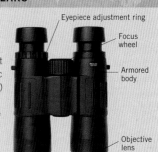

Eyepiece adjustment ring
Focus wheel
Armored body
Objective lens

Traditional-style binoculars *use a porro prism design. This simple optical arrangement is rugged and offers great value to the beginner. The widely separated objective lenses help to produce an excellent three-dimensional image.*

Waterproof optics, *a rubber-clad body, and retractable eyecups give these porro prism binoculars good all-weather performance. The lenses are made of low-dispersion glass to maintain color accuracy. Coatings on the lenses minimize internal reflections.*

Compact models, *such as this 8x23 porro prism design, are highly portable and ergonomically designed for maximum comfort when held in one hand. The small objective lens, however, limits the brightness of the image.*

Roof prism *binoculars have a straight body. They are slender and compact, but the prism is more complicated than in porro prism binoculars, so the glass and manufacturing need to be of a higher quality, reflected in their higher price.*

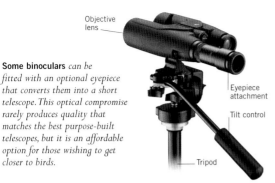

Some binoculars *can be fitted with an optional eyepiece that converts them into a short telescope. This optical compromise rarely produces quality that matches the best purpose-built telescopes, but it is an affordable option for those wishing to get closer to birds.*

Objective lens

Eyepiece attachment

Tilt control

Tripod

commonly used for birding. Larger numbers may seem appealing, but greater magnifications may be difficult to hold steady and field of view decreases. Also, as the objective lens increases, the binoculars become much heavier. This is very important, as you will have them around your neck for hours. Special harnesses that distribute the weight over the shoulder can help, but if binoculars are too heavy, they may be left behind. When choosing binoculars, bear in mind that the focus wheel will be in constant use; you should be able to turn it effortlessly with just a fingertip, without having to move your whole hand.

How to use binoculars

Song or other vocalizations are often the first clue that a bird is present. To increase your success at locating birds, it sometimes helps to cup hands to ears to determine where

The slightest jolt *is magnified by binoculars. Leaning against a solid object, such as a tree or wall, helps to stabilize the image.*

BINOCULARS AND GLASSES

People who wear eyeglasses often find that viewing through binoculars results in a poor image. This is because the eye is too far from the binocular eyepiece and light can enter from the side. A raised finger or thumb helps block out this stray light, but the edges of the image may still appear blurred or dark. To avoid this problem, purchase binoculars with eyepieces that are adjustable for eyeglass wearers.

Normal eyesight   Adjusted for eyeglasses

song is the loudest. Once you detect a gentle movement, it is time to carefully lift your binoculars. The secret of keeping the bird in sight is to face the bird, keeping your head and body still. With eyes locked on the bird and without moving your head, lift the binoculars to your eyes. You should find that you are looking straight at the bird.

This approach works much better than searching the general vicinity of activity, hoping to spot the bird randomly. For extra stability, wedge a finger against your forehead, or your thumb against your chin, or rest your arms against a window ledge or tree branch.

When walking outside, carry your binoculars on a strap around your neck, where they will be ready for action at all times. Clean the eyepieces as needed, taking care to blow off sand, or use a soft brush first before wiping with lens tissue. When leaving a cool room to go out into warmer weather, leave the binoculars in their case a few minutes before you need them. This reduces the degree of fogging that occurs as water condenses on the cold lenses.

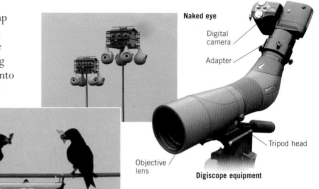

Naked eye
Digital camera
Adapter
Tripod head
Objective lens

Digiscope equipment

Scopes and tripods

Spotting scopes are low-power telescopes ideal for watching birds. They are usually used for looking at birds in open country, especially those at greater distances such as hawks and shorebirds. They are, however, also ideal for seeing the fine detail of birds at closer range.

Digiscope view

Digiscoping gives amateurs equipped with a scope and a digital camera magnifications of up to 100x. Certain models are more suited to digiscoping than others; check on the Internet for the most up-to-date advice.

Most birdwatcher models provide a magnification of about 22x or more. The downside of larger magnifications is that greater power results in more exaggerated vibrations caused by shaking hands. Therefore, telescopes should be firmly supported on a tripod, beanbag, or window clamp.

Many telescopes have a fixed focal length, but those with zoom lenses provide greater flexibility. As with binoculars, the brightness of the image depends, in part, on the diameter of the objective lens. When making a selection, it becomes necessary to balance light intake with bulk. Fluorite lenses, designated fluorite or ED, greatly increase image brightness, but add significantly to cost.

Spotting scopes may be fitted with straight or angled eyepieces; the former are easier and more intuitive to "aim" at a distant bird. Angled telescopes offer other advantages: they are far more comfortable to use when mounted on

All scopes come equipped with a screw bracket that allows them to be fixed to a standard camera tripod. Angled scopes are more comfortable for low-level viewing. This position gives the greatest stability.

a tripod, especially when keeping low to the ground; and the view of a bird is easier to share between people of different heights.

Observing with a spotting scope

Getting the most from a telescope takes a little practice. Lining it up with a bird presents the first challenge due to its inherent narrow angle of view. The most effective technique is to look along the casing of the telescope to roughly align it with the bird, and only then to bring your eye to the eyepiece.

Always keep your eye directly in line with the eyepiece; if it is off-center, the image you see will be vignetted or in soft focus. (Maintaining a direct line is harder than it sounds, especially if using a straight telescope fixed to a tripod.) Also, try viewing through your telescope while keeping both eyes open; not only will this ease eye strain but you will be aware of other birds as they enter your peripheral field of vision.

MAGNIFICATION

Binoculars and telescopes magnify the image that you see with the naked eye, but will not improve the image on a dull or misty day. A standard pair of binoculars may magnify the image by eight times, while a telescope gives a far higher magnification of 30x or more. Magnifications that are too high will result in a blurred image unless the telescope can be held very steady.

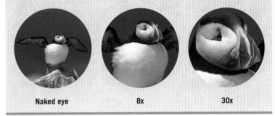

Naked eye   **8x**   **30x**

Digiscoping

The widespread use of digital cameras and digital video cameras in recent years has put still higher magnifying power in the hands of the telescope user. By attaching the zoom lens of a digital camera to the eyepiece of a telescope (see opposite), it is possible to achieve magnifications equivalent to those produced by a (very costly and cumbersome) 3,000mm lens on a conventional 35mm camera. The high-quality images produced by this technique, known as digiscoping, can be viewed and edited quickly, so adding a new dimension to birdwatching.

CHOOSING TELESCOPES AND ACCESSORIES

Most birdwatchers favor angled, compact telescopes (right) over straight models. They do, however, take a little getting used to, because you do not look straight at the bird.

Objective lens   Eyepiece

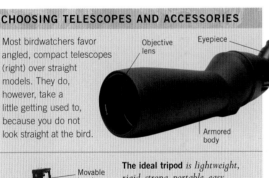

Armored body

Movable head

Telescoping leg sections

Rubber feet for grip on smooth surfaces

The ideal tripod *is lightweight, rigid, strong, portable, easy to set up, and tall enough for comfortable viewing. It has a "fluid head," that allows smooth movement with one control.*

Most telescopes *have changeable eyepieces. Wide-angled eyepieces of 20x to 30x are good for general use; 40x eyepieces are good for long-distance work, and zoom eyepieces give more versatility.*

Standard 30x eyepiece   Zoom eyepiece

A clamp is especially useful *for a permanent position in a hide or other observation point. The telescope can be mounted quickly when needed in a hurry and the clamp provides a very firm base.*

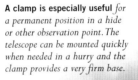

Setting the shutter *to a high speed (1/250 second or more) reduces the effects of camera shake, which can be very noticeable when using a long lens. High shutter speeds also help to "freeze" the motion of birds in flight.*

Changing the aperture *(the diameter of the metal-bladed iris within the camera lens) affects the amount of light reaching the film. In tandem with shutter speed, setting the aperture gives control over exposure.*

A flashgun *can illuminate a subject in low light or complete darkness, but is just as useful in daylight, when it can light birds in deep shade, or create more pleasing effects when used to "fill in" dense shadows.*

Even equipped *with a long telephoto lens, you will need to get within a few yards of a bird to get a frame-filling shot. This will tax your field skills far more than everyday birdwatching. Sit-and-wait tactics and bird blinds will help.*

Exposure controls and autofocus controls

A camera records an image when light, focused by the lens, falls on to a film (or a CCD, the digital equivalent of film). The amount of light reaching the film must be carefully controlled to achieve the correct exposure; too much light results in pale, washed-out pictures (overexposure); too little light produces dark, muddy images (underexposure). Many people are content to set their camera to automatic or "program" mode and allow its onboard computer to sort out exposure and focus. In most situations this produces acceptable results, but understanding the effects of different exposure

Photographing birds

Bird photography can become a compelling pastime, though it requires time, patience, and investment to achieve the best results. The key to capturing outstanding bird images is getting close. For this, you will need a telephoto lens (sometimes called a "long" lens), and a camera to which it can be fixed, or a digital camera with a long zoom range. From the many film camera formats available, most bird photographers choose 35mm SLR cameras. "35mm" refers to the size of the film used in the camera, while "SLR" stands for Single Lens Reflex – meaning that you view the scene and take the photograph through one lens. What you see in the viewfinder is (more or less) what appears in your photograph. SLR cameras are convenient because they have interchangeable lenses, so one camera body can take both wide-angle and telephoto pictures. Telephoto lenses favored by bird photographers have focal lengths of 300–600mm (giving angles of view of 6° and 3°). They are capable of recording high-quality frame-filling images of birds; however, they are not only costly, but heavy and bulky.

For the photographic novice, a digital camera may be a better choice. The images it produces are visible immediately, and, with no need for film and processing, its operating costs are much lower. Basic digital cameras may cost more than their film equivalents, but they provide greater magnifying power for the price.

FILM CAMERAS

35mm Single Lens Reflex cameras offer the best compromise between portability, affordability, and quality. Invest in a good long lens with a focal length of 300–500mm or a "long" zoom lens.

Camera body

Shutter release

Autofocus lens

Wide-angle lens

Zoom lens

A 24mm *wide-angle lens and a medium-range zoom— say 70-210mm, plus a long telephoto will cover most photographic situations.*

Pan and tilt head

Telescopic legs

A tripod *is essential for preventing camera shake when using a long lens. Buy the heaviest and sturdiest that you can bear to carry.*

Birds will approach *a fixed observation blind, like this converted shed, to visit feeders. Mount your camera on a sturdy tripod—and wait.*

settings on your camera will help you make more creative images. Even if you own a fully automatic camera, it is worth occasionally setting it to "manual" mode and experimenting with the exposure settings for yourself. Some autofocus lenses are good for catching birds in flight, but can be annoying at other times as objects in the foreground easily confuse them.

Making light work

Most photographs of birds are taken in natural daylight, but it is worth assessing the "quality" of the light before pressing the shutter. For example, diffuse sunlight, filtered through thin clouds or patchy leaves, is ideal for capturing a naturalistic portrait of a bird. Morning and evening light illuminates a bird from the side, adding interest (and a golden color cast) to your pictures, while overhead light

A zoom lens on a digital camera may magnify an object 3x with optical zoom, while the digital zoom capability adds another 4x magnification. However, digital zoom greatly decreases quality.

in the middle of the day tends to be less flattering. Direct sunlight produces dense shadows that can appear as ugly "black holes" in a photograph; firing a flash set to a low power can help "fill in" these shadows to produce a more balanced image. Flash can also help to "freeze" a bird in motion.

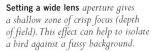

Setting a slower shutter speed *allows a bird's movement to "paint" the scene. Used creatively, blur gives atmosphere to an otherwise ordinary image.*

Setting a wide lens *aperture gives a shallow zone of crisp focus (depth of field). This effect can help to isolate a bird against a fussy background.*

The burst of light *from a flash lasts as little as one ten-thousandth of a second. It freezes the fastest action and allows every feather to be seen in sharp relief.*

Understanding bird behavior

Your backyard is an ideal place to observe bird behavior. Birds visit every day, engaging in activities that vary throughout the year. Keeping a close watch on these visitors reveals the complexities of their behavior and the reasons for their sometimes surprising actions.

Barn Swallows

The daily round

BIRDS ARE MOST NOTICEABLE when they are active: feeding, flying, singing, displaying, or fighting. They are especially visible in spring and summer when they set up territories, find mates, build nests, and tend their broods. Preening and bathing occur throughout the year and occupy much of a bird's time, as does resting.

Cycles of activity

During a normal day outside the breeding season, a bird has two main activities: it has to feed, which it does in bouts through the day, and it must maintain its feathers in good condition by preening and bathing.

The first meal of a bird's day is particularly important because it helps replace the fat used up through the night to keep warm. However, a watch of birdfeeders shows that birds are not in a hurry to start feeding at the very earliest hours of daylight. They may gather in nearby trees to preen and sing, but do not begin to feed until it is fully light. Perhaps they cannot see well enough in the dim morning light to detect approaching predators, or locate food effectively.

Birds do not all become active at the same times. Robins and blackbirds, for example, are early risers, and are usually the last to disappear as dusk gathers, while gulls and starlings leave gardens and parks early in the afternoon

Birds preen and sing in the early light of dawn. Here, a Florida Scrub Jay uses its beak to preen the feathers under its wing following a bath.

A Gray Catbird *sings to defend its territory and is a member of the dawn chorus. A few minutes after waking up, it flies to a perch and sings for at least an hour.*

Foraging is an activity *that takes up a large part of a Northern Mockingbird's day. It does not feed continuously, but retires after each meal to rest on a perch or take part in other activities, such as preening, between bouts of eating.*

A Winter Wren sunbathes *with it wings spread and body feathers raised to allow the sun's rays to penetrate. Sunbathing not only warms the body on a cold day, but is also thought to help with feather care.*

to return to their roosts when it is still light. In developed areas that are illuminated by street and security lighting, birds may sing and sometimes even feed through the night. House Sparrows, for instance, may extend their day by catching moths attracted to streetlights.

Times of stress

A bird loses its free time twice during the year: once during the breeding season, when it struggles to feed its chicks and rear them to independence, and again in the winter, when its own survival becomes a struggle. Not only are there fewer daylight hours in the winter, but food is often in short supply and harder to find, and extra rations are needed just to maintain body temperature in cold weather. As a result, small birds may have to spend most (if not all) of their daylight hours looking for food.

Keeping clean

When not feeding, birds devote much of their time to keeping their feathers in top condition. Air trapped between the feathers gives them their insulating and waterproofing qualities; when feathers are damaged, insulation and waterproofing are impaired, and flight becomes more strenuous. The barbs that hold the feather vanes together become "unzipped" by daily wear and tear, and the bird must zip them back up using its bill. Preening consists of gently nibbling or stroking the feathers one at a time with the closed bill so that splits between the barbs are zipped. Nibbling and rubbing also removes dirt and parasites (such as feather lice and mites), and arranges feathers back into

This chart shows *how a male Red-breasted Nuthatch spends a spring day. Nearly two-thirds of its time is spent looking for food. At this time of year, it also has to patrol its territory, singing and driving off other males.*

- Resting
- Singing
- Foraging
- Other
- Aggressive encounters
- Flying
- Preening

position. At intervals during preening, the bird squeezes its bill against the preen gland at the base of its tail to collect preen oil, which he spreads in a thin film over the feathers; the oil is believed to kill bacteria and fungi.

Birds dislodge external parasites from their bodies by bathing; most will ruffle their feathers in a convenient pond or puddle, but some indulge in dust baths or even "bathe" in the smoke from a chimney or fire. Many birds occasionally indulge in "anting." They either allow ants to crawl through their feathers, or they hold ants in the bill and rub them in their feathers. The function of anting is unknown, but the formic acid from the ants' bodies may kill parasites.

This Black-headed Grosbeak *bathes in a garden pond, but a gutter or puddle will often do. After its bath, it will fly to a safe perch and ruffle its feathers to settle them into place.*

Like other birds, *Barn Swallows set aside time every day for a thorough, systematic preen, which keeps the plumage clean and tidy. The bill— in conjunction with scratching and fluffing movements—is used to arrange the feathers.*

Outside the nesting season, *Starlings gather in the afternoon before flying in flocks to roosts where they spend the night. They also have smaller day roosts where they preen between periods of foraging.*

Annual cycle: spring

LIFE RETURNS TO THE BACKYARD as the days get longer and warmer. Spring bulbs and other plants provide nectar to feed the first insects—welcome meals for early returning migrants. Food can be scarce, so birds often have to be resourceful about finding it. The increased volume of song signals the start of the new breeding season, establishing pair bonds and territorial rights.

Window-fighting occurs most often in spring. A bird will see its reflection in a window and peck at its apparent rival.

Renewed activity

Spring is a time of change and uncertainty for backyard birds. As temperatures rise, spells of frost and even snow can threaten many species, especially insect-eating birds such as tanagers and thrushes. Late frosts can also kill flower buds and leaves, damaging fruit crops and exposing nests to gales, predators, and rain. Extreme weather can chill eggs and flood young in open, cup-shaped nests. Even nestlings in nest boxes are not immune; their parents try to keep them warm by brooding for longer spells, even though they need to spend more time foraging for food for themselves. Species furthest north often use feathers and even fur to line their nests. If the weather is poor, swallows will hunt over lakes and rivers where early insects congregate, and form nesting colonies only when the weather has improved.

Some resident birds such as chickadees, nuthatches, and titmice that visited winter feeding stations begin to return to nearby natural habitats. The timing for nesting depends largely on the availability of food, especially insects and other invertebrates, which are full of the proteins necessary for rapid development of feathers and muscles in nestlings.

Throughout spring, birds are increasingly seen in pairs, arguing over territorial boundaries or in courtship. Songs and calls are used to deter rivals and establish pair-bonds, and it is the best time of year to hear the dawn chorus when birds reassert their territorial rights.

Birds come into breeding condition as the days lengthen, although the exact timing of egg-laying is influenced by temperature and food.

Birds come into breeding condition based on length of day and temperature. Here, a female American Redstart removes a fecal sac from a chick, a behavior that helps keep the nest clean.

WINDS OF CHANGE
Several North American warblers winter in southern states. Like other migratory species, the timing of their migration depends on weather conditions, especially wind. Spring migrants rely on strong southerly air and they wait for these winds to commence migration. Gale force winds, however, can devastate flocks during migration.

Willow Warbler

Male Indigo Buntings *return from their tropical winter homes in mid-spring, often showing up in backyards. They may visit feeders soon after the migration.*

A few Yellow-rumped Warblers *winter in northern states and provinces, eating berries of poison ivy, bayberry, and sumac, but more migrant birds appear in the spring, arriving from their wintering grounds.*

Territorial displays *are common in spring, but aggression soon subsides so that the birds can devote time to rearing their families.*

Cedar Waxwings *live in flocks for most of the year, but by late spring they begin pairing off for the nesting season. Only adults have the red, waxy tips to wing feathers that give waxwings their name.*

Male Yellow Warblers *and other songbirds spend much of their time singing to defend their territory and to attract a mate. Males looking for a mate sometimes have different songs than those with mates.*

93

Annual cycle: summer

SUMMER IS THE CLIMAX TO THE NESTING SEASON. Bluebirds are busy raising their second brood, while late-nesting birds such as Cedar Waxwings and American Goldfinches are beginning to build nests and lay eggs. Although insect and seed foods are plentiful, summer can be just as hard as winter. Heat, drought, and unseasonal weather can kill young birds and affect the ability of their parents to recover from the stresses of rearing young.

Female Red-winged Blackbirds *supply most of the food for nestings, providing a diet comprised mostly of insects.*

Times of plenty

A few late migrants such as the Blackpoll Warbler may linger at the start of summer, but the garden now becomes the preserve of breeding populations. Fresh foliage supports hordes of insects, spiders, and other invertebrates that most birds need to rear their young. In early summer, lawns are a good hunting ground for robins, but drier summer days result in earthworms retreating deeper into the soil. If left uncut, the lawn soon becomes dotted with dandelions and clover, attracting pollinating insects and providing seeds.

Bird families are a common sight in summer, when parents bring their broods off the nest and continue to feed them until they learn to survive on their own. Young birds,

which can usually be recognized by their shorter wings and tails and high-pitched calls, may gather in conspicuous flocks. Starlings fly in tight formation and settle noisily in trees, and mixed flocks of chickadees and titmice work their way through trees by late summer, often accompanied by nuthatches and Brown Creepers. Travelling in numbers gives these inexperienced birds greater safety from predators and a better chance of finding food.

As nesting comes to an end in the latter half of summer, the garden goes strangely quiet. Their work done, some birds will retire to the shelter of the undergrowth as they complete their summer molt, before reappearing later with fresh winter plumage.

Nesting is timed *so that young birds hatch when food supplies are most abundant. Different strategies have evolved in different species to maximize survival of the young. Bluebirds lay their eggs early in the year, from March onward. Their nestlings are fed on the early summer flush of caterpillars and other insects.*

Great Crested Flycatchers *begin laying later in the season, from May to June. This allows their young to be fed on large insects such as dragonflies that are abundant in midsummer.*

Sharp-shinned Hawks *lay their eggs in late May, but the long incubation period of up to 35 days means that the chicks may not hatch until early summer. By this time, the young of other species have fledged, providing an excellent food resource for the nestling hawks.*

WEATHER WATCH

The fortunes of garden birds are tied to the weather: a heatwave can bake the soil hard, making it difficult for robins to extract earthworms from the ground, but hot, sultry weather is a boon for swallows, martins, swifts, and gulls, which feed on swarming flies and ants. Heavy rain is disastrous for chickadees, which feed their young on caterpillars. The caterpillars are washed off the leaves, so parents are forced to search for other, less suitable, prey. This takes longer so they cannot brood the nestlings to keep them warm in the cool conditions.

Most birds nest *as early in the season as possible. Birds migrating early can claim the best habitat; unseasonable weather can doom these early starts, however, forcing birds to renest.*

Most young birds *are fed by their parents after they have left the nest. The extra food helps them complete their development and learn to feed for themselves. Their noisy begging is a common summer sound.*

A fledgling *Rose-breasted Grosbeak accompanies its parent on the stand of a bird table. While it is still dependent, the fledgling learns where to find food by closely observing its parent in action.*

Prolonged heat *bakes the ground hard and sends worms deeper into the soil, out of range of probing beaks. Water may also become scarce; regularly check the levels of water in birdbaths and scrub them clean.*

The late summer *molt is a time of stress. Usually all flight and body feathers are replaced. Flight is more strenuous and birds invest much energy in growing new feathers.*

95

Annual cycle: fall

FALL IS AN EXCELLENT TIME to observe backyard birds. After their summer molt, many birds sport new plumage, making identification more difficult for some species because winter plumages often lack distinctive plumages necessary for courtship. Fall migrants are passing through, numbers swelled by the recent crops of fledglings. Winter visitors begin to arrive, hard on the heels of departing breeding species.

The size of the fall berry *crop has a significant effect on numbers of visiting birds. Backyards with berry-bearing trees and shrubs, such as hawthorn and dogwoods, attract diverse species in years when natural foods are scarce in the countryside.*

Fall activity

Fall signals the end of the nesting season for most birds, although late-nesting species such as goldfinch and waxwings may have broods well into September. Goldfinches may delay their breeding to late summer and fall because of the importance of thistle seed, a favorite food that is also used as a nest lining. Likewise, Mourning Doves and Rock Pigeons may have late broods, feeding their young on "pigeon's milk" (see page 133).

For most species, fall is a time dominated by migration. In this season, the diet of most insect-eating birds such as warblers, vireos, tanagers, and thrushes expands to include fruits rich in lipids. Flowering dogwood, spicebush, and sassafras are among the many plants that rely on birds to distribute their seeds. Many plants contain high proportions of lipids in the fruits surrounding the seeds. These act as an enticement for birds to consume the fruit. Lipids are stored as fat deposits on the keel of the breast and under the wings and back. These fuel reserves can amount to 25–50 percent of a bird's body weight. Such reserves provide energy for flights of hundreds of miles without stopping.

Food balance

When natural food is plentiful in woods and hedgerows, relatively few birds visit backyard gardens. Beech mast and acorns attract titmice, nuthatches, and woodpeckers; conifer seeds feed crossbills, siskins, and woodpeckers. Bluebirds, robins, and other thrushes feed mostly on berries at this season. Likewise, sparrows and even flycatchers shift their diet to include the fruit of vines such as Virginia creeper and poison ivy.

Many trees, especially oaks and conifers, usually produce good crops of seeds or berries in alternate years and this affects the pattern of bird visits to the garden. In lean years, gardens fill with birds, and feeders need to be replenished frequently to keep up with demand.

Fall provides birdwatchers with a great diversity of species to observe, as populations of nesting species and winter visitors change over. Most small birds migrate at night, so vigilant birders should use their ears to listen for migrants. Many species such as thrushes have distinct night flight calls. Post-breeding dispersals of southern species such as Blue Grosbeaks and Yellow-breasted Chats wander northward in the fall before heading to southern climates for the winter. Also, watch the sky for large birds such as eagles, cranes, and geese that migrate during daylight, especially in northerly winds.

In fall, *American Robins feed largely on fruit such as crabapples and hawthorn. At this season, even warblers, vireos, and flycatchers eat lipid-rich fruit to build fat reserves for migration.*

Swallows *may linger in backyards well into the fall, waiting for shorter days and a north wind to help transport them to southern climates.*

Scarlet Tanagers *are named for the male's spring plumage, but during fall males molt their scarlet plumage for more cryptic greens for the non-breeding season.*

Chestnut-backed Chickadees *return to the garden in fall, having nested in surrounding woodland; groups of 5-10 flock and roost together throughout winter. These flocks disperse the following spring.*

Bird song, *such at that of the Wood-thrush, is largely absent in the fall, but the calls of night migrants are distinct, especially on clear nights when migration is particularly common.*

Birds such *as the Bohemian Waxwing consume most fruit with a high fat content by mid-fall, leaving low-fat fruits such as rosehips, hawthorn, and crabapples until winter and spring.*

Annual cycle: winter

WINTER IS A DIFFICULT SEASON for many backyard birds. Long
nights, extreme temperatures, and accumulated snow force most
birds to migrate to milder climates to find food, many retreating just
south of persistent snow cover, ready to return north as soon as possible.
Locally, extreme winter weather brings resident species such as chickadees
and woodpeckers out of the woods and into backyards where they visit feeders.

Cold and mortality

Short winter days mean that foraging time is drastically cut,
and small birds have to spend almost all of their waking hours
searching for food. Low temperatures do not in themselves
endanger birds, as long as birds have a good supply of food
and enough shelter in dense shrubs and conifers. When
supplies of food run short, and coverings of ice and snow make
finding food difficult, mortality rates of all birds, from wrens
to herons, can soar. This is one of the best times to attract
large numbers of birds to garden feeders. Feeder birds are
typically the most common species, but some unexpected
visitors may turn up, especially in winter when finches from
the far north such as Pine Siskins, crossbills, and redpolls
venture into gardens. Crabapples are especially attractive at
this season, providing food for Pine Grosbeaks and waxwings.

A slow change comes over some
birds during the course of the winter.
After their late summer molt (see page 95),
birds reappear with new feathers, often fairly drab non-
breeding plumages. Towards the end of winter, the males of
some species slowly take on their courtship dress. Sometimes
this change occurs from a molt of body feathers—as in the
American Goldfinch, but it may also result from feather wear.
For example, male House Sparrows develop their black bib
by wearing off the tips of the drab winter breast feathers,
exposing the jet black base to the feathers. Likewise, starlings
of both sexes lose their star-spangled look of winter by
wearing off the white tips of the feathers. As days increase
in length, some birds obtain brighter colored beaks; for
example, starling beaks change from black to flashy yellow.

Winter crow roosts are organized hierarchically: the more
dominant birds occupy roosts on the leeward side of trees
where they get better protection from icy winds.

RARE NORTHERN MIGRANTS

Persistent winter storms can blow coastal birds, such as the
Atlantic Puffin, far inland, where they can end up stranded
and may even visit backyards. Disorientated and prevented
from feeding (they usually catch small fish, such as sand eels
and herring), their fat reserves soon become depleted, and
the birds are too exhausted to fly. Even with assistance, their
emaciated condition means that they are unlikely to survive.

Air trapped in the feathers is a good insulator. Many birds, like this chickadee, fluff up their feathers in cold weather, giving them a much rounder appearance.

Brown Creepers, along with other small birds, conserve heat by roosting in the shelter of holes and crevices. By roosting in groups, huddling against neighbors, they can cut heat losses by one-third.

Cedar Waxwings feed on crabapple fruit on a snowy day. Berries are an easy and available source of winter food. Some birds, such as robins and mockingbirds, defend favorite trees, chasing off rivals.

The Red-winged Blackbird was once found mainly in freshwater marshes, but it is now common in agricultural fields and backyard feeding stations.

Ice prevents water birds like mallards from feeding and allows predators to reach their roosts. In icy conditions, they often migrate to search for open water, or try to find food on land.

99

Migration

BIRDS ARE ON THE MOVE THROUGHOUT their lives. Every day, they commute between their roosting and feeding grounds, and every year they may move between their summer and winter homes. These seasonal journeys vary in length. Some birds move short distances from a woodland breeding place to a backyard, while others travel thousands of miles across continents and oceans.

Purple Martins are among the champion migrants. They often gather in flocks containing thousands of birds before migrating to their winter home in Brazil, where they also occupy massive roosts, sometimes in large cities.

Incredible journeys

Every spring, we can witness one of earth's greatest wildlife spectacles without leaving our own backyards. Migration watchers eagerly await the southern flows of spring wind that signal the return of migrant birds from their winter in warmer latitudes. Watch for martins, swallows, and swifts darting overhead, for warblers and flycatchers flitting in newly opening foliage, and listen for the first tanager or cuckoo. Then, at the end of summer, these birds slip away again and we watch juncos and redpolls arrive as they escape harsher climates.

Despite the huge expenditure of energy required to travel sometimes hundreds or thousands of miles, migration has clear benefits for many species. These mainly revolve

Robins are winter visitors *in Florida, but head north in the spring to breed, usually to Canada, but they have been known to go as far north as Alaska, and even the Arctic.*

around the need to find good supplies of food. It is wrong, however, to think that they are driven to migrate by hunger. Birds prepare for migration before food runs out, eating more and laying down fat to sustain them throughout their journey. Once ready to fly, they set off when wind and weather are favorable.

Most small birds migrate by night and are not likely to be seen, while larger birds travel by day. Birds leave their breeding grounds in fall in a fairly regular order. Swifts and other birds that rely mainly on a supply of insects depart early, while Tree Swallows manage to linger, eating late insects supplemented by fruit from bayberries and coastal myrtle. A change to a vegetarian diet when insects are in short supply enables some warblers to delay departure for a few weeks and some, such as the Yellow-rumped

Blue Jays are partial migrants. *Some migrate while others are resident all year round. Migrating birds stock up on berries before departure.*

Warbler, may stay in North America for the winter. Most others migrate far to the south. About 200 species, about 35 percent of all North American landbirds, migrate south of the US, mostly to Central America and the Caribbean islands, for the winter.

In spring, birds hurry back to establish territories and make the most of the summer plenty. Swallows spread northwards through North America as temperatures increase, in a steady advance of about 25 miles (40km) per day, unless cold weather or a headwind holds them up.

Birds are sometimes seen when they stop to rest during migration. Many of these transients are common birds, but anything may turn up, especially birds from Latin America and the Arctic. Spring and fall can therefore be exciting times of the year, offering the chance to observe species not usually seen in the backyard. These visitors may stay for a few days to feed, rest, or wait for a tailwind, before they continue on their long journeys. In some winters, there is a sudden invasion of birds known as an "irruption." This dramatic event occurs when the food supply fails in the birds' summer homes. Bohemian Waxwings, for example, irrupt from Canadian forests when crops of mountain ash fail.

Fruit on trees and shrubs is especially important for migrating birds' first return to their breeding habitat, where late winter storms may have created a layer of snow on the ground. Winter-persistent fruit such as crabapples, bayberry, and highbush cranberry are often life-savers for winter-stranded robins, phoebes, and waxwings.

ACCIDENTAL MIGRANTS

Migrating birds sometimes become caught up in storms and get swept off course, appearing thousands of miles from their normal routes. European birds such as Fieldfare caught in storms on their southward journey can find themselves in New England and the Canadian Maritimes.

MIGRATION ROUTES

Rose-breasted Grosbeak

Bobolink

Scarlet Tanager

Scarlet Tanagers *migrate from their wintering grounds in South America to eastern North America. They return to South America in late September.*

Rose-breasted Grosbeaks *perform a remarkable loop migration each year, flying non-stop from Arctic breeding grounds through the Canadian Maritimes, straight through to southeastern South America. In the spring, they migrate inland over the prairies.*

Bobolinks *migrate over land on their northward migration to coniferous forests in Canada and Alaska, but migrate non-stop over open ocean from southeastern Canada and the northeastern United States to their winter home in northern South America.*

Flying

A BIRD'S BODY IS BEAUTIFULLY designed for flight, combining lightness with controlled muscular strength and efficient metabolism. Flight confers the great advantage of speed, but uses large amounts of energy (about 10–15 times as much as walking) so birds must find plenty of food to fuel their activity. Through evolution, the shape of the wings and tail of each species has been matched to a specific lifestyle.

Keeping airborne

Some birds, such as wrens and mallards, must flap their wings continuously to stay in the air, but many others reduce the cost of flight by gliding whenever possible. Economy is more important than speed when searching for food or traveling long distances, so while gulls flap regularly when flying from their roosts to feeding grounds, they glide in slow, energy-saving circles when scanning the ground for food. Likewise, Red-tailed Hawks circle on outstretched wings in thermals (rising air found over farm fields and towns). Birds like chickadees and finches cannot glide well enough to exploit thermals, but save energy by using "bounding" flight, folding their wings between bouts of flapping to reduce drag.

The spread wing *and tail feathers of this starling give maximum aerodynamic control for landing at the nest.*

AIR SPEEDS

Most birds have two, or sometimes three, flight speeds. A bird that normally flies at 19mph (30km/h) may average 25mph (40km/h) on migration and as much as 31mph (50km/h) when evading a predator. The table below gives average flight speeds for several North American species.

Barn Swallow	20mph (32km/h)	Pheasant	34mph (55km/h)
Winter Wren	20mph (32km/h)	Mallard	42mph (68km/h)
European Starling	21mph (34km/h)	White-crowned Sparrow (max)	44mph (71km/h)
Herring Gull	25mph (40km/h)	Peregrine Falcon (stooping)	224mph (360km/h)
Great Blue Heron	27mph (44km/h)	Common Eider	47mph (75km/h)

Take-off and flight control

Like a plane, a bird has to achieve a minimum speed to achieve flight. From a standing start, the wings are swept to and fro to create an airflow over the flight surfaces, as the bird leaps into the air.

Deep wing beats get the bird hovering just clear of the ground for a split second before it lifts away. Larger birds, which cannot generate enough power to hover, employ a different strategy; they drop off a perch, spread their wings, and allow gravity to do the work, or, if on the ground, run a few steps to take off. When landing, the bird has to lose as much speed as possible without tumbling from the air. Small birds slow

Barn Owls have large, *broad, rounded wings that enable them to fly at low speeds with little effort. Their special downy flight feathers result in near-silent flight.*

Ring-necked Pheasants *spend most of their time on the ground. Sometimes they need to fly quickly to escape a predator and catapult straight into the air, powered by short, broad wings. Their muscles are designed for short bursts of speed.*

Hummingbirds, *like this Anna's Hummingbird, regularly hover while foraging for nectar or when feeding their young. Larger birds, such as the American Kestrel, "hover" or remain in place by flying into the wind at a speed equal to that of the wind.*

Large birds, *such as this Great Blue Heron, require huge amounts of energy to take off from the ground. Once in flight, they have a leisurely flight pattern with occasional glides. In flight, recognize herons by the way they retract their neck into their shoulders, with trailing legs and broad, rounded wings.*

down until they are hovering on whirring wings, and then gently touch down.

Larger birds such as hawks and eagles swoop slightly below their intended perch and then climb to lose speed. Alternatively, they land on the ground with a thump and run for a short distance to lose momentum.

A bird's flying style has important but subtle effects on its biology. Swifts and swallows, for example, are similar-shaped birds, but they have very different flight patterns. Swifts hunt for flying insects by circling in the air, alternating bursts of flickering wing beats with long glides. In contrast, swallows often fly near the ground with a less economical, flapping flight. Barn Swallows use their longer tail to aid their nimble maneuvers. This permits them to capture larger and faster insects than swifts do.

Feeding

A BIRD'S ENERGY REQUIREMENTS ARE HIGH, and finding adequate supplies of food is vital for survival. Ample food is the fuel for growth, movement, and keeping warm. In the nesting season, the search for food is particularly intense as males engage in energetic courtship and territorial behavior. Females at this season require extra food to produce and incubate eggs, and sustain both themselves and their young.

Birds are remarkably *quick to discover new feeding opportunities. Robins will sometimes take dried raisins from baskets.*

Bill shape

The size and shape of a bird's bill often gives the best clue to its diet. Crows, starlings, and gulls have "general-purpose" bills that enable them to take a wide variety of foods, but other birds are equipped with specialized bills that enable them to exploit certain types of food with great efficiency. In the finch family, for example, Pine Siskins have slender bills for probing deep into the heads of thistles to extract seeds, while grosbeaks have stout, sharp-edged bills that are effective at plucking buds and crushing and peeling seeds and fruits. Despite these specializations, most birds eat a surprisingly varied diet, using their beaks to eat many kinds of foods throughout the year. For example, woodpeckers and flycatchers use their specialized beaks to eat fat-rich berries, a necessity for building energy reserves for migration and winter survival.

The American Robin *has a general-purpose bill, which suits its highly varied diet.*

The Chickadee's *short bill is perfect for picking tiny insects out of crevices.*

The Chestnut-sided Warbler *uses its long, fine bill for picking up tiny caterpillars.*

The American Goldfinch *manipulates seeds in its conical bill, removing the husks.*

The Mallard's *broad bill is fringed with fine plates that sieve food from water.*

Most birds use *their beaks to obtain a remarkably varied diet. This female Red-winged Blackbird, for example, has collected a beakful of insects for her nestlings, even though she has a seed-eating beak that is well adapted for eating weed seeds.*

The Song Sparrow and Great-crested Flycatcher *feed their young on a high-protein insect diet. Sparrows feed their young on flies and other small insects, while the larger flycatcher can deliver dragonflies.*

The bluebird *adapts its diet to eat foods that are abundant in different seasons. Like most landbirds, it feeds mainly on insects during the spring and summer, changing to fruits, seeds, and nuts from late summer onwards.*

The economics of feeding

Birds usually work to obtain the best nutrition for the least effort, and they will often change their feeding strategy to adapt to changing environmental conditions and time of year. Food that is not used to fuel activity is stored in the body as fat: reserves for times of scarcity, and for energy-intensive activities, such as breeding and migration.

Birds focus their attention on the best-available food at any time, feeding until supplies are exhausted. Most birds that habitually visit feeders eat a wide variety of natural foods. Seeds and invertebrates are the food of choice for many birds because they are rich in carbohydrates, fats and proteins. However, birds that normally rely on these foods may choose

to gorge on fruit when there is a dense, easily gathered crop. The time saved by not having to search for food more than compensates for the lower nutritional value of the fruit.

Most species that winter in northern latitudes store (cache) food during abundant times. This habit rewards them during winter months. Some have remarkable memories for finding food weeks or months later, even when it is covered by up to 18in (45cm) of snow. Clark's Nutcrackers are unusual in that they communally store food. In the fall, flocks of these jay relatives store pine seeds and hazel nuts. The next spring members of the flock share the stored food. Caching is also common among feeder birds, including chickadees, titmice, and nuthatches. Watch carefully for these birds storing individual sunflower seeds.

FEEDING STYLES

The Sharp-shinned Hawk *hunts in the air for smaller birds. Quarry is eaten on the ground or on a stump, with the hawk standing with both feet on its victim, drooping its wings to form a "tent."*

The Canada Goose *is one of few large birds that can survive on nutrient-poor grasses, rushes, leaves, and stems. It uses its broad bill to pull up roots and crush harder vegetable matter.*

The Yellow-rumped Warbler *feeds by taking insects and invertebrates from leaves and tree trunks. It favors flies, beetles, and midges, but will happily take berries at the end of summer.*

The Snow Bunting *eats seeds from low-growing plants, manipulating them in its bill to remove the inedible husks. It takes insects and spiders too, but only in the breeding season.*

The Common Redpoll *has a small, pointed bill that can pick tiny seeds from the ground or from plants. When it visits in the winter, they feed on birch and alder seeds, and eat nyger seed at feeders.*

shifting much of their diet to agricultural crops and road kills. Perhaps the most famous example of birds adapting their diet to changing circumstances is that of cream-stealing from milk bottles. In Britain, milk bottles with foil caps are delivered to the doorstep. Blue and Great Tits, Magpies, and even Great Spotted Woodpeckers pierce the caps and steal the cream. They probably learned to open the cap accidentally as they searched for natural food, using the same technique as they apply to hammering open nuts. These examples demonstrate that birds learn from each other, and how new behaviors may be carried forward between generations.

Birds and fruit

Many gardeners become outraged when birds raid prize fruit crops, but the fact is that fruit is designed precisely to be eaten by birds. From cherries and elderberries in summer to hollies in winter, fruits provide birds with food for a large part of the year, and in return, birds provide fruit trees and bushes with an excellent means of dispersing their seed. The fleshy pulp of each fruit contains starchy sugars that protect the seed within, and sometimes fats that are especially attractive. A glossy, colorful coat makes the whole package more visible and attractive to birds such as thrushes, warblers, vireos, mockingbirds, and waxwings that eat the fruit and then disperse the undigested seeds in their droppings. Plants like hawthorn produce seeds tough enough to

Although Red-winged Blackbirds *can do damage to commercial crops such as corn, most of their food consists of insects and weed seeds such as this bristlegrass.*

Woodpeckers also cache food, especially acorns. Among this species, the Acorn Woodpecker is remarkable for the extent of its caching instinct; sometimes groups will store 50,000 acorns in a single tree. Nuts are the most usual food to be hidden because they are nutritious and store well. Even northern owls such as the Northern Hawk Owl and Saw-whet Owl store frozen mice in tree cavities. Hidden food may be left for weeks before the owner returns to claim it; biologists believe that a bird remembers the exact location of its food cache by reference to nearby landmarks, but this does not easily explain how birds find food buried by leaves and snow.

The diets of many common garden species have changed over the years as birds have learned to exploit new food sources. Nuthatches typically feed upside down, clinging to tree trunks, but now regularly hang on suet bags and do not hesitate to take food from bird tables. It is likely that they first discovered this new food by observing chickadees and titmice that typically feed from hanging branches.

Birds are remarkable in their abilities to recognize new feeding opportunities. Scavenging species such as Herring Gulls and American Crows are especially adaptable. Herring Gulls once fed mainly on schooling fish and invertebrates plucked from the intertidal zone. But now they benefit from garbage dumps, fishing waste, and dumpsters. Crows occupy a similar scavenging role on land, but they too have adapted to a human-shaped landscape by

Specialist feeders *need careful consideration in the garden. Planting Purple Coneflower will attract goldfinches (above), while mature conifers may draw in crossbills (left).*

FOOD AND HUMAN ACTIVITY

Herring Gulls, *common coastal scavengers, benefit from food at garbage dumps. They gather every day, sometimes having flown many miles from their roosts. These huge supplies of food have caused populations of gulls and crows to increase dramatically. Some become pests when they turn to other sources of food and their droppings can be a nuisance.*

Commercial fishing activity *has increased dramatically since the end of the 19th century. The intestines of gutted fish from a catch are discarded in huge quantities, helping the populations of gulls to expand. Now that fish stocks are depleted, these ravenous species are eating other seabirds such as terns and eiders.*

Earthworms and other insects *are a major part of the robin's diet. Originally a woodland bird, this versatile species adapted its natural foraging behavior of feeding on forest floors to exploit earthworms in new habitats such as lawns. Most earthworms are not native and are often super-abundant—a boon to adaptive robins.*

withstand the digestive system of almost any bird, while yew seeds are coated with an unpalatable poison that causes the bird to spit out rather than swallow the seed.

Fruits and berries are an important source of winter food for many birds. Robins will gorge on fall hawthorn and Bohemian Waxwings are known to eat at least 500 cotoneaster fruits in the course of a single day. Sometimes a mockingbird or robin defends its private fruit tree against all comers. The effort is worthwhile because the bird stands to keep its secure food supply, but it may be overwhelmed if a flock of fruit-eaters invades. Then the "owner" has no option but to join them in stripping the tree of its fruit as fast as possible.

Taking on water

Although birds do not sweat and their excretory systems are designed to conserve fluid, they constantly lose water through respiration and in their droppings. Some water is released when metabolizing or "burning" fat, so birds can survive for a while on dry seeds; and insectivorous birds take in water with their juicy food. Nevertheless, all birds need regular topping-up with water and, in warm weather, they may need to drink several times a day.

Most garden birds employ one of two drinking techniques (see below). Swallows, however, are an exception; they drink at ponds and lakes by swooping over the surface and taking a mouthful of water without landing.

Birds like the Eastern Bluebird, *which feed on juicy foods such as earthworms, only need to drink water in the hottest weather.*

Most garden birds, *such as this starling, drink by taking a sip from a pool and then tilting their heads back to swallow.*

Doves and pigeons *drink by dipping their bills in a pool and sucking up the water, as if through a straw.*

Voice

VOCAL COMMUNICATION between birds of the same species is often surprisingly sophisticated. They sometimes use astonishingly intricate songs to establish territories, deter rivals, and attract mates. Yet the subtleties of bird communication are largely indistinguishable to the human ear. Many birds also have an extensive "vocabulary" of basic calls, used especially when they are living together in flocks or as families.

The meaning of song

Song varies greatly between birds, from rich and varied repertoires, to sequences of simple notes, but all species use it to broadcast one of two basic messages: "Go away!" (to repel rivals) or "Come here!" (to attract a mate). Singing is largely a male activity, and is most intense at the start of the breeding season, when birds are setting up territories.

Most landbirds use song to establish territorial boundaries and sing vehemently if a stranger of their own species sings from within their claimed borders. When a bird's territory includes the backyard, it is easy to observe the function of bird song. Male mockingbirds, for example, sing loudly from rooftops to announce their presence, which functions to keep other male mockingbirds from claiming a piece of the territory.

For many species, song is not only important for defending a territory, but it is also the principal method

of attracting a mate. Female songbirds usually select their mate on the quality of their songs. Older males have time to build larger repertoires of songs over the years and long-lived males are good choices for mates as they are healthy and have shown that they have survived. Well-established males typically have territories with plenty of food, so they promise to be the best providers for a family. A rich and varied song may also be the sound equivalent of elaborate plumage—like the peacock's train—designed to dazzle the female and induce her to accept the male.

Some birds reduce or stop singing completely once a pair has formed, while others continue as a means of strengthening the pair-bond. A bird's song is partly inherited from its parents but the songs of neighboring

Scarlet Tanagers *returning from the tropics race back to nesting habitat to claim prime territories. Males soon select a territory, which they defend by singing.*

Bobolinks deliver *their warbling song while in special "song-flights." After take-off, the male spirals steeply upwards, singing loudly. He descends more slowly, gliding down in larger, slower spirals.*

Some species adopt *a characteristic pose when singing, which can be a useful aid to identification. House Wrens often cock their tail in the air when singing; their loud bubbling song a familiar sound.*

The Red-bellied Woodpecker's *"song" is not made vocally but by repeatedly striking a tree trunk or branch with its bill. It "drums" in a series of short bursts, each lasting less than a second, to announce its presence in spring.*

A Mallard keeps *her brood together with quiet quacks, which the young learn to recognize before they hatch out of the egg. The ducklings utter high-pitched cheeping to keep in touch with their mother.*

Crows and ravens *look similar, but they sound very different. Ravens have a much more varied vocabulary of hoarse croaks and cackles. In contrast crows give their distinctive "caw" call.*

pairs also influence nestling birds. Young songbirds grow up listening to the males of their species singing from surrounding territories and use this memory to compose their own song. For this reason, individual birds within the same species often have local dialects that are distinct from more remote populations of the same species.

Communicating with calls

Bird calls are distinct from song. They are simple sounds, used throughout the year, which are delivered by a bird to coordinate the behavior of others. Black-capped Chickadees, for example, have winter flock calls that help to keep the winter group together. Each flock has its own distinct call that helps the group come together and avoid mixing with neighboring flocks. These flock calls help the birds assemble and stay warm at night and during extreme weather, as well as watching for predators. As a small flock of chickadees makes its way along a hedge searching for insects, for example, they give their flock call to group together. We cannot distinguish one flock call from the next, but chickadees can readily do it. Each year the flock will create a new distinct flock call unique to a specific group.

Alarm calls alert other birds to a potential threat. When a cat tries to sneak up on a bird table, its attempt to catch a feeding bird is often frustrated by a simple, harsh "scolding call" from a vigilant neighbor. Birds of all species recognize this sound and immediately fly up to safety, and often rally to attack and chase the predator. The alarm calls of most backyard birds have a generalized quality that birders sometimes imitate to obtain better views. It works best when birds are already giving excited chip sounds.

SONG-POSTS

American Robins have a melodic, caroling song. The male advertises his territory by singing from tall trees, utility poles, rooftops, and other tall structures. By observing the birds singing in your garden over a few weeks and recording where you see each bird singing, it is possible to create a rough map, like the one below, of the song-posts around your garden. Like most songbirds, robins make the rounds of their song-posts in early morning as prominent members of the dawn chorus. They also sing at dusk.

By singing *from prominent perches around the backyard, a male robin defines the borders of its territory.*

● Song-post

Territory

A TERRITORY IS A PATCH OF GROUND that a bird defends against intruders to preserve a precious commodity—typically food or a place to breed. Territories are usually held only for the duration of the breeding season. The Barred Owl, however, usually defends its territory throughout the year and may stay in one location for its adult life. Territories are also created around rich food supplies.

An American Goldfinch *shows off its broad, black breast-stripe to threaten another goldfinch that is invading his territory.*

Size and survival

Defending a territory costs time and energy. Yet many birds are prepared to make the investment because having exclusive rights to a feeding and nesting area is invaluable—indeed survival and successful breeding may be impossible without it. Territorial behavior also improves survival rates by helping birds to avoid predators. Consider a nest predator, such as a grackle: when it locates a nest, it will take eggs and then search nearby for more of the same; it is far less likely to be successful if the nests are well-spaced by large territories.

The territories held by many garden birds tend to be large in area, simply because they need to contain sufficient food for the breeding pair plus their offspring. A pair of thrushes, titmice, or wrens, for example, holds an area that covers several suburban backyards (this explains why there are fewer birds to be seen in a backyard during the breeding season than at any other time of year). Other species hold smaller territories, and must venture beyond their boundaries in search of food. Some hole-nesting species, such as Purple Martins, and colonial birds such as gulls, defend only a small area that immediately surrounds the nest.

The sizes of territories occupied by birds of the same species are similar, but territory size is also dependent on the abundance of food. In years where supplies are plentiful, birds need a smaller area in which to rear their young and so defend smaller territories, with the result that more

Many species conduct *territorial "song fights," matching the song of their rivals for several minutes; these help to set the boundaries of the territories.*

birds can squeeze into a given area. However, when food is scarce, territories must be larger to ensure adequate food, so fewer birds are able to breed.

Setting up a territory

Competition for breeding space is fierce among birds, so males begin to stake out their territories as soon as the weather improves after winter. Among migrant species, the males return before the females in order to claim their space. The male alone usually defends territories, but the female may occasionally help. The male deters rivals

TERRITORY SIZE
The extent of a territory varies between species, and is elastic within a species, depending on habitat quality.

	25–30ha (65–75 acres)	**Barred Owls** *hold their large territories throughout the year. They become familiar with the terrain, moving easily in darkness.*
	1–1½ha (2½–3½ acres)	**Eastern Bluebirds** *have separate territories in winter, but meet to establish a mutual breeding territory in spring.*
	½–1ha (1–2½ acres)	**American Robins** *defend territories that meet all their needs in the breeding season, but relinquish them in winter.*
	1 sq.m (1¼ sq.yd)	**Tufted Titmice** *defend the immediate area around the nest, but remain sociable when feeding in large flocks.*
	Nest only	**Pairs of swifts** *defend a small area around their nesting cavity and defend a feeding territory in the air.*

Goldfinches *feed in flocks that gather at good sources of food. Competition develops and dominant birds drive away the others with threats.*

Two Barn Swallows *fight for dominance. A submissive bird recognizes its inferiority and retreats before a fight starts, but fights between birds of equal rank can be fierce.*

A **Barn Owl** *surveys its territory from the entrance to its nest. It defends a small area around its nest and roost, but its hunting ground overlaps those of its neighbors.*

through singing, aggressive displays, and sometimes by fighting. Physical contact between birds is most common when they first assert their ownership of a patch of land; after a short period, neighbors recognize one another and warning songs and displays are sufficient to deter intruders.

Maintaining boundaries

With vigilance, it is possible to map the boundaries of bird territories within your backyard. Watch out for song-posts (see page 109), which are typically located on the borders of a territory, and make a note of locations where you spot disputes between neighbors. Sometimes, however, the extent of a territory is not clear. Late in the breeding season, once a territory has been established for some time, the resident bird often relinquishes its hold on the territory and becomes tolerant of neighbors encroaching on its space.

Likewise, birds will not typically chase away others of the same species from birdfeeders, even if they occur within their territories.

Non-breeding territories

Most territories are abandoned at the end of the breeding season, but non-breeding birds will also defend space, even on the wintering grounds. Robins and mockingbirds defend trees or bushes containing crops of fruit, but stop defending when a flock descends on the tree. Some birds, such as starlings, defend roosting locations and maintain a space around themselves while sleeping in the roost. These birds can be seen jostling for space when they line up on buildings as night falls. Likewise, swallows and Rock Pigeons sitting on utility wires defend a little "personal space" around themselves while they are sitting.

Flocks

WHILE SOME BIRDS are mostly solitary, others live or feed in large flocks. Groups of millions of Red-winged Blackbirds may congregate at fall roosts in wetlands, and American Crows assemble in roosts in thousands. Such concentrations offer advantages such as protection from predators and exchanging information about finding food, but aggregations also bring new risks such as exposure to disease.

Starlings space out *evenly along a roof and chimneys. The distance between birds prevents them pecking at one another and preserves harmony.*

Keeping a distance

All birds maintain a clear personal space around themselves —the "individual distance"—that prevents collisions when a flock takes to the air. Such distances also minimize conflict and disturbance when feeding. Starlings, for example, space themselves out on a lawn when hunting so that each bird can creep up on worms undetected. The extent of a bird's individual distance depends on its circumstances and lifestyle, and on its place in the pecking order that is usually established through a series of skirmishes. Individual distance is sometimes reduced to allow contact, such as when mating or huddling for warmth in a roost. Species that are normally solitary sometimes group together for specific purposes; Tree Swallows, for example, aggressively defend the space around their nest box, but they are quick to join migratory flocks in the fall.

Avoiding predators and finding food

In some ways, flocks can be thought of as a single organism: feeding, moving, and surviving together. There are many advantages to communal living. For a start, a bird in a flock is less likely to be taken by a predator (such as a falcon) than a solitary individual. Many pairs of eyes can keep careful watch for approaching danger, and flocks have been shown to take off fractionally sooner than single birds when threatened. Flocks confuse and deter predators. A diving hawk knows that it could get damaged in a collision with birds in a flock, and it is hard for the hawk to concentrate his attack on a single target if he is surrounded by the swirling shapes of many potential targets.

Another advantage of living in a flock is economy in feeding. Birds need to spend less time scanning their surroundings for danger and so can devote more energy to the important task of feeding. Finding food also becomes more economical, because rather than wasting precious time searching for food singly, it is far easier to keep an eye out for neighbors

A flock of sparrows *feeds on millet in a raised table feeder. The birds keep their distance from one another so they can feed peacefully.*

who have a good supply, and simply fly over to join them. This is especially important for seabirds that flock to schools of fish, but group attraction likely works in the backyard as well, especially around birdfeeders and trees and shrubs that have ripe fruit. Flocking is a particularly useful strategy in winter when food is especially hard to find. Mixed flocks of chickadees, titmice, nuthatches, and Brown Creepers stay together, sharing resources and all watching for the ever-stealthy hawks that are looking for their own next meal.

Flocks on the move

Many birds form flocks in order to migrate, but the exact advantages of traveling in a group are unclear. Avoidance of predators is an unlikely explanation because most birds migrate at night, but traveling in flocks may make it easier for juvenile birds to find their way, particularly if experienced "pathfinder" birds are in the group. Another explanation is aerodynamics; individual birds expend less energy when moving in a group than singly because the group experiences less aerodynamic drag.

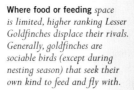

Where food or feeding space is limited, higher ranking Lesser Goldfinches displace their rivals. Generally, goldfinches are sociable birds (except during nesting season) that seek their own kind to feed and fly with.

Collisions are rare as a tightly packed flock of starlings circles before going to roost. The birds are alert to the slightest movements of others. The flock wheels in precision when one or two birds decide to alter course, and a wave of movement passes along the mass of birds.

House Sparrows are gregarious birds that live in small, loose colonies. Here, a group of sparrows settles down to roost in an urban tree on a winter's night.

Courtship

PARADOXICALLY, COURTSHIP AND PAIR-FORMATION have much in common
with territorial behavior—the songs and displays used in defending
territories are often the same as those used to attract a mate. Courtship
involves more than bringing birds of two sexes
together. It allows birds to select the best partner,
and, by feeding their mate during courtship, males
demonstrate their ability to provide for a family.

The size of a male House
*Sparrow's black "bib" indicates
his status. Females look for this
marking when selecting a mate.*

Prepared for parenting

Birds normally maintain a certain amount of space between
one another in order to prevent conflict (see page 112).
But for breeding to take place, a male and female must
come into intimate contact, first to fertilize the eggs and
then to feed and care for their nestlings. Courtship is the
necessary process that breaks down the barriers between
the birds by reducing their natural aggression toward one
another. Behavior related to courtship is very distinctive.
For most of the year, birds keep a deliberately low profile
to avoid predators, but when courting, males make themselves
obvious to attract females. This is a risky strategy, but one
that is necessary for successful reproduction.

At the beginning of the breeding season, males
typically start by attacking females, simply because
their instinct is to drive intruders from their
territories. Females overcome this aggression by
holding their ground and acting submissively, so
gradually establishing their presence. The males
switch to courtship behavior and the bond
between the pair begins to form. In some
species, this is almost instantaneous, but
in others, it may take more than a week.

Choosing a mate

Courtship permits birds to choose the
best possible mate for successful family
life. As a general rule, female birds
select the male. They assess males
according to several criteria,
including quality of song and

display ritual, size, and color, which indicate individuals with
good genes and parenting skills. One of the attributes that
a female bird looks for in a potential mate is age: an older,
more experienced male has already proved his ability
to survive hard times and find food, so is likely to make
a good father. Mature males
may signal their age with

Male and female Tree Swallows
*look very similar. Behavior
displays help the pair to recognise
members of the opposite sex.*

a more elaborate song than younger birds; and older males tend to display more vigorously and pursue females with more determination than younger birds.

Female Barn Swallows assess the suitability of males by the length of their tail feathers, while female Winter Wrens choose a mate based on his skill at nest-building. Males that build nests well-hidden from predators are especially attractive. A female bird does not necessarily choose to stay with the first male to court her; she may visit several before making a choice. If the female pairs with a male in one breeding season, there is a good chance that she will pair again with him in the next, if only because the two birds return to the same place to nest and so meet again. But this varies from one species to the next. Familiarity and experience with last year's partner helps courtship to proceed rapidly and nesting to start early. This is an advantage in some species, such as chickadees, because the earliest clutches of eggs yield the most young.

Courtship feeding

Male birds of diverse species present females with gifts of food. This "courtship feeding" helps to strengthen the bond between the pair, but also helps the female to assess the qualities of a prospective mate; a male that brings her plenty of food should be good at feeding her young. Courtship feeding also provides the female with the extra food she needs for breeding. Small birds may require 40 percent more food to form eggs, so the extra meals provided by her mate are vital to the female's diet. Courtship feeding often continues during incubation, so the female can spend more time on the nest.

PAIRING UP

Some birds pair for a single season, while others seek out the same mate, year after year. House Wrens may have two or three partners over the course of a nesting season, while Mute Swans pair for life. Usually, once birds haveformed a pair, they are inseparable before egg-laying; they feed and roost together, and male songbirds follow their mates while they are collecting nest material. This is not so much a sign of devotion as insurance that he alone will be the father of her young. On the other hand, males sometimes take advantage of any lapses in a neighbor's vigilance. Females are also known to seek out extra-pair matings.

Tree Swallows *often have different mates each year; woodpeckers and nuthatches are monogamous for many years.*

After pair formation, *but before egg-laying, the male Mallard follows his mate closely, never letting her out of his sight.*

Female Song Sparrows *listen to singing males to help determine the fitness of their prospective mate. As in most species, this is one of the ways females select their mate.*

A female Northern Cardinal *accepts an offering from her mate. Such feeding precedes egg-laying and continues through incubation. Courtship feedings help to secure the pair bond and provide nutrients for the eggs.*

Mutual preening *(also called allopreening), seen here in a pair of Rock Pigeons, helps to maintain the pair bond as well as serving a necessary grooming function.*

Nesting

ALL BIRDS LAY EGGS, and most go to great lengths to craft a successful nest. Acting largely by instinct, birds build a nest, incubate the eggs, and then rear their family to independence. As a rule, birds that leave the nest shortly after hatching, such as terns and pheasants, have simple nests whereas species whose young remain in the nest until they can fly typically build more elaborate structures.

Site selection

In late winter and spring, garden birds are often seen hopping from twig to twig along hedges or among bushes and climbers. Most such birds are foraging for food, but some are prospecting for nest sites. In most species, nest site selection and construction are the responsibilities of the female. In woodpeckers and kingfishers, both sexes excavate the cavity. By contrast, male wrens typically build multiple nests; females select the nest of preference and add the lining.

The criteria that birds use to select a nest are little known. Birds that build cup-shaped nests usually search for a configuration of branches where three or more branches arise creating a crotch to secure the nest. Protection from predators and shelter from the elements are other considerations, although birds often nest in surprising places such as window sills, porches, and foundation shrubbery—

Male House Wrens build several nests. The female inspects these and adds a lining to the nest of her choosing.

sometimes near active doorways. Birds may select such locations because they are safer from foxes, raccoons, and other predators that are typically shy of approaching where they smell humans. Birds may also nest in exposed places where overzealous gardeners have cleared away undergrowth that offers shelter and nesting opportunities.

Nest construction

Nests come in all shapes and sizes, from the bulky stick structures of osprey and herons to the intricate balls of lichen, spider webs, and plant fiber built by hummingbirds. Most common garden birds build cup-shaped nests, but several kinds prefer to nest in holes. Nests are built using the bill (sometimes assisted by the feet) as a tool, and can take up to three weeks to complete. As a rule, building a nest takes longer at the start of the season because the more likely inclement weather may interfere.

The most difficult part of nest construction is making the foundation—providing a firm anchor for the nest. When a female hummingbird starts building a nest, she first makes secure anchor points by wrapping strands of spider web around twigs. She then adds moss and grass, until she has built up a firm

Tree Swallow nests are relatively secure from predators and weather, but such sites are scarce. In contrast, hummingbirds nest in locations that are exposed but plentiful.

cushion. Sitting on this pad, the bird works still more material into place before forming the cup shape of the nest by pushing with her breast and pressing with her feet until the materials become felted together.

Considering the time and energy invested in building a nest, it is surprising that very few are used for more than one brood, even if more broods follow in the same year. Each brood gets a new nest, probably to minimize the problems caused by feather lice and other nest parasites, or simply because the nest is squashed by the first brood of nestlings or destroyed by wind and weather. Even well-built nests of orioles and vireos that last the winter are not reused. In contrast, large stick nests of hawks, herons, and crows are often used in successive years and may be occupied by other species. Magpies typically use their well-built nests from one year to the next, and robins, bluebirds, and other smaller birds use abandoned nests for shelter during storms.

Eggs and laying

Formation of the eggs inside the female's body starts several days before laying. The fertilized eggs, consisting mainly of yolk, move down the oviduct where they are coated in albumen (egg white) and finally shell. Egg production places great demand on the female; she needs extra food to manufacture the eggs. Extra calcium for the shells may need to be taken from her bones. It is not surprising that females of some species become less active before laying and roost at night in the nest so that they use less energy to keep warm.

A White-headed Woodpecker *makes a nest hole in a dead tree. Male and female excavate the cavity and share incubation responsibilities. Both parents also feed the young.*

NEST DESIGNS

Male Marsh Wrens *build several incomplete, oval-shaped nests of wet grass, rushes and cattails, and anchor these to standing cattails or shrubs that emerge from 1–3ft deep marshes. Females then choose one of the nests for her eggs, completing it with a lining of fine grass, plant down and feathers.*

Female Hooded Warblers *select a nest site and do all or most of the building. Usually she chooses a patch of deciduous shrubs under forest canopy. Located 1–4ft above ground, the nest is an open cup of dead leaves with shreds of bark, lined with fine grass, spider webs, plant down, and animal hair.*

Cliff Swallows *often build their nests under the eaves of a roof. The pair spends days collecting hundreds of balls of wet mud from the edges of a pond or puddle and sticking them together over a framework of grass stems. Nests are replaced each year.*

Female Bobolinks *usually build their nest in a slight depression in the ground. Like many ground-nesting species, the eggs are beautifully detailed with scribbles and specks of olive and brown that help to hide them from predators such as foxes and raccoons.*

In the few days that pass between building the nest and the start of egg-laying, the female concentrates on feeding. Most garden birds lay their eggs in the morning at 24-hour intervals, but herons, owls, and swifts lay at longer intervals. If the clutch is lost, through predation or destroyed by weather, most birds are able to lay a replacement clutch, especially if the loss occurs soon after egg-laying.

Clutch size usually depends on the general health and food available to the female, as well as environmental conditions. In bad weather, swifts lay two, rather than three eggs, while owls and kestrels may not even attempt to lay if there is a shortage of mice. There is also variation with climate and geography. Birds in northern countries lay more eggs than those in the south. For example, Scarlet and Western Tanagers typically lay three to five eggs, while resident tropical tanagers usually lay just two eggs. The number of clutches laid in one season also depends on food supply. Chickadees, which depend on spring caterpillars to feed their young, usually manage a single brood in one year, while robins, which have a more varied diet of worms and insects, can rear several broods.

An incubating parent *like this Red-eyed Vireo will often slip off the nest if a predator approaches. It is better to lose the eggs and start again than to risk injury.*

Incubation

Birds are warm-blooded animals, and the chicks developing inside eggs need to be kept warm by their parents. Shortly before the eggs are laid, parents shed feathers from their breast to leave a patch of bare skin, known as the brood patch. The rich supply of blood vessels to the brood patch enables it to serve as an efficient heating surface for transferring body heat to the eggs.

For most backyard birds, incubation is carried out by the female alone, but some species such as woodpeckers divide the incubation more equally, with males typically

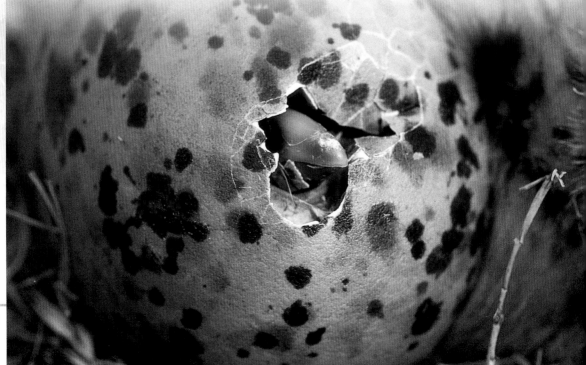

A hatching chick *pecks a hole through its shell using its horny egg tooth. Hatching chicks also grow powerful muscles on the back of the neck that permit them to push the egg tooth against the shell interior. Hatching takes from hours to days, with the chick completing the exhausting task by forcing the cap off the egg.*

EGGS AND NESTS

Just as the type of nest, size of clutch, and number of broods varies for sound, adaptive reasons from species to species, so too does the size, shape, and color of the eggs. For example, the eggs of birds that use open nests are often well-spotted or streaked for camouflage, while the eggs of hole-nesters are white for visibility.

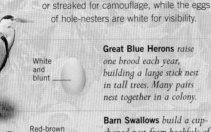

White and blunt — **Great Blue Herons** *raise one brood each year, building a large stick nest in tall trees. Many pairs nest together in a colony.*

Red-brown spots — **Barn Swallows** *build a cup-shaped nest from beakfuls of mud and grass. It is typically located on small ledges against vertical surfaces.*

Smooth, glossy surface — **A robin's nest** *is a cup of grass, twigs, and plant material. It usually raises 2–3 broods per year, or up to 5 in exceptional years.*

Greenish speckles — **House Sparrows** *build untidy, domed nests from dry grass or straw. Clutch size is 4 eggs on average, and they lay 2–4 clutches per year.*

Smooth, olive brown — **Herring Gulls** *nest on open ground and roofs, where their nests are little more than mounds of vegetation. They lay a clutch of 2–4 eggs.*

Purple speckles — **Song Sparrows** *often raise 3 broods per season across most of the US. Their grassy, domed nests are concealed in taller vegetation.*

Variable speckling — **Cedar Waxwing nests** *are messy structures, made of sticks, mud, and dung. The birds lay a single clutch of up to 8 eggs in one year.*

Buff or bluish — **A Mallard's** *nest is a shallow dip in the ground, lined with down from the female's breast. It lays 1 large clutch of up to 18 eggs per year.*

incubating at night and females by day. In these species, both sexes have a well-developed brood patch. Most birds do not remain on the nest continuously when incubating, but take regular breaks to feed, defecate, and indulge in bouts of preening. Before settling to incubate the eggs, the adults of most species ruffle their feathers to expose the brood patch. At intervals, they typically stand up and poke the eggs with their bill to shuffle them. This has several functions: it allows air to circulate so the embryos inside the eggs can breathe (air diffuses through the egg shells), and rearranges the eggs so they are evenly warmed to within a few degrees. Egg turning also aids embryonic development.

Timing

The eggs in a clutch are laid at a rate of about one per day, but the adult birds do not begin incubation in earnest until the clutch is complete. This results in the eggs hatching simultaneously. Owls, birds of prey, and a few other species are exceptions to this rule; incubation starts as soon as the first egg is laid, and they consequently hatch in sequence at the same intervals as they were laid. This arrangement helps to insure that at least the oldest chick will have ample food during lean food years.

Parent birds *typically remove the egg shell from the nest soon after hatching. This keeps the nest clean and reduces the risk of a predator spotting the nest because of the white inner side of the egg shell.*

Growth and independence

THE YOUNG OF SONGBIRDS, pigeons, woodpeckers, and birds of prey (known as nestlings) hatch in an almost helpless state and stay in the nest until they are ready to fly, while the young of gulls, coots, and quail leave the nest soon after hatching. Even under the protection of their parents, these inexperienced birds face the most hazardous time of their lives.

Early days and parental care

When nestlings hatch, they are weak and unable to maintain their body temperature, so they must be brooded almost continuously by their parents. As they grow stronger, they are left alone in the nest for longer periods while the adults forage for food. Brooding resumes at night and in bad weather until the nestlings are well developed.

Feeding the family keeps the parents busy all day, and even males that played no part in nest-building or incubation now help their mates by bringing food. Insects and other invertebrates, such as spiders, snails, and worms are the favorite food for young garden birds. Even

A parent bluebird *removes the fecal sacs of newly hatched birds to keep the nest clean and secure.*

Some birds have "helpers" at the nest. For example, about half of all Florida Scrub Jay pairs are assisted in rearing their young by previous broods that defer their own breeding. American Crows and Acorn Woodpeckers also have helpers.

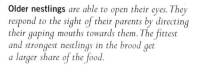

At first, nestlings *cannot open their eyes or direct their gape. They raise their heads and open their beaks when they detect vibrations in the nest. The parents simply push food into their brightly-colored, gaping mouths.*

Older nestlings *are able to open their eyes. They respond to the sight of their parents by directing their gaping mouths towards them. The fittest and strongest nestlings in the brood get a larger share of the food.*

Most birds *continue to feed their young after they have left the nest. The fledglings follow their parents and so learn how to find different kinds of food and rich feeding grounds.*

the vegetarian finches give their young some animal food, because it contains more of the nutrients needed by growing bodies. Animal food is also rich in fluids, so young birds do not need to drink. However, collecting insects is hard work for the parents, particularly in bad weather.

Fledging and flight

By the time the nestlings grow feathers and are ready to fly, they have grown to a size at which they are almost bursting out of the nest. Leaving the nest is a priority, because young birds are less vulnerable to attack when out in the open than when confined in the nest. The time taken to fledge varies between species, but in general birds raised in open cup-shaped nests fly at an earlier age than those raised in the greater safety of tree cavities or soil burrows. Even within a species, fledging time depends on the abundance of food and the number of mouths that the parents have to feed.

For the first few days after leaving, most fledglings do not fly, but rest quietly in a secluded spot, such as a dense hedge or bush, where they wait for their parents to bring food. The fledglings are easily recognized on the ground, because their tails and wings look stumpy and they lack the effortless grace of their elders. Songbird fledglings usually also have a bright patch of skin at the corner of their beak, a remnant of the nestling's open-mouthed gape.

As their feathers complete their growth, young birds become more confident. They follow their parents and save them the effort of flying to deliver each beakful of food. Young grackles, for example, can often be seen following their parents as they forage on the lawn; the adults have only to turn to push the food into a waiting mouth. The time necessary for young to reach independence from their parents varies considerably between species. Swifts, for example, are independent from the moment they fly, while Great Horned Owl young receive feedings from their parents for three months after leaving the nest.

Survival of the fittest

Many young, inexperienced birds die shortly after leaving the nest, especially in times of food shortage or bad weather. Fledglings are more vulnerable to predators and are at a particular disadvantage when competing with older birds, which always dominate the choicest feeding spots.

A study of Song Sparrows in San Francisco found that of 100 eggs laid, only six sparrows were alive a year later and 43 percent of these died in each subsequent year.

A fledgling's ability to fly is instinctive, even if it has never fully extended its wings in the nest before its first flight. Parents do not "teach" their young to fly, but practise helps.

FLEDGING TIMES

The chart below compares fledging times for cavity nesting and open cup nests of birds about the same size.

Number of days from leaving the nest to independence

American Kestrel	30–31 days
Mourning Dove	12–14 days
Northern Flicker	25–28 days
Gray Catbird	10–11 days
Hairy Woodpecker	28–30 days
American Robin	14–16 days
Red-winged Blackbird	11–14 days
Starling	21 days
House Sparrow	14–17 days
Downy Woodpecker	20–25 days

UNWITTING CARERS

Brown-headed Cowbirds are renowned for laying their eggs in the nests of other species, and fooling the foster parent into rearing their young. Cowbird young typically hatch earlier and grow faster than their hosts. Cowbirds are known to parasitize more than 200 other kinds of birds! Species that have blue or green eggs such as thrushes and catbirds usually remove cowbird eggs from their nests.

Bird profiles

Identification is an essential skill for any backyard birdwatcher, and learning bird characteristics is a satisfying end in itself. The profiles on the following pages describe North America's most common backyard birds, including their feeding and nesting behaviors.

Western Scrub-jay

Recognizing birds

BIRD IDENTIFICATION IS A SKILL that can be honed by study and experience, but which can take a lifetime to master. Appearance and song give the most immediate clues to a bird's identity, but location, season, and habitat are also important factors to consider. In time, and with patience, bird identification becomes as straightforward as recognizing human neighbors.

The Northern Cardinal's *distinctive crest and large orange bill are unique.*

Feathers are *arranged around defined feather tracts. Try to learn the names of these tracts.*

Crown
Nape
Mantle
Back
Coverts
Tertials
Secondaries
Upper tail coverts
Tail
Under tail coverts
Vent
Primaries
Belly
Flank
Breast
Throat

White-throated Sparrow

Median coverts
Greater coverts
Primaries
Wingbar
Secondaries
Tertials
Primary coverts
Rump
Outer tail feathers

White-throated Sparrow in flight

Reliable signs

Most species have "absolute" characters that will identify them—a robin's russet-red breast or the stumpy tail of a wren, for example. However, birds rarely present themselves in textbook poses that afford us good views of their diagnostic markings. Also, relying on a single characteristic to identify a bird is usually unreliable. Color and plumage pattern may change over the course of a year and size may be difficult to judge in the absence of a sense of scale. Shape is trickier still, because a bird can fluff or sleek its feathers, extend its neck, or spread its wings and tail to change its profile.

Rather than focusing on single characteristics, seasoned birdwatchers talk about the "jizz" of a bird, which is an amalgam of its basic physical appearance, behaviour, and personality. It allows them to identify birds just as we recognize

To assess a bird's *size, it is useful to compare it to other, familiar "reference" species.*

RELATIVE SIZES

15"
12"
9"
6"
3"
0"

Chickadee
House Sparrow
American Robin
American Crow
in

Song is as reliable *a method of identifying birds as field marks. Yellowthroats are often heard long before they are seen.*

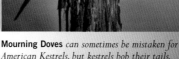

Mourning Doves *can sometimes be mistaken for American Kestrels, but kestrels bob their tails, a behavior that quickly distinguishes them.*

our friends: from their walk, the way they hold their bodies, or from some small but characteristic mannerism.

Books and articles, and birdsong on CD and video, will familiarize you with a bird's features, behavior, and sounds, but there is no substitute for hours of observation in the field (or your backyard). You will learn to differentiate the fluent, swooping flight pattern of a swallow from the flickering, jerkier wingbeats of a Purple Martin. Repetition and attention to detail will distinguish the distinct phrases of the robin's song from the whistling run-on of a Rose-breasted Grosbeak's.

Behavior is *very helpful for identifying this female American Goldfinch. Although there are many kinds of small yellow birds, the habit of clinging onto plant stems and feasting on seeds is typical of goldfinches.*

ABOUT THE BIRD PROFILES

The following pages describe 100 of the most common North American backyard birds, giving details of their size, shape, color, voice, and behavior. Distribution maps (see below for key) show the seasonal range of the species; the letters below the maps indicate the months the bird can be seen in North America.

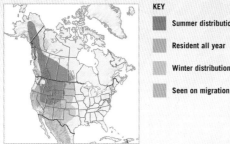

KEY

Summer distribution

Resident all year

Winter distribution

Seen on migration

Cooper's Hawk

THESE LONG-TAILED PREDATORS are lured by feeding stations, where they attack concentrated groups of feeder birds. Ground-feeding birds such as doves, flickers, jays, and sparrows are especially vulnerable to these magnificent predators. Although they cause chaos when they are present, they usually stay for just a few days.

Backyard predators

Adult Cooper's Hawks have a blue-gray back with fine rust-colored barring on their breast and belly; immatures are brown above with dark brown stripes below. Females are larger than males, but male Cooper's Hawks may overlap in size with female Sharp-shinned Hawks. Like other accipiters, Cooper's Hawks have a distinctive flight pattern of several quick flaps followed by a glide, but in migration they often soar with little effort. These bird-eating specialists have longer legs, toes, and talons than other raptors, features that help to snag fleeing birds in dense brush.

Stealth hunter

Cooper's Hawks must eat the equivalent of one Mourning Dove every day or two. This could ravage feeder populations, including European Starlings, Dark-Eyed Juncos, and House Sparrows, except that Cooper's Hawks also feed on mammals and reptiles. They typically hunt from hidden perches in low, shrubby habitat, while Sharp-shinned Hawks hunt from higher perches in more open habitat.

Both Cooper's and Sharp-shinned Hawks *have rounded wings and long tails. Distinguish Cooper's by its rounded tail and large head. First-year birds are striped underneath.*

IN THE BACKYARD

■ If hawks visit your feeders, stop feeding for a week or two to reduce the concentration of birds.

After capturing prey, *Cooper's Hawks typically spread their wings and tail over their catch to keep it from escaping.*

Accipiter cooperii
Accipitridae

Relatively large head

Rusty underside

Long, rounded tail

Stiff and choppy wingbeats

Crow-sized body

LENGTH 14–20in (35–50cm)

WINGSPAN 31in (77cm)

JFMAMJJASOND

VOICE A rapid *kek, kek, kek.*

EGGS Usually 4–5 (3–6) white or blue-white eggs with splotches appearing about halfway down the egg.

REARING Both incubate; 32–36 days' incubation; fledging 27–34 days; fed by male and female.

Sharp-shinned Hawk

SHARP-SHINNED HAWKS FEED ALMOST EXCLUSIVELY on small birds. They are wonderfully adapted for this diet, with rounded wings and a long tail that help them change course quickly as they maneuver through dense brush and forest in pursuit of agile prey. Watch for them migrating over open country during fall and spring.

Viewed from below, *the Sharp-shinned Hawk has a relatively small head and square tail. This contrasts with the large head and rounded tail of the Cooper's Hawk.*

Bush wacker

They resemble Cooper's Hawks in body shape, but Sharp-shinned Hawks are smaller than their crow-sized relative; more the size of a Rock Pigeon. Tail shape is a good way to separate the two species. The Sharp-shinned Hawk has a square tail, whereas the Cooper's Hawk has a round-tipped tail.

Although Sharp-shinned Hawks will sometimes lurk quietly in dense brush like Cooper's Hawks, they are also known for their habit of "bush-wacking" small birds. In this behavior, they make short flights over bushes and treetops to spook prey from

hiding, then they dash after their next meal. They may suddenly appear at feeders, sometimes snagging small birds in mid-air or from feeder perches. These chases often scatter feeder flocks into nearby windows. Tragically, these chases frequently

end with fatal window collisions for both the hawk and its prey. At birdfeeding stations, the prey consists of Mourning Dove, Blue Jay, European Starling, Dark-eyed Junco, Pine Siskin, House Finch, and House Sparrow.

Adult Sharp-shinned and Cooper's Hawks are blue above with rust color below. They typically perch in sheltered habitats such as forests and shrublands, and only rarely sit out in the open.

Accipiter striatus
Accipitridae

Head and neck proportionally smaller than Cooper's

Short, rounded wings

Dark back

Slim tail

Rusty-barred breast

Slightly notched or square folded tail

LENGTH 10–14in (25–35cm)
WINGSPAN 23in (57cm)

VOICE A high *kik, kik, kik.* Like Cooper's Hawk's, but shriller.
EGGS Usually 4–5 (3–8) dull white eggs with splotches of rich brown about halfway down the egg.
REARING Female incubates; 32–35 days' incubation; fledging 24–27 days; fed by male and female.

J F M A M J J A S O N D

IN THE BACKYARD

■ If possible, position feeders within three feet of a window. Birds frightened from such feeders by hawks are less likely to build lethal momentum if they strike the glass.

California Quail

THE CALIFORNIA QUAIL AND ITS DESERT RELATIVE, the Gambel's Quail, are perky western ground birds that often parade into backyard feeding areas in groups of 20 or more. Males give loud, territorial calls most often at dawn and dusk; covey calls help to reunite scattered members of the group.

The Gambel's Quails *looks similar to the California Quail, but it has a dark belly patch without a scaled pattern.*

Topknot visitors

California Quails frequent parks and rural areas west of the Rockies. In winter, family groups join together to form coveys of 20 to 50 birds. Both sexes have the striking "topknot" head plume that bobs as they strut. The covey members usually roost together in trees at night, but typically split into smaller groups during the day. Coveys offer protection from predators, and the huddled birds at night share body heat. When a predator threatens the covey, the group scatters into the air or it may flee on foot into tangled brush. California Quails sometimes live within cities, where they frequent brushy areas in parks and the suburbs, often surprising residents by strolling across lawns.

Gambel's Quails (*Callipepla gambelii*) are desert relatives of the California Quail, found only in the Southwestern US. Like California Quails, they may visit feeders, but they make the most of their visits in the early dawn and late afternoon. Gambel's Quails can survive with little water, but they readily take water when it is available. Like other quails, they also require sprouted greens, especially clover and other legumes.

California Quails *are readily recognized by their distinctive head plume and scaled pattern below.*

Callipepla californica
Odontophoridae

Short black plume curving forward from the crown

Rather long-tailed for a quail

Black and white face and throat pattern

Chicken-like body

LENGTH 9–11in (23–28cm)
WINGSPAN 14in (36cm)
VOICE Three-syllabled

J F M A M J J A S O N D

qua-quer'go, chi-ca'go. Light clucking calls.
EGGS Usually 10–12 (10–15) dull white eggs with brown spots and blotches. Two or more females may lay in the same nest.
REARING Female incubates; 18–23 days' incubation; fledging 10 days; both parents tend chicks.

IN THE BACKYARD

■ Where outdoor cats frequent backyards, provide safe opportunities for quail on raised platform feeders at least several feet off the ground. Although quails are usually ground feeders, they roost in trees.

Northern Bobwhite

FEW BIRDS SAY THEIR NAME AS DISTINCTLY as the Bobwhite. Males announce their presence as reliably as a rooster greeting the dawn with the emphatic "Bob White" whistle. The performance may occur throughout the day, especially in the evening. Both sexes give emphatic covey calls.

Dust bathers

Like other quails, bobwhites are particularly fond of dusting, especially where they find dry, sunny soil. This behavior helps to remove feather mites and other parasites, and serves as an aid to maintaining immaculate plumages. Bobwhites require habitat containing brushy fencerows or hedges and bare soil, where they scratch for weed seeds and insects. Dense pasture grasses are not favored.

Bobwhites and most other quail are becoming increasingly rare. Many factors affect their numbers—including changes in agricultural practices such as fewer shrubby fencerows and less spilled grain—but losses to predators are also a major factor. Small predatory mammals such as raccoons, fox, and skunk are often abundant near farms and even in cities. The ground-nesting habits of the quail make them especially vulnerable to feral and domestic cats, particularly near cities and suburbs.

Bobwhites frequent *borders of woods and fields, especially where they find disturbed soils near agricultural land.*

The male Bobwhite *(left) is easily distinguished from the female by the bold black-and-white patterns on their heads.*

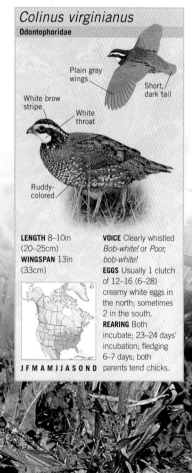

Colinus virginianus
Odontophoridae

Plain gray wings

White brow stripe

White throat

Short, dark tail

Ruddy-colored

LENGTH 8–10in (20–25cm)
WINGSPAN 13in (33cm)

J F M A M J J A S O N D

VOICE Clearly whistled *Bob-white!* or *Poor, bob-white!*
EGGS Usually 1 clutch of 12–16 (6–28) creamy white eggs in the north; sometimes 2 in the south.
REARING Both incubate; 23–24 days' incubation; fledging 6–7 days; both parents tend chicks.

IN THE BACKYARD

■ Bobwhites are not regular feeder visitors, but coveys sometimes approach for their favorite foods of millet, cracked corn, and milo. Plant rows of clover and till strips along hedgerows and brushy forest edges, letting weeds grow in the disturbed soil.

Ring-necked Pheasant

FIRST INTRODUCED FROM ASIA to California in 1857, these colorful members of the chicken family are now established throughout most of the northern United States, especially in the prairie states. Although many are reared and released for hunting, wild populations are self-sustaining in many areas.

Brilliant colors

Male Ring-necked Pheasants are spectacular birds that stand on their heels, throw their heads back like a rooster, and broadcast their discordant blast, followed by loud wing-flapping. Males have green heads and necks, a red wattle, and often white neck-rings. In contrast, females and juveniles are smaller and drab brown. Male pheasants are more often seen in gardens than females, in part because they are more conspicuous and also more eager to defend their territory. Often several females form a group in association with a single male, who defends his harem from rival males.

Females lay 10–12 eggs in a depression, but sometimes they lay in the nests of other ground-nesting birds such as ducks, domestic hens, quails, turkeys, and grouse. Young pheasants usually stay with the female and receive protection from predators for about their first month. When threatened, the female may perform a broken-wing act, in which she hobbles away from the chicks, distracting predators such as foxes.

Pheasants mainly forage for food by scratching on the ground, but also clamber in trees for buds and fruit. They eat a range of foods, especially grain and other seeds and acorns, but also insects, snails, worms, and the occasional small mammal and lizard.

Male Ring-necked Pheasants *display their spectacular plumage to attract mates and intimidate rivals. The discordant call is often followed by wing-flapping.*

Hen Ring-necked Pheasants *incubate the eggs and brood the chicks. Each male may have several females in his harem.*

Phasianus colchicus
Phasianidae

Metallic green head

Red face

Copper-colored body

White neck-ring in some races

Pale rump patch

Tail long, pointed, barred, trailing tail

LENGTH 20–35in (51–89cm)
WINGSPAN 27–35in (69–89cm)

VOICE Male song is a loud *kork-kok*, to which the female replies with a *kea-kea*.
EGGS Typically 10–12 (6–15) olive-brown, unmarked eggs.
REARING Female incubates; 23–25 days' incubation; fledging 12 days; fed by female.

J F M A M J J A S O N D

IN THE BACKYARD

■ Pheasants sometimes visit rural gardens to take grain, bread, and kitchen leftovers. They also eat insects, snails, and worms.

Mourning Dove

NAMED FOR ITS MOURNFUL SOUNDING CALL, the Mourning Dove is the only North American dove found in every state and province. Mourning Doves can raise six broods per year, more than any North American bird, a living reminder of the now-extinct Passenger Pigeon, whose numbers filled the skies until the late 1800s.

An appetite for seeds

In winter, Mourning Doves live in small groups, frequenting farm fields, railroad tracks, and backyards, feeding almost entirely on small seeds and grains. Unlike most birds that include large numbers of insects in their diet, Mourning Doves are almost exclusive seed-eaters. The stomach of one was found to hold 7,500 seeds of yellow wood sorrel; another held 17,200 grass seeds. Flocks of 50 to several hundred occur on agricultural land, but smaller flocks are the rule at backyard feeders. At birdfeeders, they eat cracked corn, millet, canary, and sunflower seeds.

Early nesting

In late winter, Mourning Doves begin to pair, starting to nest long before most other species, sometimes when snow still lingers. The pair builds a loose nest of sticks, usually in a conifer about 5–25ft (1.5–7.5m) from the ground, but sometimes they choose peculiar nest locations, such as windowsills and roof gutters. They take regular incubation shifts: males incubate the two-egg clutch by day, and females at night.

Mourning Doves are able to keep themselves on cold winter days by ruffling their plumage. This can also cool them down in summer.

Mourning Doves are robin-sized, with a distinctive small head and a long, pointed tail.

Zenaida macroura
Columbidae

Gray underwing

Wings uniform brown above

Long, pointed tail with large white spots

Pale bluish orbital ring

Gray-brown overall

Buff belly

Black spots on back

Long, pointed tail

Smaller and slimmer than rock dove

LENGTH 12in (30cm)
WINGSPAN 18in (46cm)
VOICE A hollow, mournful *coah, cooo, cooo, coo.*
EGGS Usually 2, occasionally 3, unmarked, white eggs. Often 2 or more clutches.
REARING Both incubate, on day/night shifts; 13–14 days' incubation; fledging 12–14 days; fed by male and female.

J F M A M J J A S O N D

IN THE BACKYARD

■ Provide nesting cones for Mourning Doves in forked branches of conifers. Cut cones from a 12in (30cm) square of fine-meshed hardware cloth. Where cats are a threat, provide food on raised platforms.

Rock Pigeon (Feral Pigeon)

THE ANCESTORS OF ROCK PIGEONS (Feral Pigeons) once lived in European sea cliffs. Now they usually frequent urban canyons and barnyards, where tall buildings and towering silos serve as sea cliff equivalents. Rather than nesting in sea caves, these adaptable birds nest on windowsills and squeeze into rooftop attics. They are famous as "homing pigeons," and are often bred for racing.

Columba livia

Columbidae

Purple-green sheen to neck and breast

Large, white spot on bill

Reddish pink legs

Variable plumage color

Some have double wingbars

Dark bill

Compact body

LENGTH 12–14in (30–36cm)
WINGSPAN 25–27in (63–69cm)

VOICE The low, cooing *ooor-ooor* or *o-roo-coo* is a familiar sound in city parks and streets.
EGGS Usually several clutches of 2 smooth, glossy white eggs.
REARING Male and female incubates; 16–19 days' incubation; fledging 25–26 days; fed by male and female.

J F M A M J J A S O N D

Rock Pigeons are stockier and shorter-necked than other pigeons. There is enormous color variation, but all have a white, fleshy spot (cere) above the beak.

City dweller

Few birds are more easily recognizable than the Rock Pigeons that live in our towns and cities. Some individuals resemble more closely their wild ancestors: these birds are blue-gray with two distinctive black bars on each wing. However, plumage colors range from all-black to all-white, with countless shades of brown and gray. All variants have a large, white, fleshy patch—the cere—at the base of the bill. Rock Pigeons in city parks are often very tame, especially where they are fed regularly, and they can become a problem when they foul buildings. Yet their courtship behavior, colorful plumage, and friendly character

provide an opportunity for even the most urban-bound people to connect to wildlife in positive ways.

Paired for life

Young Rock Pigeons spend their time in flocks, but pairs retain their nesting territories and often live together all year round, even when they are not breeding. Like their wild ancestors, Rock Pigeons usually mate for life, and pairs may nest at any time of year if conditions are favorable, although fewer nest during the winter months.

The male courts the female by driving her away from the rest of the flock and performing bowing displays, or by flying close behind her when she takes off. The female, with the assistance of the male, builds the nest

When displaying to females, male Rock Pigeons inflate their throat, fluff their plumage, and parade around females.

of twigs or grasses. The chosen site is often on a ledge or in a hole in a building within easy reach of an available food source. Both parents help to incubate the eggs and feed the nestlings, continuing to do so for about ten days after fledging. Like other pigeons, Rock Pigeons feed their nestlings entirely on "pigeon milk," a secretion from the crop that is rich in protein and fat, for the first ten days after hatching.

Indiscriminate scavenger

City-dwelling Rock Pigeons scavenge for any edible meal; in rural areas and barnyards, they feed on the seeds of crops and plants, and on green leaves, buds, and invertebrates.

In times past, city pigeons relied on spilled grain from horses' nosebags but nowadays it is fast-food outlets that provide largesse. Many urban pigeons take at least some of their food from handouts in city parks and squares. It is not uncommon for some

Rock Pigeons typically live in groups of 20 or more; in flight, their shape resembles that of a falcon.

birds to learn to recognize individual providers and to approach these people when they see them appear.

PigeonWatch is an international research project involving people of all ages and locations in a real scientific endeavor. The data is crucial for research, and PigeonWatchers learn all about this bird.

Able to adapt to a wide range of city and farm environments, Rock Pigeons occur throughout North America, often congregating in city parks.

133

Screech-owls

SCREECH-OWLS ARE SECRETIVE and easily overlooked. They usually nest in old woodpecker cavities, but readily accept large bird-houses for roosting throughout the year. Screech-owls are most abundant in sparse woods, streamside forests, and mesquite deserts, but often reside in suburban backyards if they find suitable nest boxes.

Night owls

Screech-owls start feeding soon after dusk and may continue throughout the night, eating insects, small mammals, and birds. Look for telltale evidence of their diet in the regurgitated pellets of feathers and bones, and debris left from their meals in nest boxes.

Two species

Screech-owls begin nesting in February in southern states, but nesting is delayed until July in far northern habitats. Females do most or all of the incubation, while the male provides her with food. Both members of the pair feed the 4–8 young, which leave the nest about 27 days after hatching. They prefer to nest in abandoned flicker cavities, often in sycamores along streams. In the southwest, they often nest in Saguaro cavities. Eastern Screech-owls have gray, red, or brown plumages and a trilling call. Western Screech-owls (Otus kennicottii) are usually gray or brown; their call is a series of short whistles.

Parent Screech-owls *often close their eyes when delivering food to chicks, to insure that their eyes are not injured by their eager young.*

A young Screech-owl *eagerly awaits the return of its parents for a meal. After leaving the nest, young remain dependent for several weeks.*

Otus asio
Strigidae

Underside relatively strongly barred

Ear tufts, may be inconspicuous on young

Pale greenish or gray bill

Whitish bill tip

Two color phases: reddish brown and gray

LENGTH 7–10in (18–25cm)
WINGSPAN 20in (50cm)

J F M A M J J A S O N D

VOICE A mournful whinny or wail; tremulous, and descending in pitch; sometimes a series on a single pitch.
EGGS Usually 4–5 (2–7) all white eggs.
REARING Both incubate; 26 days' incubation; fledging 27 days; fed by male and female.

IN THE BACKYARD

■ Create a Screech-owl trail in forests, orchards, or other habitats where large cavities are scarce by hanging nest boxes at least 10ft (3m) from the ground. Place several inches of wood chips in the box.

Anna's Hummingbird

THESE ARE THE MOST ABUNDANT and widespread hummingbirds on the Pacific coast of North America. Anna's Hummingbirds often frequent human-modified habitats and are thus a familiar sight in backyards and parks. This adaptable species is also commonly found in open woodland and shrubby areas.

Calypte anna
Trochilidae

Wings appear blurred as they fly

Gray-edged tail feathers

Tail held stationary and in line with body

Long, sloping forehead

Short, straight bill

Dark head with pale eye-ring

Red crown and throat

LENGTH 3–4in (9–10cm)
WINGSPAN 4in (13cm)

J F M A M J J A S O N D

VOICE Song consists of squeaking, grating calls; feeding call is *chick.*
EGGS Usually 2 (1–3) pure white eggs.
REARING Female incubates; 14–19 days' incubation; fledging 18–23 days; fed by female.

Easy to identify

Anna's Hummingbirds are bigger than most other hummingbird species within their range. Identify them by the short, straight beak, which is proportionately large for the body size. Males are easy to differentiate from other western hummingbirds, as they are the only species with an iridescent rose-red gorget (throat) and crown. Females resemble several other western species, but have a husky build, gray breast, and patch of rose-red in the center of the throat.

Winter nesting

During the courting season, males stake out a territory over a patch of flowers with a rich supply of nectar.

An immature and female Anna's Hummingbird lacks the male's brilliant throat and crown, though it does show a little red on the throat.

They then begin to advertise their presence above the flowers with a towering vertical flight that ends in a J shape. Females enter the territory, where mating occurs, and then depart to build a nest. For this they use plant down and spider webs, then decorate the exterior with lichens.

Unlike other hummingbirds that nest in the United States, Anna's is not migratory. Courtship and nesting begin in November and December, and the cycle is complete by late spring. After breeding, they occasionally wander as far north as Alaska.

IN THE BACKYARD

■ Increase hummingbird traffic in your garden by providing a shallow, puddle-like pool with clean water. Use a glass pie pan or nonporous flowerpot dish. Replace the water twice each week.

The adult male Anna's Hummingbird is the only hummingbird with a brilliant red throat and crown. They are common visitors to backyard feeders and flower gardens.

Ruby-throated Hummingbird

THIS IS THE ONLY HUMMINGBIRD to frequent eastern North America. It is named for the male's dazzling red throat, but the flashy color is apparent only in a certain light and the male's throat more often appears black. Unlike the males, females and young, who typically outnumber adult males, have white throats.

Marathoners

Despite their tiny size, Ruby-throated Hummingbirds perform a marathon fall migration from southern Canada to Central America, crossing the Gulf of Mexico or skirting its border. They arrive along the Gulf Coast in March, then work their way northward, arriving in Canada by the first week of May. Soon after, males begin displaying to attract females with dramatic aerial dances that consist of pendulum-like, 180° swings. Pairing is promiscuous, with each male attempting to attract many females.

Knotlike nest

The Ruby-throated Hummingbird's nest is about the size of a half-dollar; just large enough to hold two white eggs the size of small beans. The female usually locates the nest on a forked branch 5–20ft (1.5–6m) from the ground. The nest resembles a small knot, constructed of plant fibers, held together with spider web and often lined with stem-fuzz collected from ferns. As a final touch of camouflage, the female uses spider webs to attach large, green lichens to the outside of the nest.

Hummingbirds readily visit gardens to feed on natural nectar sources from native plants such as this trumpet honeysuckle (Lonicera sempervirens).

IN THE BACKYARD

■ Provide terraced native plantings for hummingbirds, including trees, shrubs, vines, and garden flowers with tube-shaped red, orange, and yellow flowers.

After mating, *females build their nests and raise their young without help from males. They often return to the same site the following spring.*

Archilochus colubris
Trochilidae

Longer tail than Black-chinned with deeper notch

Glowing, fiery red throat, which appears black with backlighting

Iridescent green back

Forked tail projects beyond wingtips

LENGTH 3–3½in (8–9cm)
WINGSPAN 4½in (11cm)

VOICE Calls are squeaky and high. Male in aerial display gives a hum as he moves in a wide arc.
EGGS 2 white eggs; occasionally 2 broods.
REARING Female incubates; believed to be 11–14 days' incubation; fledging 14–28 days; fed by female.

J F M **A M J J A S O N** D

Rufous Hummingbird

WHEN IT COMES TO SETTING MIGRATION RECORDS, the Rufous Hummingbird wins the prize. This pugnacious and noisy bird, notable for chasing rivals with great vigor from feeding areas, flies from its nesting habitat in southern Alaska to central Mexico, a distance of up to 3,000 miles (4,800km).

Fuel-efficient

These tiny dynamos are masters of energy efficiency. They burn calories and oxygen at an extraordinary rate, pumping blood with a proportionately larger heart than other hummers have. They also have special blood and muscle characteristics that permit them to beat their wings at 45 beats per second.

Although they weigh less than a quarter, Rufous Hummingbirds can fly 500 miles (800km) without stopping to refuel. They may stay at a rich feeding area for two weeks, increasing their weight by 50 percent before continuing the next leg of their migration. Rufous Hummingbirds conserve energy by roosting at low elevations, where they find more moderate temperatures, and then buzz back to feeding areas at higher elevations by day. Rufous Hummingbirds can also reduce their body temperature at night to further save energy.

Sapsucker associates

Like Ruby-throated Hummingbirds, Rufous hummers time their migration to coincide with the opening of certain flowers and the migration of sapsuckers. These sapsuckers are especially important for Rufous Hummingbirds as there are relatively few flowers available in Alaska when the hummers first arrive. Holes drilled by sapsuckers provide a predictable source of sweet sap in early spring.

This male Rufous Hummingbird *is feeding on red hot poker, (*Kniphofia uvaria), *a favorite perennial garden flower.*

The female Rufous Hummingbird *lacks the distinctive red throat of her male counterpart and often has a green back.*

Selasphorus rufus
Trochilidae

Flaming orange-red throat

Outer tail feathers usually broader than Allen's Hummingbird

Bright red-brown back

White breast

The only North American hummingbird with a red back

LENGTH 3½in (9cm)

WINGSPAN 4⅓in (11cm)

VOICE Call a high, hard *chip tyuk*.
EGGS Usually 2 pure white eggs.
REARING Female incubates; 12–14 days' incubation ; fledging 20 days; fed by female.

J F M A M J J A S O N D

IN THE BACKYARD

■ Native columbine, bleeding hearts, and Solomon's seal provide food in early spring. Also, plant red-flowered currant and salmonberry as well as mountain ash, which is a favorite tree for sapsuckers.

Downy Woodpecker

THE SMALLEST WOODPECKERS in North America, these perky, short-beaked, black-and-white tree-clingers are especially fond of nuts and suet. They are very similar in appearance to the robin-sized Hairy Woodpecker, but the latter has a proportionately longer beak. Males of both species have a red patch on the back of the head.

Dominant males

The diminutive size of the Downy Woodpecker permits it to hang on stems of goldenrod, where it pounds the ball-shaped galls to extract fly larvae. Before they begin the laborious process of excavation, they determine the quality of the fly larvae by giving the gall a light tap and listening for a response. The appetite that Downy Woodpeckers have for suet probably derives from their fondness for insect larvae, as both suet and insect larvae are rich in fat.

The mated pair usually stays together through the winter, with the male showing dominance over the female. The preferred foraging habitat is treetops, where the bark is thinner and it is easier to dig deeper holes for insect grubs. The males usually chase the females from the tops of trees, relegating them to feed lower down. In late winter, when food is

Downy Woodpeckers are often seen hanging upside down, as they feed on swaying plant stems such as this sunflower head.

scarce, pairs may temporarily split up, which permits the female to forage in better habitats. Even at feeders, there is often tension between the pair, especially in mid-winter. As spring approaches and the pair become more territorial, they reunite and there is less squabbling.

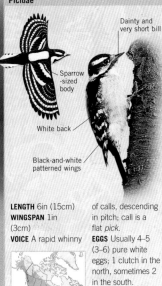

Picoides pubescens
Picidae

Dainty and very short bill

Sparrow -sized body

White back

Black-and-white patterned wings

LENGTH 6in (15cm)
WINGSPAN 1in (3cm)
VOICE A rapid whinny

J F M A M J J A S O N D

of calls, descending in pitch; call is a flat *pick*.
EGGS Usually 4–5 (3–6) pure white eggs; 1 clutch in the north, sometimes 2 in the south.
REARING Both incubate; 12 days' incubation; fledging 20–25 days; fed by male and female.

IN THE BACKYARD

■ Hang raw beef-kidney suet in a mesh bag, or use a commercial suet feeder. Avoid using suet when temperatures climb well above freezing because the fat will turn rancid and stain plumage.

Distinguish Downy Woodpeckers *from the similar Hairy Woodpecker by their short bill—it is only as long as the distance from the base of the bill to the back of the eye. Adult males have a red patch on their nape.*

Hairy Woodpecker

SIMILAR IN APPEARANCE to the Downy Woodpecker, Hairys are distinguished by their hefty bills, the length of which equals the distance from the back of the head to the base of the bill. Both sexes defend their territory in winter and spring with a drumming that is louder, faster, and somewhat shorter than that of the Downy.

Raw suet is a favorite food of Hairy Woodpeckers. It is easy to make a wire feeder like this and attach it to a tree.

Beetle detector

Hairy Woodpeckers sometimes use their large beaks to pound a tree trunk with a series of side blows. This may send echoes into the trunk, helping to detect the presence of beetle larvae. Sometimes they hold their beak in the excavated hole, apparently feeling or listening for the movement of prey. At other times they use their beak to remove flakes of bark, looking for hiding insects. Males typically excavate deep into wood, while females do more picking at the surface.

At feeders, Hairy Woodpeckers favor suet, peanut-butter, and sunflower seeds. They usually feed peacefully with other feeder birds, but the behavior of the male changes if another male appears, when they threaten the intruder with head and tail swaying from side to side. Females are greeted similarly, except with the tail spread.

Lifelong residents

Hairy Woodpeckers usually occupy the same territory, with the same mate, for life. Males do most of the nest-cavity excavation, typically choosing a location in the top of a dead tree.

IN THE BACKYARD

■ Leave at least one tall, dead tree on your property and leave some dead branches on living trees. These are necessary for nesting and roosting cavities, and or drumming posts.

The male Hairy Woodpecker *has a patch of red on the back of his head. Juveniles of both sexes have red on their foreheads in July and August.*

Picoides villosus
Picidae

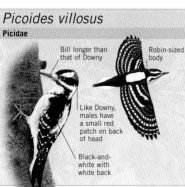

Bill longer than that of Downy

Robin-sized body

Like Downy, males have a small red patch on back of head

Black-and-white with white back

LENGTH 9½in (24cm)
WINGSPAN 15in (38cm)
VOICE Call is a Kingfisher-like rattle; also a flat *pick*.
EGGS 1 clutch; usually 4 (3–6) pure white eggs.
REARING Both incubate; 11–15 days' incubation;

fledging believed to be 28–30 days; fed by male and female.

J F M A M J J A S O N D

Red-bellied Woodpecker

RED-BELLIED WOODPECKERS are named for the seldom-seen patch of red on their lower belly. Both sexes have red on the nape, and the male has red extending over the head to the base of the beak. They closely resemble Golden-fronted Woodpeckers (*Melanerpes aurifrons*) and Gila Woodpeckers (*Melanerpes uropygialis*) of the Southwest.

The male Red-bellied Woodpecker has a vermillion red nape, crown, and forehead; females have only a red nape.

Acorn hiders

Red-bellied Woodpeckers are most common in wooded bottomlands along rivers, swamps, and mixed groves of conifers and deciduous trees. However, they also regularly venture to birdfeeders and backyard habitats if there are trees or shrubs near the feeder. They drill into wood to extract the larvae of wood-boring beetles, but often feed on berries and nuts. They also store acorns, nuts, insects, and fruit pulp for later meals. Often they hide their caches with vegetation to reduce the chance of theft by Pileated

Woodpeckers, who frequently rob their hidden reserves. Both parents help to excavate the nesting cavity, which they normally locate in a partly decayed limb. The parents take turns brooding the young for the first week after hatching. Both feed the chicks, which leave the nesting cavity when they are about 26 days old, and usually continue to feed their young for the next six weeks. Their population is increasing as their range expands northwards, perhaps due to the warming climate.

The Red-bellied Woodpecker's namesake patch is often visible as the bird clings to feeders to eat suet and other foods.

IN THE BACKYARD

■ At garden feeding stations, Red-bellied Woodpeckers favor suet, nuts, whole corn, and peanut-butter. Offer whole corn by pressing it onto a spike driven through a board that is strapped securely to a tree trunk.

Melanerpes carolinus
Picidae

White patch on wings

Barred upperside

Red cap covers crown and nape

Zebra back pattern

Speckled rump

LENGTH 16–19½in (41–50cm)
WINGSPAN 29in (74cm)
VOICE Call is *kik-kik-kikkik—kik-kik*, like that of a flicker, but louder and irregular.
EGGS Usually 4 (3–5) white eggs.
REARING Both incubate, the male at night; 15–18 days' incubation; fledging 26–28 days; fed by male and female.

J F M A M J J A S O N D

Pileated Woodpecker

THIS UNMISTAKABLE, CROW-SIZED WOODPECKER exists in every US state and throughout southern Canada. Both sexes have a striking red crest; the male also has a red forehead and red whisker marks. In flight the Pileated Woodpecker displays a bold, black-and-white wing pattern.

Drumming and feeding

The pair requires a large, forested territory, where they remain through the year. Males defend the core of the territory with drumming and a loud, trumpeting call that is reminiscent of a jungle scream from a *Tarzan* movie. Males without mates drum more often than those with mates; the sound is produced by repeated striking of the bill against a tree trunk or branch. Larvae from termites, ants, and wood-boring beetles comprise about 75 percent of the Pileated Woodpecker's diet. Typically, they feed on large trees, excavating oblong cavities deep into the heartwood. These cavities are often big enough to enclose the bird completely. More than any other woodpecker, they also feed on decaying, fallen trees. In the fall and winter, they build fat

The call of the *Pileated Woodpecker is reminiscent of a flicker's, except that it is slower and lower-pitched.*

reserves by changing to a diet of acorns and fruit. Occasionally they visit feeders for suet.

Nesting

Male Pileated Woodpeckers typically roost in the nesting cavity prior to incubation and continue occupying the cavity at night, taking the nocturnal incubation shift. Females incubate by day, and both sexes brood and rear the young. They are among only a few birds known to retrieve eggs after the loss of a nest. In one well-documented case, a female returned to her nest after a storm to find the nesting tree broken off, exposing her eggs. Within 20 minutes, she had carried the eggs in her bill to a new nesting site.

Dryocopus pileatus
Picidae

Prominent, flaming red crest

All black back

Flashing white underwing areas

Long-necked with broad wings

LENGTH 16–9½in (41–50cm)
WINGSPAN 29in (74cm)

VOICE Call is *kik-kik-kikkik—kik-kik*, etc; resembles that of a flicker, but louder, and irregular.
EGGS Usually 4 (3–5) white eggs.
REARING Both incubate; 15–18 days' incubation; fledging 26–28 days; fed by male and female.

J F M A M J J A S O N D

IN THE BACKYARD

■ Leave fallen trees on the ground and ensure that some large dead trees remain standing. Encourage grapevines, Virginia creeper, and sumac to provide fall and winter foods.

Pileated Woodpeckers *typically excavate deep, oblong feeding channels to expose carpenter ants and beetles deep within trees.*

Northern Flicker

THESE GROUND-FEEDING BACKYARD WOODPECKERS are easily identified by their bold white rumps, which they flash as they take wing. Presumably this startles predators, such as Cooper's Hawks, which follow the target only to lose their prey when the woodpecker abruptly lands, folding its wings over the rump. Most flickers belong to two subspecies of the Northern Flicker: the Yellow-shafted has an eastern distribution, the Red-shafted occurs in the west.

Colaptes auratus
Picidae

Brownish head with gray or brown crown

Black or red mustache

Black patch on chest; spotted below

Conspicuous white rump

Golden yellow or red under the wings and tail

LENGTH 12–14in (30–35cm)
WINGSPAN 20in (50cm)

VOICE Calls are a loud *klee-yer*, and a squeaky *flick-a, flick-a*.
EGGS Usually 5–8 (3–12) glossy white eggs.
REARING Both incubate; 11–14 days' incubation; fledging 25–28 days; fed by male and female.

J F M A M J J A S O N D

Ground feeders
Flickers frequently feed on the ground, hopping over lawns and other open habitats such as forest floors and fields. Insects make up about 75 percent of their diet, and ants comprise more than half of their prey. Flickers also eat grasshoppers, crickets, wasps, beetles, and other flying insects, which they can capture on the wing—a surprising talent for a woodpecker! The remainder of the diet consists of fruits and berries, mainly dogwood, Virginia creeper, hack-berries, pokeberries, elderberries, and serviceberries. They also eat sumac fruits, including those from poison sumac and poison ivy.

Flickers have *brown backs and a black breast patch. Males from the east have yellow feather shafts and a black whisker mark.*

They seldom come to feeders, but sometimes snack on suet and peanut-butter mixtures.

Nesting
Males usually select the nest site and do most of the excavation on the trunk of a dead tree that typically rises from bushes. Such snags may have 25 or 30 old nesting holes, but they also reuse nesting cavities from previous years. The nest is located between 2ft (60cm) and 90ft (27m) off the ground and contains fresh woodchips in the bottom. More than most other woodpeckers, flickers also use nest boxes. Both sexes incubate the eggs, with the male taking the night shift and both parents helping to raise the brood on a diet of regurg-itated insects. Nesting cavities created by flickers are used by many other species, but they are especially important for Buffleheads, a small tree-nesting duck of the Canadian lakes.

The roosting sites are usually within a mile of each other, but stay within an area of about half a square mile. Studies of flickers carrying

Western Northern Flickers *typically have red feather shafts; males have red whisker marks.*

transmitters have shown that males usually sleep in a different roosting location every night: hanging onto a tree, under the eaves of a building, or in a tree cavity.

Flickers have declined in abundance over the past 30 years. Several factors are likely to have contributed to this, including the regrowth of secondary forest throughout much of the eastern part of their range, which causes the loss of favored shrublands and fields. Control of fire ants with insecticides is probably taking its toll in the southern US, where most flickers winter. Also, introduced European Starlings can drive flickers from nesting cavities.

Hungry nestlings *beg for food from their father, who is identified by his distinctive whisker marks.*

Female flickers, *which can be distinguished by their lack of whisker marks, assist with excavating the nesting cavity.*

IN THE BACKYARD

■ Leave nesting snags for flickers and hang nest boxes; plant shrubs such as elderberry, serviceberry, and dogwoods.

Chimney Swift

ALTHOUGH CHIMNEY SWIFTS look like swallows, they are more closely related to hummingbirds. Both groups have tiny feet and stubby legs. Although they once nested in hollow trees, Chimney Swifts now nest and roost almost exclusively within chimneys and similar man-made structures.

During fall *migration, hundreds of chimney swifts sleep together in communal roosts within chimneys and smokestacks.*

Nesting

Although many pairs sometimes nest together within airshafts of large buildings, most swifts have solitary nests within small chimneys, where they nest within a few feet of the top. Here they usually lay 4–6 white eggs. Young swifts stay in the nest longer than most other birds their size and typically fly from the nest when they are about three weeks old. Chimney Swifts have tiny, hooked beaks, but a huge mouth which they open in flight to capture flying insects such as beetles, flies, and ants. As their name suggests, Chimney Swifts are built for speed in the air, with pointed wings resembling those of a falcon.

Gregarious roosting

During migration, large numbers come together to roost at night in big industrial chimneys. Such roosting concentrations are spectacular, with hundreds of birds circling the roost for an hour before dark, then pouring into the chimney at dusk, like smoke entering the shaft.

Chimney Swifts attach their small, cup-shaped nest against the inner wall of a chimney, silo, or open well with glue-like saliva.

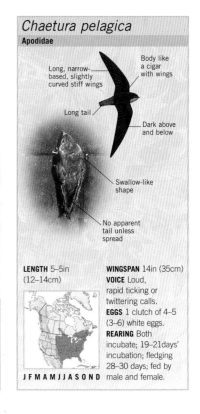

Chaetura pelagica
Apodidae

Body like a cigar with wings

Long, narrow-based, slightly curved stiff wings

Long tail

Dark above and below

Swallow-like shape

No apparent tail unless spread

LENGTH 5–5in (12–14cm)

WINGSPAN 14in (35cm)
VOICE Loud, rapid ticking or twittering calls.
EGGS 1 clutch of 4–5 (3–6) white eggs.
REARING Both incubate; 19–21days' incubation; fledging 28–30 days; fed by male and female.

J F M A M J J A S O N D

IN THE BACKYARD

■ If Chimney Swifts frequent your chimney, avoid using the fireplace in the spring as the heat and gases may kill the parents and young.

Eastern Phoebe

IDENTIFY EASTERN PHOEBES by their upright posture and tail-wagging behavior. Like other insect-eating birds, they migrate from northern habitats in winter, typically wintering in southern states, which helps to explain why they are among the first migrants to return in the spring.

Sayornis phoebe
Tyrannidae

Wagging tail

No eye rings

No wing-bars

Gray-brown body, size of large sparrow

Dark, long tail

Large, dark head

LENGTH 6–7in (16–18cm)
WINGSPAN 10in (25cm)

J F M A M J J A S O N D

VOICE Song is a burry, well-enunciated *phoe-be* or *fi-bree*; call is a sharp *chip*.
EGGS Usually 4–5 (3–8) white eggs with sparse spots. Often 2 clutches.
REARING Female incubates; 16 days' incubation; fledging 15–16 days; fed by male and female.

Shelf nesters

Phoebes once nested mainly along stream-bank cliffs and overhangs, but these adaptable birds now usually occupy porches, eaves and rafters of houses, barns, and sheds. Often they locate the nest near a doorway that is in regular use, demonstrating their tolerance for humans.

The substantial nest is built from pellets of mud and grass with an outer covering of moss; they line the nest with hair and fine grasses. Phoebe nests are often parasitized by Brown-headed Cowbirds. If the cowbird lays its egg first, the phoebe may abandon the nest. Phoebes may occasionally renovate old nests or build onto Barn Swallow nests. The birds that build new nests may have smaller clutches than those that adapt old nests.

Eastern Phoebes are named for their raspy-toned call, which repeats "phoebe." Their tail-wagging habit is another clue to identity.

Western cousins

Black Phoebes (*Sayornis nigricans*) exist in California and southwestern states. They frequent backyards, open woodland, and canyons. Like Eastern Phoebes, they perform the distinctive tail-wagging behavior.

Black Phoebes are common southwestern birds, frequenting habitat similar to that of their eastern cousin. Like the Eastern Phoebe, they are easily recognized by their tail-wagging.

IN THE BACKYARD

■ Plant sumac and bayberries for winter food; blackberries, blueberries, elderberries, and hackberries for summer food. Provide a 6inx6in (15cmx15cm) nesting shelf and secure it under eaves or a similar overhang.

Blue Jay

THESE STRIKINGLY BEAUTIFUL blue-backed birds are easily recognized by their erect crest and prominent black necklace. Once a bird mainly of wilderness forests, Blue Jays have adapted to the suburbs and cities, and are frequent visitors to backyard feeders. Like other members of the crow family, they are inquisitive and intelligent.

Most of the year, Blue Jays live in boisterous flocks, but when they are nesting they become remarkably quiet.

Cyanocitta cristata
Corvidae

Bold, white spots on tail and secondaries

Crest

Broad, rounded wings

Pale blue upperside

Black necklace

Whitish or dull gray underside

LENGTH 11–12in (28–30cm)
WINGSPAN 16in (41cm)
VOICE A harsh slurring *jeeah* or *jay.* Calls include a musical *queedle, queedle.*
EGGS Usually 4–5 (3–7) olive or buff eggs marked dots and spots. One clutch in north, 2 or 3 in south.
REARING Both incubate; 16–18 days' incubation; fledging 17–21 days; fed by male and female.

J F M A M J J A S O N D

Oak planters

Blue Jays readily consume acorns and beech and hickory nuts. Although many animals eat acorns, only jays regularly carry the nuts far (more than several hundred yards) from the parent tree. For this reason, many species of oaks and other nut-bearing trees may depend exclusively on Blue Jays for long-distance dispersal of their seeds. Only jays routinely carry and bury acorns. Although some Blue Jays are resident throughout the year, others migrate, especially in years when there are few acorns available.

Blue Jays also eat a wide variety of insects, fruit, and the eggs and young of smaller birds.

Secretive near nests

Both males and females of the pair break off sticks and weave their nest, which often includes moss, bark, lichens, and paper. They locate the nest in shrubs, vines, or low trees, usually 10–15ft (3–4.5m) from the ground. Although jays are known for their noisy, boisterous behavior throughout most of the year, when nesting they become generally silent, except that they will dive at intruders approaching the nest.

Steller's Jays (*Cyanocitta stelleri*) resemble Blue Jays in body shape and crest, but have a black head and crest. They frequent western mountains and coastal conifer forests.

The Steller's Jay is the western counterpart of the Blue Jay. Like Blue Jays, they often eat the eggs and young of other species.

IN THE BACKYARD

■ Provide whole peanuts, cracked corn and sunflower seed. To ensure sunflower feed for small birds as well as for jays, place seed in feeders that limit access, such as those with weighted doors, no perches, or within cages.

Western Scrub Jay

NAMED FOR THEIR HABIT of frequenting scrub-oak forests, Western Scrub Jays are familiar backyard residents throughout much of the west. The Pacific Coast population is brighter blue than the interior population; they are also bolder and become so tame that they will take peanuts from the hand.

Feeding and caching

Feeding stations located near the territories of several Scrub Jay families may host a number of family groups at the same time, while a sentinel sits high, watching for predators. At feeders, these birds can consume huge amounts of sunflower seeds: one observer counted a Scrub Jay eating over 100 seeds in a half-hour. Such collections are transported and buried for later retrieval—a behavior called caching. Like crows, Scrub Jays also collect and cache shiny objects such as pieces of china, glass, and spoons.

Acorns and pine seeds make up about 50 percent of the Scrub Jay's diet. The birds prefer caching whole acorns and pine seed rather than cracked or insect-infested foods,

apparently because intact foods store better. Such seeds also have a greater chance of germinating, hence the Scrub Jay's important role in the spread of oak and pine forests. The balance of their diet is mostly animal life, especially insects, but Scrub Jays also eat the young of small birds, mice, and lizards.

Nesting

Females build a bulky stick nest 2–12ft (0.5–3.5m) off the ground and the male feeds the female while she incubates. Young Florida Scrub Jays (*Aphelocoma coeulescens*)—restricted to scrub habitat in central Florida—help parents feed subsequent broods for several years before nesting for the first time.

Whole peanuts *are a favorite food for Western Scrub Jays. Jays often store food for later meals.*

Scrub Jays readily visit backyard birdbaths. Ideally, these baths should be no more than belly-deep for the birds.

Aphelocoma californica
Corvidae

Wingbeats are quicker and stiffer than those of Stellar's Jay

Whitish or bluish undertail coverts

Gray-blue or brownish back

Blue breast band

White or gray underside

LENGTH 11in (28cm)
WINGSPAN 15in (38cm)
VOICE Call usually a harsh, rising

J F M A M J J A S O N D

shreeeeeenk, but may include low clucking or clicking sounds.
EGGS Usually 3–4 (2–7) pale green eggs with spots and dots of dark olive, or red with spots of red-brown.
REARING Female incubates; 15–17 days' incubation; fledging 18–19 days; fed by male and female.

IN THE BACKYARD

■ Plant Gambel's Oak and Pinyon Pine and dense brush for nesting. These favorites provide shelter for nesting and a steady source of acorns and pine seeds.

American Magpie

THIS UNMISTAKABLE MEMBER of the crow family is easily identified by its bold black-and-white plumage and an iridescent, dark green tail that is longer than its body. In flight, it flashes large white wing patches. American Magpies are found throughout much of the West, north to Alaska. The Yellow-billed Magpie (*Pica nutallii*) looks similar except for its yellow bill, and its range is restricted to Central California.

Pica hudsonia
Corvidae

Black wings with blue-green sheen

Black bill

Long, dark, iridescent tail

White belly, black breast

White wingtips with black streaks

Black head and back

Broad, rounded wings

Long trailing tail

LENGTH 17–18in (43–46cm)
WINGSPAN 20–23in (50–58cm)

VOICE Calls can include a harsh *kyack* and a repeated *shak-shak-shak*.
EGGS 1 clutch, of 7 (3–9) eggs spotted and flecked with brown.
REARING Female incubates; 18 days' incubation; fledging 24–30 days; fed by male and female.

J F M A M J J A S O N D

Magpies are rarely *confused with other species. They remain in their territories year round and some individuals never wander far from the locations where they hatched.*

Bold in their feeding *habits, magpies feed on a great variety of plant and animal foods, including velvet from antlers. Velvet is very nutritious, being made up of blood vessels enclosed in skin and covered with fine hair.*

Nest-building may start in winter, with both adults of the pair contributing to the work. The ideal nest sites are thorny trees, but some birds may even build nests on the ground.

Territories and flocks

American Magpies frequent scattered trees in open country, trees along streams, and tall thickets. They occur in croplands, pastures, and sometimes occupy suburban backyards. They defend their home territory throughout the year, but territorial birds often leave during the day to join foraging flocks elsewhere. Outside the nesting season, magpies travel in small family flocks of 6–10 birds, but winter groups may increase to 50 or more. Sometimes individual birds wander eastward in the fall, especially when food supplies are scarce.

Feeding

Magpies spend much of their time on the ground, walking with a graceful swagger and holding their grand tail in the air. Insects are an important part of the diet, especially in the fall when the birds consume grasshoppers. Like crows, magpies eat roadside carrion and scavenge among the leftovers,

Agile when feeding on the ground, magpies move with a distinctive high-stepping walk interspersed with brisk jumps. Their bills are strong enough to strip meat from carcasses.

Juvenile magpies closely *resemble the adults, although they have shorter tails and their plumage is less glossy.*

consuming meat, flies, and pupae. They are so agile that they can feed alongside a coyote or wolf, while keeping a safe distance from the predator. These adaptable birds glean ticks from the backs of elk, mule deer, and bighorn sheep, and also eat the young of small birds, mice, snakes, grain, and fruit.

Like other members of the crow family, magpies cache food. Sometimes they make temporary caches of meat within 100yds (90m) of a dead animal, and later move the prey to a more secure location. This strategy secures the maximum amount of food in the shortest time and helps them to survive periods of winter food shortages.

Well-built nests

Magpies nest in small, scattered colonies along streams and thickets. The nest is typically a bulky mass of sticks located 2–4ft (60–120cm) above the ground. It is usually held together with a mud base. Typically the nest has a dome of spiny branches with entrance holes that lead to a nest cup of rootlets, fine plant stems, and horsehair. The female builds the nest from materials brought to her by her mate. The nest is so well built that it has lasting value for magpies and other birds. Magpies often reuse the nest year after year, while robins, bluebirds, and others use abandoned nests for shelter during storms. American Kestrels, Sharp-shinned Hawks, Mourning Doves, herons, and grackles claim old magpie nests for raising their own families.

IN THE BACKYARD

■ Meat scraps are preferred, but magpies also eat peanuts in the shell, peanut-butter mixes, and suet.

American Crow

AMERICAN CROWS FREQUENT OPEN and forested habitats across North America. They are often accused of agricultural damage and the destruction of small birds, but in fact they feed mainly on discarded grain, agricultural pests, and carrion. American Crows and ravens are among the most intelligent of all birds.

Corvus brachyrhynchos
Corvidae

Broad wings when gliding

Black bill

Large head

Short tail

Large, compact tail

LENGTH 17–21in (43–53cm)
WINGSPAN 39in (98cm)

VOICE A loud *caw*, *cah* or *kahr*.
EGGS Usually 4–6 (3–9) gray-green eggs spotted with brown and gray. 1 clutch in north, 2 in south.
REARING Both incubate; 18 days' incubation; fledging 28–35 days; fed by male and female.

J F M A M J J A S O N D

Helpers at the nest

Crows that nest in Canada are usually migratory, but crows in the United States are typically resident through the year. Crow families maintain a large nesting territory shared by the adult pair with some of their offspring from the past several years. Young crows remain with their parents to help raise additional broods in subsequent years. These helpers actively participate in building the nest, incubating eggs, and feeding nestlings. In winter, crows typically leave their nesting territory in the late afternoon to join large roosting flocks. These vary in size from a few thousand to more than 200,000 birds.

Crows have remarkably *varied diets, in part because of their universally adapted bills. Carrion is high on their list of favorite foods. They usefully clean up animals killed on highways.*

American Crows *have remarkable family lives, and deserve a better reputation than they usually receive.*

Danger patrols

Crows work together to watch for danger. They often have a sentinel perched atop a tall tree while others are feeding. They are quick to detect predators such as Great Horned Owls, which they mercilessly harass. If these large owls were to stay in their territory overnight, they might kill roosting crows.

Northern Ravens (*Corvus corax*) are found throughout Canada, Alaska, and western United States. Ravens differ from crows by their larger size, their habit of soaring like hawks, and their long, wedge-shaped tail.

IN THE BACKYARD

■ Crows (and most other birds) are susceptible to West Nile Virus, a deadly mosquito-transmitted disease. Clean bird-baths every few days to provide a fresh water supply. This will reduce the risk of infection.

Tree Swallow

TREE SWALLOWS ARE STEELY BLUE or green above and glistening white below. Most species of swallows migrate to South America for the winter, but Tree Swallows winter in the southern United States and Mexico. The shorter migration means an early return to nesting areas, where they take residence soon after the snow melts.

Tachycineta bicolor
Hirundinidae

Broad-wings

White below

Steely blue-green-black above

Wingtips reach tail tip

LENGTH 5–6in (13–15cm)
WINGSPAN 14in (36cm)
VOICE Song is *weet*, *trit*, *weet*, presented with different variations; call is *cheet* or *chi-veet*, call is a liquid twitter.
EGGS Usually 1 clutch of 4–6 white eggs.
REARING Female incubates; incubation usually 13 days, but may be 16; fledging usually in 20 days, may be 16–24; fed by male and female.

JFMAMJJASOND

Varied diet

Feeding mostly on flying ants, beetles, and flies, at times Tree Swallows also eat bees, wasps, and grasshoppers. They are very adaptable in their feeding habits, sometimes landing on beaches and shores to consume tiny insects and sand "fleas" (crustaceans) from the ground. In cold weather, when insects are scarce, they switch to fruits such as bayberry, and seeds from bulrushes, sedges, and smartweed.

Violet-green Swallows *look similar to Tree Swallows, but they have a green back, and the white on their flanks extends upwards towards the tail. They live only in western states.*

Named for their habit *of nesting in tree cavities, these colorful birds readily accept nest boxes. Dimensions suitable for bluebird boxes are also ideal for Tree Swallows.*

Cavity nesting

Originally restricted to woodpecker cavities, tree swallows now readily use artificial nest boxes. Females do most of the nest building, using fine grasses with a lining of white feathers that insulate the eggs during the extreme cold days of early spring. Males may have two mates at the same time, and usually have different mates each year.

Violet-green Swallows (*Tachycineta thalassina*) occur in the western third of North America, from Mexico to southern Alaska. They resemble Tree Swallows, with white above the eye and an emerald-green back with violet wings. Unlike Tree Swallows, they feed almost entirely on flying insects.

IN THE BACKYARD

■ Provide white chicken feathers in a hanging basket for swallows. In early spring locate pairs of clean nest boxes (the same size as for bluebirds; see page 35). Separate them by about 20ft (6m) to provide for both tree swallows and bluebirds.

Purple Martin

IN JANUARY, AFTER WINTERING IN BRAZIL, some male Purple Martins claim nesting houses on the Gulf coast while other males move north, taking up residence at the northern edge of their range in April. Females typically arrive after the males. In flight, the starling-sized martins alternate flapping and soaring, thus saving on energy. Their liquid warble is one of the most cheerful voices in the spring sky.

Metal or wooden *martin houses, like this one below, can accommodate many pairs, but they also attract starlings and House Sparrows.*

IN THE BACKYARD

■ Hang Purple Martin nesting gourds and broadcast the dawn call of the male martin to help establish the colony. Place mirrors inside some holes. Gourds and martin recordings are available from the Purple Martin Conservation Association: www.purplemartin.org.

Progne subis
Hirundinidae

Long head

Short bill

Dark head and body

Long, pointed tail

LENGTH 7–8in (18–20cm)
WINGSPAN 18in (45cm)
VOICE Throaty, rich

JFMAMJJASOND

tchew-wew, or *pew*, *pew*. Gurgling song ends in a succession of low, rich gutturals.
EGGS Usually 1 clutch of 4–6 (3–7) pure white eggs.
REARING Female incubates; 15–18 days' incubation; fledging 26–31 days; fed by male and female.

This subadult male Purple Martin, *identified by his purple-speckled throat, is guarding the entrance hole to his nest cavity, trying to attract a mate.*

Colonial nesting

Throughout most of their North American range, these large swallows nest only in artificial boxes and gourds, but some Florida and Pacific Coast Martins still nest in the ancestral manner: in rock crevices and dead trees riddled with woodpecker cavities. Martins are colonial in nesting habit, choosing sites where there are many suitable nesting places, but such sites are naturally scarce and usually vulnerable to predators. Martin houses are attractive alternatives to natural sites, but they also attract House Sparrows and European Starlings, competitive resident species that often claim the houses while martins are absent.

Gourds for martins

Native Americans lured martins to their camps by hanging hollowed gourds. Martin experts now consider gourd-shaped housing preferable to the classic multiple-compartment houses. When given a choice of such houses or gourds, martins usually choose gourds, while European Starlings and House Sparrows tend to prefer houses.

It is simple to make your own martin housing with bottle gourds. Dry gourds 8–14in (20–35cm) thoroughly. Cut a 2⅛in (5cm) entrance hole through the middle of the side and a hole large enough to reach in for cleaning out the seeds just below the neck. Cut an opaque lid of a plastic kitchen storage container to size, using silicon caulk to hold the lid in place for the season. Then drill ⅝in (1.5cm) holes in the bottom of the gourd for drainage and a set of ¼in (6mm) holes through the top of the neck to attach a line to suspend the

Plastic SuperGourds are readily *used by martins for nesting; competitive starlings and House Sparrows are less likely to use gourds.*

gourd from a tall pole. Finally, paint the exteriors with white latex paint to reflect heat. (Plastic "gourds" are also available.)

Mount gourds and martin houses atop a pole approximately 14ft (4m) tall. Position the pole in an open area at least 40ft (12m) away from overhanging limbs or buildings as raccoons and other predators may use these to gain access to the nests.

If possible, place the house near open water, such as a pond, river, or lake. Lower the nesting structures in the fall after martins depart to keep sparrows and starlings from claiming the housing. Clean and store them for the winter.

Family life

Both sexes build the nest from mud, grass, leaves, twigs, and shreds of bark and green leaves. Females do all of the incubation and males guard the nest in her absence. Young can fly when they are 26–31 days old. Parents feed the young a diet of flying insects. Once airborne, the family departs the house for the season. During July and August, martins gather in enormous pre-migratory roosts in preparation for their southward journey. These sleeping roosts can often number from 25,000 to one million birds.

This subadult *pair of Purple Martins is selecting a nesting chamber in a gourd. They are nearly a year old and are likely to be breeding for the first time.*

Barn Swallow

ONCE PRIMARILY A CAVE AND CREVICE NESTER, these long-tailed swallows now mostly nest in the shelter of barns, sheds, and porches. They fly with swift, effortless grace over fields, marshes, and ponds in search of flying insects. Sometimes they follow tractors, catching grasshoppers, crickets, and dragonflies.

Hirundo rustica

Hirundinidae

Long, slender, pointed wings

Wing tips pulled back at the end of stroke, not much gliding

Deeply forked swallow-tail with white tail spots

Dark throat

Blue-black above

Cinnamon-buff or rich orange below

LENGTH 6–7in (15–19cm)
WINGSPAN 15in (38cm)
VOICE Call is a soft

vit or *kvik-kvik, vit-vit*; song is a long musical twitter with gutturals added at intervals.
EGGS 1 or 2 clutches with 4–5 white eggs, spotted with shades of brown.
REARING Female incubates with help from male; 3–17 days' incubation; fledging 18–23 days; fed by male and female.

J F M A M J J A S O N D

Colony nesting

Usually a colonial nesting species, Barn Swallows sometimes nest alone. They use a wide variety of nesting places but all have one common feature: an overhead roof. Barn Swallows are known to nest in farm outbuildings, under boat docks, in caves, rock crevices, lakeside cliffs, and even on slow-moving trains and boats!

Four to five eggs are laid in the nest cup, which is lined with horsehair and white breast feathers from poultry or gulls.

Family life

Both members of the pair build the nest, picking up mouthfuls of mud and mixing it with fine grass. They usually plaster the nest to a horizontal or vertical surface, sometimes using a protruding nail as an anchor. Parents take turns incubating the eggs. The young leave the nest when they are 18–23 days old, and stay with the parents for another week or more.

The parents often raise two broods each year. Swallows can drink and bathe while on the wing.

Barn swallows may have the longest migration of any North American landbird—some birds nest in Alaska and winter in southern Argentina, some 7,000 miles (11,000km) distant.

Like other swallows, Barn Swallows have tiny feet, just large enough to give them ample grip. In contrast to their tiny feet, they have huge wings for their size, and powerful breast muscles that aid them on their epic migrations.

IN THE BACKYARD

■ Install 6in (15cm) square nesting platforms in garages and sheds with an open door or window.

Cliff Swallow

ALTHOUGH SOME CLIFF SWALLOWS still nest in canyons and deep gorges, most now exist in close association to human dwellings, where they build their mud nests under the eaves of houses, barns, bridges, churches, and other similar structures. These are the famous swallows of San Louis Obispo church in California.

Feeding on the wing

Cliff Swallows have a broad distribution across North America, but they are vulnerable to cold, rainy weather in the spring, which reduces food supplies and can sometimes devastate local populations. They usually feed on the wing, consuming cotton-boll weevil, chinch bugs, flying ants, grasshoppers, wasps, dragonflies, mosquitoes, and sometimes spiders, and the fruit of junipers. Cliff Swallows resemble Barn Swallows in general color—dark blue above and light below—but are easily distinguished by their square tail, rust-colored rump, and buffy forehead. Sexes look similar.

Both members of the pair build the nest, which is usually cemented to the underside of an eave or other overhanging roof. Occasionally Cliff Swallows nest inside of barns and

Individual nests sometimes sit side by side in colonies that may contain 2,000 pairs. In other locations, some pairs nest by themselves.

other outbuildings, especially where there is abundant light. In some locations they build their nest on top of old Barn Swallow nests. The nest resembles a bottle with a 5–6in (10–12.5cm) long entrance tube that protrudes from the side.

The nest *is composed of hundreds of mud pellets, which the birds collect in their bills and transport one at a time to the nest site.*

IN THE BACKYARD

■ Encourage Cliff Swallows to nest on buildings. If falling excrement is a concern, install a "poop-catcher" board under the nests. If mud is scarce, expose clay soil near the colony and flood it with a hose to create puddles.

Petrochelidon pyrrhonota
Hirundinidae

Rusty or buffy rump
Short, square-tailed
Broad, square head
Short bill
Dark throat

LENGTH 5–6in (13–15cm)
WINGSPAN 13½in (34cm)

VOICE *Zayrp*; a low *chur*; song has creaking calls and guttural gratings.
EGGS Sometimes 2 broods of 4–5 (3–6) white eggs, spotted with shades of brown.
REARING Both incubate; 14–16 days' incubation; fledging 21–24 days; fed by male and female.

JFMAMJJASOND

155

Tufted Titmouse

AMONG THE MOST FREQUENT FEEDER BIRDS, Tufted Titmice have a jaunty look with a perky crest and large black eyes. They are energetic forest birds that have adapted well to suburbs and urban parks, especially where they find large oak and beech trees. Perhaps because of bird-feeders, they have recently expanded their range further north.

Like chickadees, *titmice take seeds, one at a time, to a nearby perch where they break open the husk, extracting the oil-rich kernel.*

Seed peckers

Titmice crack acorns and beechnuts by holding the nuts under their feet and persistently pecking until they break into the meaty interior. Caterpillars are also a favorite food; the birds extract the developing pupae from moth cocoons. They also eat wasps, beetles, ants, and many other insects. Their diet includes a variety of fruit, especially wild cherries, sumac, poison ivy, blueberries, bayberries, blackberries, elderberries, and mulberries. When given a choice at birdfeeders, titmice seem to prefer the large, striped sunflower seeds to smaller-oil seeds. They are relatively fearless of people, known to take seeds from the hand or teeth.

Cavity nester

The Tufted Titmouse's fearlessness is also apparent when they are searching for hair for their nests, as they will pluck it from live groundhogs, squirrels, and opossums. They are even known to pull hair from humans who are sitting near their nest! The nest consists of moss, leaves, fibrous bark, pieces of shed snakeskin, and hair.

Titmice are tame, *inquisitive birds, identified by their perky crest, black forehead, and orange flanks.*

Baeolophus bicolor
Paridae

Gray sparrow-sized body

Short, broad tail

Tufted crest

Dark eyes

Rust-colored flanks

Plain head with a black forehead, dark eyes

LENGTH 6in (15cm)
WINGSPAN 9in (24cm)
VOICE Song is a low, whistle and chant of *peter, peter, peter,* or *here, here, here, here*; calls are wheezy and nasal compared to those of chickadees.
EGGS Usually 5–7 (4–9) white or creamy eggs with speckling at larger end.
REARING Female incubates; 13–14 days' incubation; fledging 15–18 days; fed by male and female.

J F M A M J J A S O N D

IN THE BACKYARD

■ Use bluebird houses to attract titmice by locating the boxes in the forest interior about 5ft (1.5m) from the ground. Plant berry bushes at the forest edge; at feeders provide whole peanuts, sunflower seeds, and suet.

Juniper Titmouse

THE JUNIPER TITMOUSE and closely related Oak Titmouse (*Baeolophus inornatus*) are two species recently separated from the former Plain Titmouse. They look similar, but the Juniper Titmouse has a lower and faster rhythm to its song than the Oak Titmouse. Isolated over most of their range, these look-alike species seldom interbreed.

IN THE BACKYARD

■ Plant oak and pinyon pine; hang bluebird-sized nest boxes in forest; also provide black and striped sunflower seeds, peanuts, and peanut-butter mixes.

Oak and pine specialists

Neither species is restricted to its namesake tree. Acorns and pine seeds comprise about 80 percent of the titmouse's winter diet. The birds usually hold the nut securely between their feet or lodge it in a crevice while they pound it with their stout beak. When acorns and pine seeds are abundant, titmice spend most of their time on the ground, feeding on fallen nuts. They usually feed alone or with their mate. When acorns and pine seeds are abundant, titmice cache them for later use. In years when acorns are scarce, they become more sociable, feeding in small flocks with other species, gleaning insects from tree bark.

Titmice typically nest in abandoned woodpecker cavities, paired to the same mate for life. They usually stay near home, often within the same six-acre (2.4 hectare) territory. Young titmice disperse after they leave the nest, but only wander a few territories away. For this reason, it is likely that the same pair of titmice will keep visiting the same backyard feeders.

Baeolophus ridgwayi
Paridae

All gray

Short, broad tail

Short, pointed crest

Faint or no brown tinge on wings

Very drab, somewhat larger than Oak Titmice

LENGTH 5in (14cm)
WINGSPAN 9in (23cm)
VOICE *Tchick-a-dee-dee*, like that of the chickadees; whistled song is *weety weety* or *tee-wit tee-wit tee-wit*.
EGGS Usually 6–8 (3–9) unmarked white eggs.
REARING Female incubates; 14–16 days' incubation; fledging 16–21 days; fed by male and female.

J F M A M J J A S O N D

Juniper Titmice *are gregarious birds that form local flocks in winter. In years with abundant acorn crops, they spend more time alone or in pairs.*

Black-capped Chickadee

WHILE NEARLY ALL BIRDS abandon northern forests during the extreme months of winter, Black-capped Chickadees are remarkable for their tenacity. Special adaptations allow them to tolerate frigid temperatures, deep snow, and raging winds. Research provides insight into the importance of birdfeeders and helps us understand how these remarkable birds adapt to extreme winters.

IN THE BACKYARD

■ Mount nest boxes 1–5ft (30–152cm) off the ground in the forest. Use a cordless drill with a 1⅛in (25cm) bit to make nest hole starts in dead forest trees. Provide black-oil sunflower seeds and pure suet in feeders.

Winter survivor

Despite their tiny size, Black-capped Chickadees and their closely related cousins thrive in extreme northern habitats throughout North America. This is no small feat considering the frigid conditions and long nights that limit the amount of time for feeding. During the limited daylight of northern winters, chickadees frenetically gather food, consuming as many calories by day as they lose at night. Although they are conspicuous at birdfeeders, research in Wisconsin shows that feeder foods comprise just 20 percent of their diet, and food from feeders only affects survival during the most extreme conditions.

The Black-capped Chickadee *differs from the similar Carolina by its large white cheeks and frosting on the edges of wing feathers.*

Feeder behavior

At feeders, chickadees favor sunflower seeds and suet. Their bill is too small to shell sunflower seeds at the feeder, so they carry each seed to a nearby perch, place it between their feet and peck at the shell to expose the kernel. They may cache hundreds of seeds daily in tree-bark cracks, clusters of conifer needles, and under leaves. They not only remember where they have stored foods, but which sites they have emptied and which caches have the highest quality foods. They reclaim cached seeds, insects, and suet within 24 hours and either eat it or move it to a permanent cache. They can remember the location of caches for at least 28 days!

On frigid winter nights

Winter chickadee flocks conserve energy by huddling together in tree cavities and other shelters. Chickadees also survive the long, bitter nights by dropping their body temperatures and fluffing their feathers for near-perfect insulation. It is remarkable that almost no heat is lost, even though there may be a massive 70-degree difference in temperature between the skin and air!

Chickadees can *enlarge woodpecker feeding holes into nest cavities by removing soft wood a billful at a time.*

Black-capped Chickadees *prefer black-oil sunflower seeds. The small size and thin shell make it more manageable than larger sunflower seed.*

wood until the cavity is 6–8in (15–20cm) deep. The nest often fills the cavity, made of mosses and plant fibers.

Northern cousin

Boreal Chickadees (*Poecile hudsonica*) are at home among the spruce, balsam, and cedar forests throughout most of Canada and Alaska. This resident of northern coniferous forests occurs north to the tree line. They are slightly larger than Black-capped Chickadees, an adaptation that may help them retain body heat at temperatures as low as –49°F (–45°C).

Boreal Chickadees are resident throughout the year, though some may have short migrations in years when conifer seeds are scarce. They typically travel in small groups separate from Black-capped Chickadees and other small forest birds. They are also quieter and less active than Black-capped Chickadees, often feeding in the highest treetops where they extract seeds from cones and eat the seeds of gray birch.

Chickadees use *a wide range of tree cavities, including those created when branches break from tree trunks.*

Nesting

Black-capped Chickadees nest in abandoned woodpecker cavities or they excavate their own nest cavity through a knothole, usually choosing a site that is between 1–10ft (0.3–3.5m) off the ground. Both members of the pair excavate the cavity by removing bits of rotting

Poecile atricapilla
Paridae

White cheek

Black cap and bib

Edges of wings are brighter white than that of Carolina Chickadee

LENGTH 4–5in (10–12cm)
WINGSPAN 8in (20cm)
VOICE Song is a clear whistle, *fe-bee-ee* or *fee-bee*, with the first call higher; a clearly enunciated *chick-a-dee-dee-dee* or *dee-dee-dee*.
EGGS Usually 6–8 (5–10) white eggs, spotted with reddish brown, especially at large end.
REARING Both incubate; 11–13 days' incubation; fledging 14–18 days; fed by male and female.

JFMAMJJASOND

Black-capped Chickadees *eat many kinds of natural fruits including staghorn sumac, a staple in winter.*

Chestnut-backed Chickadee

THIS COLORFUL CHICKADEE of the Pacific coast and Sierra Nevada range is well named for its distinctive back and shoulders. Like the familiar Black-capped Chickadee, this western species is a common visitor to backyard birdfeeders where it takes sunflower seed and suet. They join winter flocks with other chickadees, kinglets, bushtits, warblers, and juncos.

IN THE BACKYARD

■ Both the Chestnut-backed and Mountain Chickadee readily visit backyard birdfeeders. They will use nest boxes with 4x4in bases and entrance holes as small as 1¼in across.

Poecile rufescens
Paridae

Relatively short and dark tail
Chestnut back
White cheeks
Chestnut or gray flanks
Black cap and bib

LENGTH 4½–5in (11–13cm)
WINGSPAN 7½in (18cm)
VOICE Call is hoarser than that of the Black-capped Chickadee; it has no whistled song.
EGGS Usually 6–7 (5–9) white eggs with sprinkle of reddish and brown dots.

REARING Information unavailable, but female does most of the nest-building.

J F M A M J J A S O N D

Both sexes use the scolding call to rally flock members when they discover a predator such as a Screech-owl. Chickadees attempt to chase owls from their territory during the day, which may give them more security at night.

Chestnut-backed Chickadees *differ from others by their chestnut-colored flanks and back as well as very white cheeks.*

Identify chickadees *by their round body shape and short, conical bill. All species have a black cap and bib. Seven species occur in North America; they are closely related to titmice.*

Treetop home

Chestnut-backed Chickadees usually live in dark, coastal humid forests from southern Alaska to the vicinity of Monterey, California. They frequent tall, coniferous forests of fir, spruce, pine, redwoods, and hemlock where flocks of 4–20 typically feed high in the treetops. They also inhabit broad-leaved woods along streams or in shrubby habitats of residential areas. Often they occur with mixed species flocks of Mountain Chickadee, Golden-crowned Kinglet, Dark-eyed Juncos, and Red-breasted Nuthatch. Watch for them clinging to seed heads and flower clusters of shrubs, and eating the fruit of salal, elderberry, birches, and dogwoods. Unlike Black-capped Chickadees, which hang upside down about half of the time while foraging, Chestnut-capped Chickadees seldom assume this posture.

Flocks and guilds

During the winter months, chickadees form flocks of 6–10 birds, including a dominant mated pair and young birds from nearby territories. Flocking is important for chickadees, as the group is more successful at detecting predators such as hawks and owls, a fact that brings other species such as titmice, creepers, woodpeckers, and nuthatches together in a loose association called a guild. Migrants such as warblers and kinglets sometimes join these flocks, taking advantage of the local knowledge of the resident chickadees. The familiar "chick-a-dee-dee" call communicates the discovery of both food and predators. When predators are nearby, the rate of the call increases. The call also helps members of the flock recognize each other from nearby flocks throughout the winter months.

Sunflower seed *is by far the favorite food of chickadees. They carry away seeds one at a time, often storing them for later feeds.*

Winter cache

Chestnut-backed Chickadees readily visit birdfeeding stations where they eat sunflower seed and suet. In the fall, they store much of the seed for later consumption in hidden caches within tree bark and other secret places. Some chickadees can store as many as 45 items an hour. In addition to seeds, chickadees cache insects, spiders, and even tiny aphids, sometimes hiding them on the undersides of branches where food is less likely to be buried by ice and snow.

Nesting

Chestnut-backed Chickadees usually nest in abandoned woodpecker cavities, especially those created by Downy Woodpeckers. They can also create nesting places by extracting soft wood from a dead snag, persistently removing it one billful at a time until they are satisfied with the outcome. Within the cavity, they typically build a bulky nest of moss, plant fibers, and animal hairs. Females do most of the nest building.

The Mountain Chickadee (*Poecile gambeli*) resembles the widespread Black-capped Chickadee except that it has a white stripe over the eye. Its range includes the Western Mountains of the US and Canada. Where ranges overlap, Mountain Chickadees usually frequent tall conifers, while Black-capped Chickadees occupy the deciduous forest at lower elevations.

Red-breasted Nuthatch

MAINLY A BIRD OF THE NORTHERN CONIFEROUS FOREST, the Red-breasted Nuthatch migrates to southern states, especially when conifer seed crops fail. It may stay throughout the year to nest, especially in plantations of Norway spruce and pines. Distinguish this species from other nuthatches by the white stripe over the eye.

Conifer connection

The Red-breasted Nuthatch feeds largely on conifer seeds, which it extracts using its long, pointed beak. A close relative, the Brown-headed Nuthatch (*Sitta pusilla*), sometimes uses a pine scale as a tool to help extract its prey. Like other nuthatches, the Red-breasted clings to tree trunks and branches, where it often hangs upside down while searching for hidden insects, pupae, and eggs.

At birdfeeders, the Red-breasted is a fierce contender for sunflower seeds, nutmeats, and suet, and is capable of driving away much larger birds. Its typical manner is to dash in, grab a sunflower seed, then fly off with the prize. It usually tucks it into a crack in the tree bark and picks at it to expose the meat. These energetic birds often cache seeds near the feeder in crevices of rough-barked trees, sometimes hiding the food with lichen or bark.

Cavity nester

These birds usually create their own nesting cavity by removing soft wood from a tree stub or branch of a dead tree, usually about 15ft (4.5m) off the ground. They also use abandoned

Hanging upside down *permits nuthatches to locate food that woodpeckers and other tree-climbing birds overlook.*

woodpecker cavities and nest boxes. Regardless of the nest site, typically they use their bill to smear pine pitch around the entrance. This is done to discourage predators.

IN THE BACKYARD

■ Provide nest boxes in coniferous forests and plantations. At feeders, these birds prefer suet, sunflower, hulled peanuts, and peanut-butter mixes.

Identify Red-breasted Nuthatches *by the black line through the eye and the reddish underside.*

Sitta canadensis
Sittidae

Stubby square-cut tail

Broad black line through eye and white line above it

Rusty underparts

Bluish back

Smaller and stubbier than White-breasted Nuthatch

LENGTH 4in (10cm)
WINGSPAN 8in (20cm)
VOICE Call is higher and more nasal

than that of White-Breasted Nuthatch: *ank* or *enk*.
EGGS 1 clutch, usually with 5–6 (4–7) white eggs heavily or sparingly dotted with red-brown.
REARING Female incubates; 12 days' incubation; fledging 14–21 days; fed by male and female.

J F M A M J J A S O N D

White-breasted Nuthatch

DECIDUOUS FORESTS ARE THE HOME of the White-breasted Nuthatch. Larger than other nuthatches, the White-breasted is usually resident throughout the year. Distinguish it from other nuthatches by its white face and dark crown, and its habit of clinging headfirst to large tree trunks as it hitches downward in search of food.

Cache thieves

The White-breast has a black crown, whereas the female has a gray crown. Males are usually dominant over their mates and sometimes displace them from birdfeeders. Both members of the pair cache sunflower seeds, which they obtain at feeders. Females tend to cache seeds further from feeders because males may steal the food. Both sexes cache more hulled sunflower seeds than seeds with hulls, perhaps because hulled seeds are more convenient to eat late in the day, just before roosting. In contrast, sunflower seeds with hulls are usually eaten earlier in the day when there is ample daylight

for the time-consuming process of finding a crevice to wedge the seed into, then hack it open.

In the forest, White-breasted Nuthatches eat a wide variety of foods, including acorns, beechnuts, and insects, which they pick from tree trunks. In winter, they join flocks of chickadees and other small forest birds, sometimes stealing cached food from members of the flock and letting the more vocal and numerous

White-breasted Nuthatches nest in *old woodpecker cavities and in knotholes that lead to rotten tree interiors.*

chickadees watch out for predators. Nuthatches can recognize the warning calls of chickadees.

Nuthatches usually retain the same mate for life and feed within a territory of 25–50 acres (10–20 hectares). They nest in abandoned woodpecker cavities and knotholes.

IN THE BACKYARD

■ At feeders, provide suet, sunflower seeds, hulled peanuts or peanut hearts, and peanut-butter mixes. Hang nest boxes and use a 1⅛in (30mm) drill bit to create cavity starts in dead forest trees.

White-breasted Nuthatches differ from Red-breasted by their all-white face. Females typically have gray foreheads; males have black foreheads.

Sitta carolinensis
Sittidae

Chestnut undertail feathers

Short, broad tail

Large slightly upturned bill

Black cap and eye, contrasting with white face

LENGTH 5–6in (12–15cm)
WINGSPAN 11in (28cm)
VOICE Song is series of soft, slightly nasal, whistled calls on one pitch; call is nasal *yank*.
EGGS 1 clutch, usually 5–8 (3–10) white eggs, with brown and lavender spots.
REARING Female incubates; 12 days' incubation; fledging 14 days; fed by male and female.

J F M A M J J A S O N D

Brown Creeper

WATCH FOR BROWN CREEPERS in forested habitats as they fly from tree to tree, spiraling upward and along lateral branches, where they pry dormant insects and eggs from tree bark with their downward-curved beak. At night, they sleep clinging to the trunk of a large tree, using their stiff, pointed tail as a prop.

Forest dweller

Brown Creepers may be gregarious when they first arrive on their wintering grounds during fall migration, but they soon become solitary, except when they join flocks of chickadees and other small forest birds. Creepers live in both deciduous and coniferous forests, but they are most common in swampy forests, especially where they find dead trees with slabs of loose, hanging bark. In their search for hidden insect prey, Brown Creepers hitch their way up trees then explore the underside of lateral branches with their long beaks. Occasionally they back up as if to take a second look as they search for weevils, aphids, bugs, ants, and spiders. At feeders, they

Brown Creepers typically construct their nests from wood chip, plant stems, and soft grasses.

eat chopped peanuts and mixes of peanut-butter, rendered suet, and cornmeal. These birds have a surprisingly musical song, one of the first heard in the early spring forest. The high, thin call is

Brown Creepers nest in crevices created when bark peels back from tree trunks. A favorite site is under large slabs of exfoliating American Elm bark.

similar to the quick trebled call of the Golden-crowned Kinglet's. The nest consists of mosses and shreds of bark with a lining of feathers of grouse and ducks. It is usually built between hanging bark and the tree trunk on a dead tree.

Certhia americana
Certhiidae

Thin, decurved beak

Small and slim

White undersides

Bold, buffy band on wings conspicuous above and below

Mottled brownish back and plumage that blend into tree bark

Stiff tail

LENGTH 5in (13cm)
WINGSPAN 7in (18cm)
VOICE Song is a thin sibilant *see-ti-wee-tu-* *ee* or *see-see-see-sisi- see*. Call is single high thin *seee*.
EGGS Usually 5–6 (4–8) creamy white eggs, speckled with red-brown.
REARING Female incubates; 14–17 days' incubation; fledging 13–16 days; fed by male and female.

J F M A M J J A S O N D

IN THE BACKYARD

■ Provide an equal-part mixture of peanut-butter, cornmeal, and rendered suet. Smear patches of the mixture deep into tree-bark crevices in order to avoid the risk of staining belly feathers.

Carolina Wren

FOUND THROUGHOUT MOST of the eastern United States, the Carolina Wren is the only wren that habitually visits backyard birdfeeders. Easily identified by their bright, reddish brown back and distinct white stripe over the eye, these bold birds sing their rollicking song throughout most of the year.

Backyard songster

Carolina Wrens frequent backyard gardens with dense shrubs and wilder places such as fallen trees and brushy areas, especially near water. The pair typically stays together throughout the year, frequenting brush piles, woodpiles, and forests with dense underbrush. The chattering males sing throughout the year, often imitating neighbors such as Pine Warblers, meadowlarks, and bluebirds.

Mostly insect-eaters, they are great friends to gardeners as they eat beetles, cotton-boll weevils, stink bugs, leafhoppers, scale insects, crickets, and grasshoppers. They also eat millipedes, snails, sow bugs, and an occasional lizard. At the northern edge of their range, Carolina Wren populations usually decline during extreme winters, especially when the ground is covered with snow, and temperatures consistently drop below 19°F (7°C).

Odd nests

Like many other species, Carolina Wrens nest in tree cavities, but they also nest in more open sites such as tree stumps, upturned roots of fallen trees and a bizarre assortment of man-made housing, including open pails, mailboxes, and even pockets of trousers left hanging on a clothes-line. Their bulky nests consist mostly of grass, inner bark, feathers, moss, leaves, and bits of snakeskin.

Wren populations decline *during extreme northern winters. Although they can fluff themselves to keep warm, snow cover and extreme temperatures make survival difficult.*

Thryothorus ludovicianus
Troglodytidae

Short, broad tail

Black cap and eye contrast with white face

Chestnut undertail feathers

Large, slightly upturned bill

LENGTH 5in (13cm)
WINGSPAN 7in (18cm)
VOICE Song is usually a clear, three-syllabled chant. It may be *tea-* kettle, tea-kettle, tea-kettle, tea or chirpity, chirpity, chirpity, chirp.
EGGS Sometimes 2 or 3 clutches, each with 5 (4–8) white or pale pink eggs, usually with heavy brown spots at large end.
REARING Female incubates; 12–14 days' incubation; fledging 12–14 days; fed by male and female.

J F M A M J J A S O N D

Male Carolina Wrens *proclaim their nesting territory with a loud, rollicking song that sounds like "tea-kettle, tea-kettle, tea-kettle."*

IN THE BACKYARD

■ Build a brush pile adjacent to some woods or in the corner of the backyard; provide suet, a blend of peanut-butter/cornmeal/ shortening, and hulled peanuts. Plant pines, bayberries, and Sweetgum.

House Wren

NAMED FOR ITS ASSOCIATION WITH HUMAN HOUSING and its ready use of bird houses, the feisty little House Wren can be distinguished from other wrens by its gray body and the narrow black bars on its wings and tail. Like other wrens, it sometimes cocks its long tail over its back. House Wrens frequent shrubby backyards and forest edges.

Gardeners' friends

House Wrens are among the best friends of gardeners, feeding almost entirely on insects such as crickets, grasshoppers, beetles, and caterpillars of gypsy moth and cabbage butterfly.

They also eat ants, bees, wasps, flies, and ticks, finding most of their prey on or near the ground.

Prolific nest builders

After spring migration from the tropics, male House Wrens select nesting territories of ½–3 acres (0.2–1.2ha) by singing from dead trees and other conspicuous places, usually near the same location where they nested the previous year. Even before females return, the male starts cramming sticks into abandoned holes, nest boxes, and a wide variety of peculiar locations such as watering pots, teapots, flower pots, old boots, and even the axles of working cars. Soon after her arrival, the female selects a male and picks

You can identify this common backyard House Wren by the slight eye ring and the barred underparts.

one of his nest starts; to this she adds a lining of feathers, hair, cocoons, and catkins. In years when food is abundant, females often leave the chick-rearing to the male and move to another male's territory to lay a second clutch of eggs.

Male House Wrens have an exuberant, bubbling song that functions to claim nesting territory and attract a mate.

IN THE BACKYARD

■ Locate multiple House Wren boxes with 1½in (4cm) diameter entrance holes near woodland borders, gardens, and shrubby fencerows; create a brush pile in the corner of the backyard.

Troglodytes aedon
Troglodytidae

Drab brown plumage

Slender, slightly decurved bill

Gray-brown body

Light eye ring

Tail often cocked

LENGTH 4–5in (10–13cm)
WINGSPAN 6in (15cm)
VOICE Series of rattles and trills ending with

descending series of bubbling trills. Call is generally low, dry, and short with soft calls.
EGGS Usually 2 clutches, each with 6–8 (5–12) white eggs, speckled with tiny red-brown dots.
REARING Both incubate; 13 days' incubation; fledging 12–18 days; fed by both or only by male.

J F M A M J J A S O N D

Golden-crowned Kinglet

THESE ENERGETIC MIDGETS are common throughout North America, but they usually frequent shrubs and treetops where they are easily overlooked. Both the Golden-crowned and the similar Ruby-crowned Kinglet *(Regulus calendula)* nest mainly in coniferous forests in Canada, western mountains of the US and in New England.

Winter survival

Ruby-crowned kinglets winter in southern US and northern Mexico. Golden-crowned Kinglets winter further north than their Ruby-crowned cousins, often frequenting conifer plantations, and male Ruby-crowned Kinglets winter further north than females. This habit makes it easier for them to race back to claim the best nesting habitat. In contrast, females, wintering further south, arrive after the males. Unlike chickadees, which can lower their body temperature while sleeping in frigid weather, kinglets cannot adjust their internal thermostats.

Instead, they take shelter in old bird nests and other protected places on cold nights. Kinglets usually nest high in a conifer, sometimes as much as 100ft (30m) above the ground.

Crown colors

The two species of kinglet are easily distinguished by other head patterns: Golden-crowned Kinglets have a black stripe running through the eye, while Ruby-crowned Kinglets have white eye rings.

Kinglets eat tiny insects and spiders, which they glean from the outer twigs of conifers and deciduous trees.

Identify Ruby-crowned Kinglets *by their white eye-ring and wing bars. The male's ruby crest is hidden under the olive crown feathers and is exposed only when the bird is agitated.*

Both Golden-crowned Kinglets *(illustrated here) and Ruby-crowned Kinglets have a nervous wing-flicking behavior—useful for identifying the birds at a distance.*

Regulus satrapa
Regulidae

Stubby tail

Yellow crown patch

Distinct white eye ring

Olive-gray above with wing bars

Tiny body

LENGTH 4in (10cm)
WINGSPAN 7½in (19.5cm)
VOICE Song consists of 3–4 high calls, several low calls, and a chant, *tee tee tee tew tew tew tew, ti-dadee, ti-dadee, ti-dadee.*
EGGS Usually 7–9 (5–11) white eggs with reddish specks.
REARING Female incubates; about 12 days' incubation; fledging about 12 days; fed by both.

J F M A M J J A S O N D

IN THE BACKYARD

■ Plant patches of spruce, pine, and hemlock; provide suet and mixes of suet and cornmeal; plant elderberry bushes for winter food.

Eastern Bluebird

MALE EASTERN BLUEBIRDS are deep, sky-blue above and orange below, with a white belly. Females look similar, except that they have a blue-gray back and lighter orange underparts. The Western Bluebird (*Sialia mexicana*) can be differentiated mainly by its chestnut shoulders and blue belly.

Male bluebirds *have a bright blue head, back, wings, and tail, and an orange breast. Typically, bluebirds are resident all year round, but migrate south to avoid severe winters.*

Sialia sialia
Turdidae

- Short tail and wings
- Smaller than robin
- Blue wings and tail
- Round-shouldered when perched
- Stout bill
- Blue with a rusty red breast, throat, and neck

LENGTH 7in (18cm)
WINGSPAN 13in (33cm)
VOICE Song is a series of 3 or 4 soft gurgling calls; call is a musical *chur-wi* or *tru-ly.*
EGGS 2 or 3 clutches of 4–5 (2–7) pale blue eggs, sometimes pure white.
REARING Female incubates; 12–14 days' incubation; fledging 15–20 days; fed by male and female. Young from previous broods may also feed nestlings.

J F M A M J J A S O N D

Bluebirds often *stun their prey by banging it on a hard surface before swallowing it or feeding it to their young. A dragonfly (as shown here) is a rare catch; more often they feed on ground-dwelling insects.*

Keen eyes
For most of the year, bluebirds feed mainly on ground-dwelling insects such as caterpillars, crickets, and grasshoppers, which they spot while perched as much as 150ft (45m) away. These insects have remarkable camouflage, so the bluebirds must have spectacular eyesight! In order to accomplish this miraculous foraging, bluebirds perch in the lower branch of an isolated tree and scan the ground looking for their next meal.

Housing shortage
Aside from their glorious color, bluebirds are appealing for their cheerful, musical song and their responsiveness to artificial housing. Artificial housing has become necessary for bluebirds because natural cavities are too often occupied by two species that were introduced from Europe, House Sparrows and European Starlings. Bluebirds are resident throughout the year in the southeastern states of the US and usually migrate further north to southern Canada.

IN THE BACKYARD

■ Establish birdhouses far from shrubs and human housing to reduce competition with House Wrens and House Sparrows. Mount the boxes off the ground. In northern states and Canada, face them east to warm them in early spring. Plant berry-producing shrubs. Provide raisins and live mealworms.

Mountain Bluebird

MOUNTAIN BLUEBIRDS are found principally in the western mountains, from Mexico to Alaska. They frequent mountain meadows from just below the timberline at 12,000ft (3,600m) to foothills, where they live among groves of cottonwood and aspen, often frequenting the vicinity of ranch buildings.

Favorite foods

Mountain Bluebirds feed mostly on insects such as ground beetles, weevils, wasps, bees, caterpillars, grasshoppers, and crickets. They typically hunt from low perches or hover over the ground before dropping to capture their prey. They also dart into the air to capture flying insects. The Mountain Bluebird supplements its insect diet with many kinds of berries, especially currants, grapes, elderberries, mistletoe, and hackberries. The male has a warbling song reminiscent of a caroling robin.

Nest competitors

Like other bluebirds, Mountain Bluebird populations have suffered from the introduction of House Sparrows and European Starlings, which compete aggressively for the limited number of natural nesting cavities such as woodpecker holes. Because these introduced species are resident near ranches throughout the year, migratory bluebirds are disadvantaged when they return to claim a nesting cavity in the spring.

Females and immatures *are gray above with a buff-colored chest, with pale blue wings and tail. In breeding plumage, the male has a stunning turquoise-blue back with paler underparts and a white belly.*

Fledgling Mountain Bluebirds *are speckled below, a reminder of their relationship to other thrushes. Soon after leaving the nest, they begin to hunt for insects, and eat berries.*

Sialia currucoides
Turdidae

Long wings and tail

Turquoise blue on upperside and paler below

Slimmer than other bluebirds

Thinner billed than other bluebirds

Whitish belly

LENGTH 7in (18cm)
WINGSPAN 14in (35cm)
VOICE A low *chur* or *phew*; song is a short, subdued warble.
EGGS Usually 5–6 (4–8) pale blue or white eggs; 1 clutch when nesting at high elevations, sometimes 2 clutches at lower elevations.
REARING Female incubates; 13–14 days' incubation; fledging 22–23 days; fed by male and female.

J F M A M J J A S O N D

IN THE BACKYARD

■ Locate nest boxes far from buildings to reduce competition with House Sparrows. Clean nest boxes in early spring. Leave the boxes up in winter as roosting places. Provide favorite berries by planting grapes, currants, and elderberries. At birdfeeders, offer dried currants, raisins, and mealworms.

American Robin

ORIGINALLY A FOREST BIRD, robins have adapted to parks, city streets, and suburbs, but they still require mature trees that offer nesting places and singing posts. Found throughout North America, most robins abandon northern latitudes in the fall and fly to the southern US, especially the southeastern states.

Identify male
American Robins by their deep russet breast color and black heads; females have a lighter orange underside and a largely gray head.

Turdus migratorius
Turdidae

Blackish tail

Blackish head and nape

Dark gray back

Brick-red breast

LENGTH 9–11in (23–28cm)
WINGSPAN 17in (43cm)

VOICE Song is a clear caroling with short phrases that rise and fall. Calls are *tyeep* and *tut-tut-tut*.
EGGS 2 or 3 clutches of 4 (3–7) blue eggs.
REARING Female incubates; 12–14 days' incubation; fledging 14–16 days; fed by female with some help from male.

J F M A M J J A S O N D

IN THE BACKYARD

■ To provide winter food and emergency food during spring snowstorms, plant sumac, crabapples and hawthorn trees. Also plant cherry trees for summer and fall food.

Territorial nature
Robins are highly territorial during the nesting season, even chasing their own reflection in windows and car hubcaps, but in the winter they live in flocks that often number in the hundreds and sometimes increase to hundreds of thousands.

Sharp eyes
Although most robins migrate, many winter in northern states, feeding on berries of fruiting trees and shrubs. At this season, fruits make up 80 percent of the robin's diet. Fruit supplies are especially important to robins in early spring as snow cover may prevent them from feeding on the ground. As snow melts, robins eat more earthworms, but these comprise only about 15–20 percent of the diet. The familiar scene of a robin standing erect with its head cocked prior to snatching a worm has led to the misconception that robins listen for their prey. In fact, earthworms often expose themselves at the surface— a fatal move when a keen-eyed robin is standing nearby.

Nesting
The first nests of the season are typically built in protected conifers; later nesting birds build in deciduous trees such as maples and elms. Others build on human structures such as gutters and eaves that are remarkably near entranceways to human homes.

Robins have adapted
well to human housing. Close proximity to human housing may offer some security from predators such as raccoons.

Varied Thrush

VARIED THRUSHES usually frequent the moist forests of the Pacific Northwest. In winter, they migrate as far south as southern California. They are robin-sized, with an orange underside, but differ from robins by a distinct black chest band, buffy stripe over the eye and wingbars. Unlike robins, they frequently visit birdfeeders.

Favorite foods

Varied Thrushes often feed on the ground and, like robins, sometimes pull earthworms from lawns; more often they forage in leaf litter, where they grab billfuls of leaves, which they toss aside as they search for sowbugs, millipedes, beetles, and other invertebrates. They readily eat acorns, but they also eat the fruit of Elderberry, Virginia Creeper, dogwoods, and Spicebush. Plant foods comprise about 40 percent of their diet during the breeding season, increasing to 75 percent in winter.

Populations peak about every two to three years then decline. Some individuals wander a long way from the Pacific Northwest and usually show up at birdfeeders, sometimes as far away as the Atlantic Coast.

Winter snows bring hard times for Varied Thrushes as food supplies are buried, and many starve. Under such conditions, they feed along roadsides and often show up at birdfeeders, where they eat mixed seeds.

Varied Thrushes *are secretive, forest-interior birds, more often heard than seen. Their ethereal voice has a reedy quality. Like other thrushes, they sing mostly at dawn and dusk.*

Nesting

Females build the nest on a horizontal branch, usually in a small fir, spruce, hemlock, or willow 10–15ft (3–4.5m) above ground. Females do all of the incubation while the male sings to defend the territory.

IN THE BACKYARD

■ Plant berry-producing shrubs that provide winter food, such as oak, madrone, and snowberry; establish clumps of conifer such as spruce and hemlock for nesting, and provide millet and cracked corn at feeders, especially when it is snowing.

Ixoreus naevius
Turdidae

Orange eye-stripe

Resembles American Robin

Obvious pale wing stripe

Short tail

Wide black band across rusty breast

Relatively long neck

LENGTH 9–10in (23–25cm)
WINGSPAN 16in (41cm)
VOICE Song is single, long whistle on one pitch, repeated every 10 seconds. Call is a short, low, dry *chup*.
EGGS Usually 2 clutches of 3 (2–5) blue eggs, evenly marked with brown spots and speckles.
REARING Female incubates; about 14 days' incubation; days to fledging unknown; fed by male and female.

J F M A M J J A S O N D

Striping over the eye *and a dark band across the chest (black on the male, gray on the female) distinguish Varied Thrushes from American Robins.*

Northern Mockingbird

NORTHERN MOCKINGBIRDS ARE RESIDENT throughout most of the US, but seldom venture far into Canada. In recent decades they have expanded their range northward, a pattern that may be linked to warmer winters and the spread of invasive multiflora rose. Their song, a varied, prolonged succession of notes and phrases, each repeated several times before changing, is often heard at night.

Mimus polyglottos
Mimidae

Pale gray overall

White underside

Conspicuous large white patches on tail and wings

Long tail and legs

LENGTH 9–11in (23–28cm)
WINGSPAN 14in (36cm)
VOICE Song is a varied prolonged succession of notes and phrases. Note is a loud *tchack* or *chair*.
EGGS Often 2 clutches of 4 (3–5) light blue or green blotched eggs.
REARING Female incubates; 12–13 days' incubation; fledging 11–13 days; fed by male and female.

J F M A M J J A S O N D

Northern Mockingbirds *frequent bushy habitats, hedgerows, and large shrubs planted around buildings. They are slender birds with long beaks, tails, and legs.*

Fruit tree defense

Mockingbirds are recognizable by their narrow body, and long tail and legs. Often they flash their wings and fan their tail to expose patches of white feathers. Such displays are usually intended to intimidate neighbors and defend nesting and feeding territories, but they may also serve the additional function of startling predators such as snakes and flushing insects, which are then snatched by the Mockingbird. Defensive mockingbirds usually sit high in favorite fruit trees, chasing away intruding fruit-eaters such as waxwings and robins.

Master mimics

Mockingbirds are remarkable for their repertoire of songs, which may include those of over 50 other species. They are also notable for nocturnal singing, especially on moonlit nights. The diversity of songs reflects the age and experience of the male. When females are selecting a mate for breeding, they listen to the quality and quantity of songs—presumably, a more diverse song repertoire and a higher quality of rendition indicate more experienced mates.

Mockingbirds may sing for remarkable, non-stop lengths of 10–20 minutes. Analysis reveals that their songs are composed of hundreds of distinct phrases, few of which are regularly repeated. Within the

repertoire are not only the songs of other birds but also a wide variety of gargles, squeaks, and warbles of their own creation. Singing is most abundant from dawn to dark, early in the nesting season. Sometimes mockingbirds sing well past dark, especially on bright, moonlit nights. Both members of the pair build the nest, usually 3–10ft (1–3m) off the ground in a fork of a tall shrub.

Primarily Mockingbirds eat flying insects that they flush from the ground by spreading their wings. Typically, they target tiny insects such as weevils and ants, but they also occasionally capture spiders, crayfish, and even

Male Northern Mockingbirds *are famed for their complex songs, composed of original and mimicked phrases, largely collected from other birds.*

lizards and tiny snakes. In addition, their diet includes fruit such as pokeberry, elderberry, and poison ivy.

Mockingbirds were often captured and sold as pets from the late 1700s to the early 1900s, but the birds (and all other native birds) are now protected by the Migratory Bird Treaty Act. After trapping ended, mockingbird populations increased and they have spread north in recent decades, a range expansion that is likely associated with the rampant spread of multiflora rose, an invasive shrub that provides favorite fruits and excellent habitat for nesting.

Mockingbirds have *elaborate flight displays: a leap from a perch while in mid-song is followed by mid-air flaps and parachuting with open wings back to its perch.*

Mockingbirds are *slender birds with long bodies and tails. The bold white wing patches are hidden while the bird is perched.*

IN THE BACKYARD

■ Plant holly, brambles, and hawthorn. Provide raisins and currants at birdfeeders, especially in the late winter when natural foods are scarce.

Gray Catbird

GRAY CATBIRDS ARE EASILY identified by their sooty gray body and black cap, and they have a surprising splash of rust color under the tail. Catbirds are named for their distinctive "meow" call. Watch for them in hedgerows and shrubby borders between meadows and forests, where they often sing from snags and dead branches.

Dumetella carolinensis
Mimidae

Blackish cap

Black tail

Slim body

Overall slate-gray underside

Chestnut undertail coverts

LENGTH 9in (23cm)
WINGSPAN 11in (28cm)
VOICE A distinctive cat-like mewing. Also a grating *tcheck-tcheck*. Song consists of disjointed notes and phrases that are not repeated.
EGGS Usually 4 (2–6) deep greenish-blue and glossy.
REARING Female incubates; 12–13 days' incubation; fledging 10–11 days; fed by male and female.

J F M A M J J A S O N D

Capable mimics
Male Gray Catbirds arrive in mid-spring, a few days before females, and immediately start singing—often from trees that emerge from hedges and thickets. When they are singing, they hold their tail down and throw back their head to claim the territory and attract a female. Males are prolific singers, often repeating their liquid phrases even after they are paired, and often at night.

Like other members of the mockingbird family, catbirds are capable mimics, sometimes incorporating renditions of the calls of jays, quail, hawks, and even whip-poor-wills within their repertoire.

Provide orange *halves on nail spikes as a juicy bait for catbirds; raisins and mealworms also lure them from their brushy habitat.*

While the male *catbird sings to defend the territory, females do most of the nest building and incubation. Both sexes provide the food.*

Food and nesting
Gray Catbirds feed almost entirely on insects, especially crickets, grasshoppers, and beetles. Their habit of favoring Japanese beetles makes them a great friend of most gardeners. They mix their largely insect diet with fruit such as grapes and blackberries.

The pair build their nest 3–10ft (1–3m) off the ground in garden shrubs or similar wild habitat. They prefer to nest near water whenever possible.

Catbirds incubate their dark blue-green glossy eggs for 12–15 days and often raise two broods in a year. They are capable of recognizing cowbird eggs and may toss them from their nest.

IN THE BACKYARD
■ Provide feeding and nesting habitat in thorny hedges of blackberries and hawthorn. Also plant holly and bayberry bushes, and allow wild grapevines and green briars to flourish.

Brown Thrasher

THESE EXTRAORDINARILY MUSICAL BIRDS live in dry, shrubby habitat in eastern states. Thrashers that nest in northern states usually migrate to the southeast for the winter. Brown Thrasher populations have declined in recent years because shrubland habitat is changing to young forest throughout most of their range.

Master composers

Although Brown Thrashers are capable of mimicking the songs of neighboring species, just like their mockingbird relatives, more often they compose original songs. With more than 1,100 song types, male Brown Thrashers hold the record among all North American birds for the variety and extent of their song repertoire. Typically, their song consists of phrases in repeating couplets.

Brown Thrashers usually feed under shrubs and trees. Beetles comprise about a third of the animal portion of their diet. During summer months, they favor blackberries and cherries, while in winter, they switch to sumac, acorns, bayberry, and holly. Also in summer, Brown Thrashers often establish territories to which they return year after year. At feeders they usually feed on the ground, eating mixed seed including millet.

Brown Thrashers occasionally nest on the ground, but usually they locate their bulky stick nest in a shrub or tree 1–10ft (30cm–3m) off the ground, eating mixed seed, including millet.

In some ways *Brown Thrashers resemble thrushes, but their long body shape and long legs are more like the mockingbird and catbird.*

Brown Thrashers *use their long beak for pushing aside and tossing leaves in search of hidden insects, spiders, and occasional lizards.*

Toxostoma rufum
Mimidae

Long, pale red tail — Wing bars
Relatively short, rather curved bill
Bright red above
Slimmer body than thrushes
Heavily striped below

LENGTH 11in (28cm)
WINGSPAN 13in (33cm)
VOICE Song resembles that of the catbird, but more musical in nature with phrases in pairs. Note is a harsh *chack*!
EGGS Usually 2 broods with 4 (2–5) pale blue eggs with many small reddish brown dots.
REARING Both incubate; 11–14 days' incubation; fledging is 9–13 days; fed by male and female.

J F M A M J J A S O N D

IN THE BACKYARD

■ Provide feeding and nesting habitat by planting a hedgerow of blackberries, choke cherries, highbush blueberry, hawthorn, and hollies; rake leaves under shrubs to decompose and create feeding areas.

European Starling

THESE RAUCOUS IMMIGRANTS were first released in New York City in 1890. Now they are found coast-to-coast and north as far as trees grow. Their squabbly nature and hearty appetites win them few friends: they displace native cavity-nesting species such as bluebirds and swallows and, typically, descend on feeders in large numbers. Yet starlings are fascinating birds to watch and, at close range, their plumage is surprisingly beautiful.

Star-spangled feathers

Glossy, blackish feathers reveal an iridescent sheen of metallic blues, purples, and greens. After the summer molt, the new feathers are tipped with buff and white, creating a star-spangled look that gives the bird its name. As spring approaches, starlings lose these white-tipped feathers, exposing the iridescent plumage below, and their bill turns bright yellow. Males have a blue-gray base to the bill; females look similar except that the base of the bill is pink.

Male starlings defend a small territory around a nesting cavity in a tree or crevice in a building. Where resident, the male will often remain

The juvenile starling *is much plainer and duller than the adult, with mouse-brown plumage and a dark bill.*

in this territory throughout winter, using the nest for roosting. Females line the nest with fine grass, feathers, and other materials, and perform most of the incubation. Both members of the pair feed the young. In fall and winter, starlings sometimes sleep within enormous roosts of blackbirds that may include over a million birds.

This star-studded, *speckled winter plumage is the source of the starling's name.*

Versatile omnivores

Starlings have a varied diet of both plant and animal food, eating mainly earthworms, ants, bees, wasps, and spiders. When feeding on lawns, a starling inspects the ground with frequent, rapid thrusts of its bill. The bill is equipped with strong muscles that force it open at each probe. Swiveling its eyes forward to peer down the hole, starlings can focus on the end of their bill to search for food, while also watching for predators from above. Fruit from trees and shrubs makes up about 70 percent of their diet, so it is not surprising that cultivated fruits such as cherries and pears are attractive. Ironically, this European native is an important disperser of invasive trees and shrubs.

Starlings are gregarious birds, flying and roosting together. These adaptable and clever birds sometimes nest in loose colonies; more often they nest in a solitary manner.

European Starlings *often fly and roost in huge flocks along with blackbirds, robins, grackles, and cowbirds.*

Sturnus vulgaris
Sturnidae

Black plumage with glossy, green-and-purple sheen

Reddish brown legs

Triangular wings

Short, square-ended tail

LENGTH 8in (20cm)
WINGSPAN 14–16in (36–41cm)
VOICE Medley of rattles, squeaks, and whistles, interspersed with mimicked calls of other species.
EGGS Usually 2 broods of 4–5 (4–7) smooth, pale blue-green eggs with slight gloss.
REARING Female incubates; 11–15 days' incubation; fledging 21 days; fed by male and female.

J F M A M J J A S O N D

Male starlings (identified by the blue at the base of their bill) collect most of the nesting material. Males build the rough nest, using these materials along with bits of plastic and other debris. The nest may also contain green leaves and flower petals that have natural insect-repellent properties. This probably protects the nestlings from deadly parasites.

IN THE BACKYARD

■ To prevent starlings from occupying nest boxes intended for native birds, be sure that openings have a diameter no more than 1⅝in (4cm). To discourage starlings at feeders, do not offer peanut hearts.

In the breeding season, the male Starling sings from a prominent perch near the nest site. His song consists of a variety of imitated calls from other birds, along with his own whistles and peculiar sounds.

Bohemian Waxwing

BOHEMIAN WAXWINGS have a circumpolar nesting distribution in conifer and birch forests, but fly south to the northern states and western mountains when food is scarce. They have a distinctive trill and in flight are similar in shape to European Starlings. The tips of the inner wing feathers exude a red waxy secretion, hence the name.

Fruit specialists

Like Cedar Waxwings, these birds can survive almost entirely on a diet of fruit. This is possible because of such distinct fruit-eating adaptations as a large liver, which helps to convert sugar to energy. Their favorite fruit includes those of mountain ash and juniper. In spring, Bohemian Waxwings also eat midges, mosquitoes, sap, and flowers. At feeders, they will eat apples, raisins, and currants.

Flocking serves the usual purpose of communication about new food supplies and predator defense, but in this species flocking may also help to dislodge territorial robins and mockingbirds that are defending rich food supplies, such as crabapple trees. Territorial robins are capable of chasing off flocks of 15 or fewer waxwings, but observers have noted large waxwing flocks swamping the territorial capacity of a solitary robin or mockingbird that would otherwise chase away smaller numbers.

Female Bohemian Waxwings *incubate the eggs, but both sexes feed the young, providing a mixture of insects and berries.*

Male and female Bohemian Waxwings build their cup-shaped nest of twigs, grass, and lichen, lining it with grass. Like many other birds of the far north, they are often tame, even landing on people. Watch for them mixed with flocks of Cedar Waxwing and robins.

IN THE BACKYARD

■ Plant fruit-bearing junipers and mountain ash, flowering crabapple trees and hawthorn with small, winter-persistent fruit.

Bombycilla garrulus
Bombycillidae

Dark wings with white bars
Yellow tip
Brown crest
Dark undertail
Upright posture
White on wings (lacking in Cedar Waxwing)
Grayer than Cedar Waxwing
Rust-colored undertail

LENGTH 7in (18cm)
WINGSPAN 12–14in (30–36cm)
VOICE Song is a quiet trilling and wheezing; call is a trilling *sirr*.
EGGS 4–6 (2–6) pale blue eggs marked profusely with blackish dots and a few squiggly lines.
REARING Female incubates; 14–15 days' incubation; fledging 14–15 days; apparently fed by male and female.

J F M A M J J A S O N D

Berries and fruit *are a major part of the Bohemian Waxwing's diet in winter; berries are picked from trees and shrubs, and fallen fruit is eaten from the ground.*

Cedar Waxwing

THESE ELEGANT BIRDS are named not only for their close association with red cedar trees and other junipers, but also for the red waxy secretion that exudes from the tips of their inner wing feathers. In some areas their food consists mainly of juniper fruit. Waxwings are among its most important seed dispersers.

IN THE BACKYARD

■ To provide winter food, plant ornamental crabapples, hawthorn, and mountain ash with small fruit that hangs on the tree throughout the winter. Avoid planting such trees near highways because the birds will consume fermented fruit and become vulnerable to traffic when drunk!

Waxy advantage

The wax that Cedar Waxwings exude from the tips of their inner wing feathers (secondaries) may serve as an indication of age. It may also be a significant factor in mate choice, because second-year birds lack the wax. Older birds seem to prefer to pair with each other rather than the younger birds, and such pairs are generally more successful at raising young. Waxwings of all ages have a bright yellow tip to their tail, except those birds that feed on introduced honeysuckles, which have orange tips. Cedar Waxwings have a delightful courtship behavior in which they pass fruit and perform a charming side-stepping behavior. They nest at irregular times of the summer, often later than most other birds. During winter, they live in flocks of 20 to several hundred. They differ from Bohemian Waxwings by the lack of white on their wings and orange under the tail feathers.

Fruit lovers

Cedar Waxwings usually prefer fruit over other foods. Even during the nesting season, when most other species feed on insects, the waxwing diet consists mainly of fruit, with supplements of ants, caterpillars, and beetles. In fall, they gorge on the fruit of palms, mulberries, and mountain

Cedar Waxwings are easily identified at a distance by their upright posture, distinctive crest, and waxy red tips on the secondary feathers of their wings.

ash. In the winter months, they feed completely on fruit, especially ornamental crabapples and hawthorn berries. In spring, the waxwings sometimes drink sweet tree sap and the nectar of maples and apple.

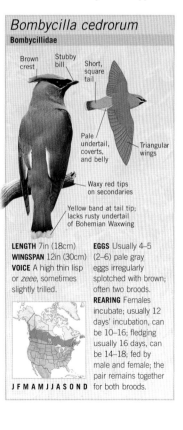

Bombycilla cedrorum
Bombycillidae

Brown crest
Stubby bill
Short, square tail

Pale undertail, coverts, and belly
Triangular wings

Waxy red tips on secondaries

Yellow band at tail tip; lacks rusty undertail of Bohemian Waxwing

LENGTH 7in (18cm)
WINGSPAN 12in (30cm)
VOICE A high thin lisp or *zeee*, sometimes slightly trilled.

EGGS Usually 4–5 (2–6) pale gray eggs irregularly splotched with brown; often two broods.
REARING Females incubate; usually 12 days' incubation, can be 10–16; fledging usually 16 days, can be 14–18; fed by male and female; the pair remains together for both broods.

J F M A M J J A S O N D

*About **70 percent** of the Cedar Waxwing's diet consists of fruit. Dried crabapples are among their favorites.*

Yellow-rumped Warbler

OF THE 54 SPECIES OF NORTH AMERICAN WARBLERS, the Yellow-rumped Warbler is the species most likely to visit backyards. They typically nest in the coniferous forests of Canada, New England, and western mountains. Unlike other warblers, they have a diet that enables them to winter in North America.

Varied diet

Most other warblers leave North America to winter in tropical latitudes. In contrast, most Yellow-rumped Warblers winter as far north as New Jersey and Washington state. Their secret for northern winters is a diet largely of bayberry and wax myrtle—coastal shrubs that produce wax-covered fruits that require special digestive enzymes, which most birds lack. Consequently, these abundant fruits are eaten by few other species. In addition to these special foods, Yellow-rumps also eat the fruit of poison ivy, other sumacs, and cedar. They benefit the plants by helping to disperse the seeds away from the parent plant where they would likely perish for lack of light and water. Like other warblers, Yellow-rumps also eat insects and switch to a mostly insect diet when they are feeding their young. At backyard feeders, they eat

Like the male, *the female is feathered in black and gold but, while the pattern is the same, her colors are paler.*

suet, mixtures of suet and seed, and peanut-butter mixtures. In winter, Yellow-rumped Warblers find safety from predators by living within flocks of other wintering species such as chickadees, titmice, and woodpeckers.

There are two subspecies: Audubon's Warblers, which have a bright yellow throat; and Myrtle Warblers, which have a white throat.

In breeding plumage, *a male Yellow-rumped Warbler flashes his distinctive shoulders and crown.*

Dendroica coronata
Parulidae

Blue-gray above

Bright yellow rump

Heavy black breast patch

Yellow patch on crown and before each wing

Stout black bill

LENGTH 5–6in (13–15cm)
WINGSPAN 9in (24cm)
VOICE Song is a loose trill similar to that of the Junco, but either rises in pitch or drops toward the end; note is a loud *check*.
EGGS Usually 4 (3–5) creamy white eggs, speckled or blotched brown at wide end. Occasionally two broods.
REARING Female incubates; 12–13 days' incubation; fledging 10–12 days; fed by male and female.

JFMAMJJASOND

IN THE BACKYARD

■ Plant clumps of bayberry (in north) or wax myrtle (south) to provide winter food. At feeders, mix equal parts of peanut-butter with cornmeal and dab into crevices in the bark and locations where side branches arise from tree trunks.

Scarlet Tanager

THE LUMINOUS RED COLOR of the male Scarlet Tanager is among the most intense colors in the natural world. Scarlet Tanagers breed throughout the northeast and upper Midwest. During the fall, they migrate to the tropics, where they mingle with South American resident tanagers and other tropical species.

Flashy display

Males return north to claim nesting territories in deciduous forests about the same time that leaves emerge. Females arrive soon afterward and select a singing male. Courtship includes an enticing display in which the male hops about on low perches, spreading his wings to flash his brilliant back and rump.

Family life

Females take several days to build a saucer-shaped nest on a horizontal branch far from the trunk. She uses twigs and coarse grass for the body of the nest, and fine grass and rootlets for the lining. The olive-plumaged female does all of the incubation, while the male continues to defend the territory with his raspy, robin-like song. Sometimes he feeds her while she incubates.

Males typically glean insects from leaf surfaces and sometimes feed on the ground; females also capture flying prey. Their diet includes insects ranging in size from tiny aphids and termites to cicadas. They also eat the fruit of wild cherries, dogwoods, wild grapes, and blackgum. At feeders, they sometimes peck at halved oranges and peanut-butter/cornmeal mixtures.

Western Tanagers (*Piranga ludoviciana*) live in coniferous and coniferous-deciduous forests of western states and provinces in mountains to 10,000ft (3,000m). Like Scarlet Tanagers, they may visit feeders for dried fruit and halved oranges, and readily bathe in birdbaths.

The cryptic olive yellow colors *of the female Scarlet Tanager permit her to hide the location of the nest while incubating.*

Piranga olivacea
Thraupidae

Jet black tail

Underside of wings white

Gray bill

Flaming scarlet body and black wings

LENGTH 7in (18cm)
WINGSPAN 11in (29cm)
VOICE Song is similar to that of American

Robin with four or five short phrases; note is a *chip-burr*.
EGGS 1 clutch of 3–5 (2–5) pale blue or pale green eggs, dotted or blotched with brown.
REARING Female incubates; 13–14 days' incubation; fledging 9–11 days; fed by male and female.

J F M **A M J J A S O N** D

IN THE BACKYARD

■ Plant blackgum, elderberries, and serviceberries; leave wild grape and Virginia Creeper in trees. Maintain large forest tracts. Provide dried and fresh fruit at feeders and clean water in birdbaths.

The song *of a Scarlet Tanager is a bury whistle, given from a lower branch of a tree. The call serves to discourage other males from entering his domain.*

Northern Cardinal

MALE NORTHERN CARDINALS are among the most admired of American birds, as evidenced by the states of Illinois, Indiana, Ohio, Kentucky, North Carolina, Virginia, and West Virginia, which claim cardinals as their state bird. For all of their gaudy color and vibrant singing, cardinals usually have a shy demeanor around feeders.

Cardinalis cardinalis

Cardinalidae

All red with a distinct crest

Stout red bill

Black patch at base of stout, triangular red bill

Long tail

Bright red overall

LENGTH 7–9in (19–23cm)

WINGSPAN 12in (30cm)

VOICE Note is a short thin *chip*; song is clear, slurred whistles; variations include *what-cheer cheer cheer, birdy birdy birdy.*

EGGS 3–4 (2–5) glossy green or blue eggs, blotched brown and purple, 2–3 clutches.

REARING Both incubate; 12–13 days' incubation; fledging 9–10 days; fed by male and female.

J F M A M J J A S O N D

Fruit eaters

The cardinal's wide gape permits it to consume a broad range of fruits and seed. In summer and fall, they feed largely on wild grape and dogwood; mulberries are a summer favorite. In winter they eat sumac. They are known to eat at least 33 kinds of wild fruit and 39 kinds of weed seeds. During the nesting season, they feed their young mostly beetles, ants, termites, and crickets, which they obtain from the ground.

At feeders, they eat black-oil and striped sunflower, hulled sunflower, and safflower seeds. Birdfeeders and warmer winters are contributing to the northward expansion of the cardinal's range. Cardinals are resident in southern states, where they sometimes form winter flocks of 50 or more. In the northern parts of its range, cardinals may retreat to warmer latitudes, but some remain in their territory throughout the year.

Singing and nesting

Unlike most songbirds, both male and female cardinals sing; the female has a softer song. Males often feed the female during courtship and while she incubates. Females build the nest in dense shrub; both feed the young.

Both members *of the pair build the nest from weed stems, pliable twigs, and bark, especially grapevines. Females do most of the incubation, which typically lasts 9–10 days.*

IN THE BACKYARD

■ Plant blackberries, dogwoods, wild grapes, hackberries, and elderberries. Provide sunflower seed and birdbaths.

In courtship, *males typically feed females, who assume a begging posture, gaping for food, with quivering wings.*

Black-headed Grosbeak

BLACK-HEADED GROSBEAKS frequent shrubby thickets, stream banks, parks, and edges of open woodland throughout the western United States. These familiar songbirds migrate to Mexico for the winter. They sometimes hybridize with Rose-breasted Grosbeaks in the plains states, where their ranges overlap.

Flight songs

In spring, males return from the tropics about a week before the females to stake out their nesting territories. Females settle into a territory where they hear the male singing, which triggers his courtship. The male courts his mate from the ground and air. The performance starts with the male perched, singing near the female. Then he leaps into the air to perform a series of flight songs. Even after incubation has started, the male continues to sing from the air.

Singing from the nest

Females usually build the nest in willows or coastal oaks from 4ft (1.2m) to 25ft (7.5m) above the ground. Both members of the pair incubate and sing to defend the territory. Sometimes they combine these tasks and sing from the nest.

They use their powerful bill to crack pine seeds and eat a wide variety of fruit, in particular mistletoe, elderberry, cherries, and blackberries. They also consume a wide range of insects including beetles, scale insects, wasps, bees, and flies.

Black-headed Grosbeaks use their powerful bill to crack open sunflower seeds and buds. They also feed on spiders and soft-bodied insects.

Only the adult male *has a black head and russet-orange patterning—and only during nesting. In fall and winter, the bold colors are replaced by sparrow-like brown stripes.*

Pheucticus melanocephalus
Cardinalidae

Very large, pale bill

Large, black head

Dull orange-brown collar and rump

Underwing coverts always pale or lemon-yellow

Dull orange-brown breast, usually finely streaked

Boldly marked black-and-white wings

LENGTH 6–7in (16–19cm)
WINGSPAN 12in (30cm)
VOICE Song is a whistled warble; call is a high, sharp *pik*.
EGGS Usually 3–4 (2–5) pale green or blue eggs, with browns and purples at large end.
REARING Both incubate; 12–13 days' incubation; fledging 11–12 days; fed by male and female.

J F M A M J J A S O N D

IN THE BACKYARD

■ Plant elderberry and blackberry bushes and cherry trees; provide birdbaths and sunflower seeds at feeders.

Rose-breasted Grosbeak

WITH A DAZZLING ROSE COLOR on the breast and jaunty black-and-white patterning, male Rose-breasted Grosbeaks are easy to recognize when they arrive in spring. Females look like oversized, plump sparrows, but their huge beak is a certain clue to their identity. In the fall the male molts into a female-like plumage.

Song and courtship

Males are the first to return after migration. They announce their arrival with a loud, robin-like caroling song, recognized by its run-on phrases, connected by slur-sounding notes. Rose-breasted Grosbeaks establish nesting territories in deciduous forests, and gardens and parks with mature, deciduous trees in late spring. When the females arrive, several males may compete for their attention, hovering above and singing in the air.

In courtship, the pair often touches bills. Females also sing, but their song is softer than the males'.

Food and family

About half of the Rose-breasted Grosbeaks' diet is insects, especially beetles, hairy caterpillars of gypsy moths, tent caterpillars, and brown-tailed moths. They also eat the fruit of elderberry and cherry, as well as elm seeds, hickory and beech blossom, and ash buds. At birdfeeders, they eat sunflower seeds.

Males sometimes select the nest site and may help the female with construction. The nest is typically located in a thicket, often near water between 5 and 15ft (1.5–4.5m) above the ground. Both sexes incubate the eggs and feed the young, which leave the nest when they are about 15 days old.

Male Rose-breasted Grosbeaks have a loud, long, robin-like call, with phrases connected without pauses; females have a softer and shorter song.

Female and young *Rose-breasted Grosbeaks lack the namesake rose color found only on summer-plumaged males.*

IN THE BACKYARD

■ Plant elderberries and cherry for summer and fall foods, and clumps of birch for nesting; provide sunflower seeds at birdfeeders and clean water in birdbaths.

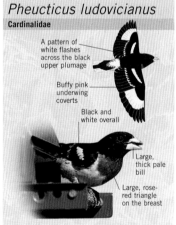

Pheucticus ludovicianus
Cardinalidae

A pattern of white flashes across the black upper plumage

Buffy pink underwing coverts

Black and white overall

Large, thick pale bill

Large, rose-red triangle on the breast

LENGTH 7–8in (18–21cm)
WINGSPAN 12in (30cm)
VOICE Song consists of rising and falling passages, like that of the robin; note is a metallic *kick* or *eek*.
EGGS Usually one clutch of 4 (3–5) light blue/green or pale gray eggs spotted with browns and purples.
REARING Both incubate; 13–14 days' incubation; fledging 9–12 days; fed by male and female.

J F M A M J J A S O N D

Indigo Bunting

INDIGO BUNTINGS OFTEN APPEAR at feeders during migration, but will abandon handouts once they set up their nesting territory. The demands of defending a territory and rearing the young dominate the schedule of this stunning finch. It lives in upland habitat, favoring the margins between forest and meadow.

Similar species

In southern states, distinguish Blue Grosbeaks (*Guiraca caerulea*) from Indigo Buntings by their larger size, brown wingbars, and heavier bill. In western states, watch for Lazuli Buntings (*Passerina amoena*), which are similar to Indigo Bunting except for orange on the chest, a white belly and wingbars. Although adult male Indigo Buntings are completely blue, they can appear black when backlit. The females are mostly brown, but have just a hint of blue in the tail.

Star watchers

Indigo Buntings live in upland habitat, favoring the margins between forest and meadow, especially where they find shrubby hedgerows. Look for them along creeks and rivers, singing from tall trees and utility lines. In the winter they migrate to Central America, where they live in flocks, frequenting haunts similar to their breeding habitat. They were the subject of innovative migration studies within planetariums, which demonstrated their ability to navigate using the North Star as a reference.

Female Indigo Buntings build their nests of woven grass with bits of snakeskin and moss in thickets of raspberry and blackberry. Nestlings are fed insects including grasshoppers, beetles, flies, and mosquitoes.

Indigo Buntings feed on berries in trees, shrubs, and on the ground; at feeders they prefer millet seed.

Passerina cyanea
Cardinalidae

Short tail

Rich deep blue, darker on head

Stocky shape

Small bill

LENGTH 5in (14cm)
WINGSPAN 8in (20cm)
VOICE Song is lively, high and strident, with regular phrases at different pitches; either *sweet-sweet* or *chew-chew*; note is a sharp thin *spit*.
EGGS Usually 2 broods with clutches of 3–4 (2–4) white or pale blue unmarked eggs.
REARING Female incubates; 12–13 days' incubation; fledging 9–10 days; fed by male and female.

J F M A M J J A S O N D

IN THE BACKYARD

■ Plant thickets of elderberry, blackberries, and raspberries along forest edges; provide millet and clean birdbaths.

Look for Indigo Buntings *in shrubby hedgerows and along creeks and rivers, singing from branches of tall trees and utility lines.*

Painted Bunting

THE GAUDY, MALE PAINTED BUNTING has a scarlet underpart and rump, an iridescent green back, and a blue head with a red eye-ring. The East Coast population nests from North Carolina to Florida, wintering in south Florida and the Bahamas, Cuba, and Jamaica. The Louisiana-to-Texas population winters south to Panama.

Passerina ciris

Cardinalidae

Violet-blue on head

Green on back

Bill slightly longer than that of other buntings

Red underparts

Red rump

LENGTH 5in (13cm)
WINGSPAN 8in (20cm)
VOICE Song is pleasant warble that resembles that of Warbling Vireo;

J F M A M J J A S O N D

note is a sharp *chip.*
EGGS May have 4 broods per year, but 2 is more common. Each clutch contains 3–4 (3–5) white or light blue eggs with brown speckles at large ends.
REARING Female incubates; 11–12 days' incubation; fledging 12–14 days; fed by male and female.

Diet and nesting

Tiny seeds of bristle grass dominate the Painted Bunting's diet. During the nesting season, they feed their young boll weevils, grasshoppers, crickets, wasps, flies, and caterpillars. Males sing from tall trees and are noted for their bold defense of the nesting territory, which may lead to bloody and even fatal fights.

Females build the open-cup nest in dense brush from dried grass, weed stems and leaves, lined with hairs, fine grass, and occasionally bits of snake-skin. Males help to feed the young.

Watchlist alert

Between 1966 and 2000, breeding populations of Painted Bunting

Unlike her male *counterpart, the female Painted Bunting is completely green—the only green finch found in North America.*

declined at the rate of 2.7 percent annually. Painted buntings are on the Audubon Watchlist (a list of species with great conservation risk) because of habitat loss, disease, and being captured from their winter homes for the songbird trade. Probably the greatest threat is the increasing loss of shrubby habitat, but the appearance of Brown-headed Cowbirds (and their accompanying parasitism) are an ever-growing threat in the East Coast region. In addition, thousands of Painted Buntings are trapped in Mexico every year to be exported to Europe.

Painted Buntings *live in habitats with weeds, brush, and trees, especially along rivers. Males may be extremely aggressive toward one another when defending nesting territories.*

IN THE BACKYARD

■ Encourage shrubby hedgerows with emergent tall trees and vines. Provide white millet at feeders and clean water in birdbaths. Do not feed on the ground where there are outdoor cats. Protect from window strikes.

Spotted Towhee

THE GREAT PLAINS separate the ranges of the more western Spotted Towhee from the similar Eastern Towhee (*Pipilo erythrophthalmus*). Until recently, both species were known as Rufous-sided Towhee. Both are shy birds that frequent shrublands and hedges, foraging and nesting on or very close to the ground.

Leaf tossers

Watch for the towhee's trademark scratching behavior. It jumps forward with its head and tail alert, then double-kicks backward with both feet to toss leaves far behind, exposing seeds and invertebrates such as beetles.

On their winter range, males from northern populations may winter in flocks with resident birds or live in flocks of a dozen or more males. Northern females winter in a warmer climate, further south than males. Unlike the males, females do not need to race back north to claim prime nesting habitat. Already in decline due to loss of habitat, towhees are also especially vulnerable to Brown-headed Cowbird parasitism.

The Spotted Towhee song is quite distinct from that of Eastern Towhees. Towhee song changes with age. The song of young males changes over time, eventually resembling that of their father. Male towhees both establish their territory and attract females with their song. Females build a cup-shaped nest either on or within a few feet of the ground, in dense shrubs.

Eastern Towhees resemble Spotted Towhees, except they have an all-dark back and the wing has only a small patch of white.

IN THE BACKYARD

■ Plant shrubs and fruit-producing trees, especially pines, oak, blackberries, wild cherries, blueberries, elderberries, hollies, and hackberries. Provide birdbaths on the ground only where they are safe from outdoor cats. Offer mixed seed and mealworms.

Pipilo maculatus

Emberizidae

White markings on wings

Long tail

Dark head

Very dark flanks

Stocky body

LENGTH 8in (20cm)
WINGSPAN 10in (25cm)
VOICE Spotted Towhees: song of identical notes starts with a stutter, ends in a buzzy trill; Eastern: repeats phrases, with variable versions of "*drink your teeee.*"
EGGS Usually 2 clutches of 3–4 (3–5) reddish speckled, creamy white eggs.
REARING Both incubate; 12–13 days' incubation; fledging 10–12 days; fed by both parents.

J F M A M J J A S O N D

Towhee populations are declining as a consequence of the widespread transition of their favored shrubland to young forest.

California Towhee

THESE BOLD, GROUND-DWELLING BIRDS are often seen scratching in backyards, picnic areas, roadsides, suburban habitats, and brushy hillsides from Oregon to the southern Baja California peninsula. In wilder habitats, they are shyer, staying tight to shrubby habitats. They are mostly brown with faint streaks around their throat.

Pipilo crissalis
Emberizidae

Stocky

Orangish rump

Pale orange-pink on underside of wings

Dusky belly

LENGTH 9in (23cm)
WINGSPAN 11in (28cm)
VOICE Song is an accelerating series of high, flat teek notes, *teek teek teek eek eekeekeekeek t-t-t-t-teek*; call is a hard, high flat *teek*.
EGGS Usually 3–4 (2–4) blue-white eggs with black spots.
REARING Female incubates; 11 days' incubation; fledging 8 days; fed by both male and female.

J F M A M J J A S O N D

Distinct species

Until recently, the California Towhee and Canyon Towhee (*Pipilo fuscus*) were considered one species—the Brown Towhee. Now, differences in ranges, behavior, song, and appearance show that these are two species. Canyon Towhees have a distinctive dark spot on their chest, a light belly, and a contrasting reddish crown. Their southwestern range (mostly Arizona and New Mexico) does not overlap with that of the California Towhee.

California Towhees are non-migratory and stay on the same habitat throughout the year. They are very territorial and readily attack their own image in windows and in the shiny hubcaps of cars. Most pairs are likely to mate for

life. The mated pair is usually seen near each other, calling if they lose sight of their mate—even a separation of 20ft (6m) may cause concern. They build a bulky nest of grass 3–12ft (1–4m) off the ground in a shrub, incorporating plant stems and lining it with bark, leaves, and animal hair. Females do the incubation and the young leave when just eight days old.

Appetite for seeds

Both California and Canyon Towhees are mainly seed-eaters, but they also eat some insects and feed these to their young. While they sometimes scratch for food, they do it without the gusto of the Eastern and Spotted Towhees.

California Towhees *are stocky and rather sluggish. They lack the dark spot on the chest and the contrasting reddish crown of the Canyon Towhee.*

American Tree Sparrow

IN THE FALL, FLOCKS OF AMERICAN TREE SPARROWS migrate from northern Canada and Alaska to fields and shrublands throughout most of the United States. American Tree Sparrows may be distinguished from several other long-tailed, rusty capped sparrows by the black spot in the middle of their unstreaked gray breast.

Weed-seed appetite

Tree Sparrows typically feed on the ground among weeds or disturbed soil. They sometimes leap up the stem to grab seeds that are still in place, sprinkling fresh seed on the ground. One Iowa study found that Tree Sparrows eat about 875 tons (800 tonnes) of seed from grass, ragweed, lamb's-quarters, and other weeds each year. This provides an important

service to farmers, who might otherwise have a greater need for herbicides to suppress such weeds.

Winter hardy!

In winter habitats, Tree Sparrows usually occur in flocks of 30–40 birds of both sexes, often associating with Dark-eyed Juncos. Within these larger flocks, groups of 4–8 stay together throughout the winter. Given ample food, they can withstand extreme cold, surviving temperatures as low as −18°F (−28°C).

During their annual migration, American Tree Sparrows may travel as far as 3,000 miles

American Tree Sparrows nest at the northern limit of tree growth and migrate into southern Canada and northern states in fall and winter.

(4,800km) between their winter habitat and nesting grounds in Northern Alaska. When flocks arrive on the nesting grounds, males set up territory and sing to attract a mate. Females build the cup-shaped grassy nest with plant stems, bits of bark and moss, and line it with a soft interior of ptarmigan feathers and lemming fur. Young leave when they are about nine days old.

Spizella arborea
Emberizidae

Two white wingbars
Bill dark above and yellow below
Solid red-brown cap
Long tail
Single dark spot or "stickpin" on breast

LENGTH 6–6½in (15–17cm)
WINGSPAN 9in (23cm)
VOICE Song is sweet and variable, usually opening with one or two high, clear notes. Note is *tseet*.
EGGS Usually 3–5 (3–7) pale blue or green, speckled with brown.
REARING Female incubates; 12–13 days' incubation; fledging 8–10 days; fed by both male and female.

J F M A M J J A S O N D

The American Tree Sparrow *is the only sparrow with a reddish crown and an unstreaked breast with a black spot.*

IN THE BACKYARD

■ Provide shrubby fencerows for cover and roosting. Leave weed heads for winter food, and provide mixed grains, especially millet, at feeders.

Field Sparrow

FIELD SPARROWS DIFFER from other rusty-capped sparrows by their pink beak and white eye ring. Field Sparrows breed throughout the eastern United States and winter in states where they can avoid persistent snow cover. They are seen at birdfeeders, but they generally prefer to collect seeds from hedgerows and fields.

Prefers shrubs

The name Field Sparrow is misleading as it suggests the birds frequent grassy meadows. In fact, they prefer old fields and pastures overgrown by sumac, brambles, and hawthorn. Unlike the similar Chipping Sparrow, they rarely nest near houses. Male Field Sparrows typically sing from the top of a shrub or small tree to defend their territory and attract a mate. The song is musical and likened to the sound made by a marble dropping on a plate of glass, repeating faster and faster until it stops. Sometimes they sing on full-moon nights.

Gentle manner

Field Sparrows are gentle, rarely aggressive sparrows that seldom quarrel, even in the congestion that they might encounter at birdfeeders.

After arriving at the nesting territory, males start singing immediately; the song declines soon after pairing with females.

Field Sparrows *are seldom found in open fields, preferring instead shrubby habitats. At feeders, they feed on millet and other grains scattered on the ground.*

They are infrequent feeder birds; more often they feed on weed seeds that they pick from the ground or obtain by hanging onto stems. They feed their young a wide range of small insects such as leafhoppers, ants, flies, and wasps.

The female builds a cup-shaped nest of coarse grass and lines it with rootlets and sometimes creates a lining from horsehair. The nest is usually located within three feet of the ground in sumac, blackberry, hawthorn, or similar low shrubs.

Spizella pusilla
Emberizidae

Pink or tan underside of wings

Relatively long tail

Pink bill

Rusty cap

Narrow light eye-ring

Plain breast

LENGTH 5in (13cm)
WINGSPAN 8in (20cm)
VOICE Song opens with sweet slurring notes, becoming a trill

J F M A M J J A S O N D

that may ascend or descend to a different pitch; note is *tsee*.
EGGS One clutch of 3–5 (2–6) pale blue-green eggs, blotched with dark brown and scrawled with black
REARING Female incubates; usually 12 days' incubation, may be 10–17; fledging 7–8 day; fed by male and female.

IN THE BACKYARD

■ Provide shrubby fencerows and let small fields, ie. 30 acres (12 hectares) or less, transition into shrub habitat with sumac and hawthorn; at feeders, scatter millet and cracked corn on the ground if there is minimal threat from outdoor cats.

Chipping Sparrow

WHERE THEIR RANGES OVERLAP, Chipping Sparrows and Tree Sparrows are easily confused. Both have rusty caps and unstreaked undersides. But fortunately for the novice birder, Tree Sparrows usually migrate north for the winter, almost the same day that Chipping Sparrows arrive from the south.

Suburban sparrow

Chipping Sparrows have readily adapted to suburbia, especially where they find tall trees for singing posts, shrubs close to houses, and closely cropped lawn. For these reasons, they are common birds in gardens, orchards, and farmyards. They also frequent the shores of lakes and streams, forest clearings, and cottonwood groves in the prairies.

Weed seed-eaters

In winter, Chipping Sparrows feed constantly throughout the day on weed seed such as ragweed, amaranth, and crabgrass every few seconds. Over the course of a winter, each Chipping Sparrow will consume about 2⅓lb (1kg) of weed seed. This is about 160 times its body weight! In most years weed seeds are very abundant, but in years when there was little rain the previous summer, seeds become relatively scarce and populations of Chipping Sparrows may decline.

Horsehair connection

About five percent of Chipping Sparrow males have two mates, an unusual habit among sparrows. Females build the nest on a branch of a conifer, such as a spruce, arborvitae, or yew, usually within about 6ft (2m) of the ground. The cup-shaped nest, made of weed stems and grasses, is often lined with animal hair such as black horsehair.

Females do all the incubation and the male feeds her while she is on the nest. Both parents feed the young a diet largely of insects, especially ants, wasps, leafhoppers, and caterpillars.

Chipping Sparrows *often feed on weed seeds in close-cropped lawns. They are common visitors to feeders, and are among the most common suburban sparrows.*

Chipping Sparrows *are among the first songsters in the dawn chorus and sometimes sing at night*

Spizella passerina
Emberizidae

Bright red cap

Black line through the eye

Gray breast

Gray rump

Relatively short, notched tail

LENGTH 5in (13cm)
WINGSPAN 8in (21cm)
VOICE Song is a simple, long trill; call is a sharp *chip*.

JFMAMJJASOND

EGGS Usually two clutches of 4 (2–5) pale bluish green eggs, dotted and scrawled with dark brown, black, and purple, concentrated at large end.
REARING Female incubates; 11–14 days' incubation; fledging usually 10–12 days; fed by male and female.

IN THE BACKYARD

■ Chipping Sparrows prefer to feed on the ground, on millet and cracked corn. Provide horsehair during nesting season.

White-throated Sparrow

BIRDS OF THE NORTHERN CONIFER FORESTS, White-throated Sparrows leave their forest home for the winter and migrate south to avoid the zone of persistent snow. Their migration usually brings them far enough south, to where they can scratch through fallen leaves in search of insects and other invertebrates.

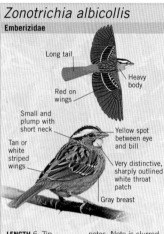

Zonotrichia albicollis
Emberizidae

Long tail

Heavy body

Red on wings

Small and plump with short neck

Tan or white striped wings

Yellow spot between eye and bill

Very distinctive, sharply outlined white throat patch

Gray breast

LENGTH 6–7in (15–18cm)
WINGSPAN 9in (23cm)
VOICE Clear, pensive whistles followed by

notes. Note is slurred *tseet* or hard *chink*.
EGGS Usually 1, but may be 2 clutches of 4–6 (3–6) creamy or bluish white eggs dotted with browns.
REARING Female incubates; 11–14 days' incubation; fledging usually 8–9 days, may be 7–12; fed by male and female.

JFMAMJJASOND

Winter territories

White-throated Sparrows have distinct winter territories to which they return year after year. At their winter home, they develop a peck-order rank within each age and sex group. The dominant birds can be identified by their tendency to sing more frequently and to feed nearest to shrubs, where they are more protected from predators.

Crown color

These birds have two plumage types: some have white stripes over the crown, while others have tan crown stripes. The more brightly colored birds are not necessarily males, but white-striped birds tend to be dominant over their tan-striped counterparts. Usually a bird with white-striped plumage will pair with a tan-striped mate. White-throated

Adults with a white *crown stripe may be either male or female and typically pair with a tan-striped adult.*

IN THE BACKYARD

■ Plant shrubby dogwoods, elderberries, and Spicebush to provide fall foods. During migration and winter, provide millet and cracked corn on ground feeders located near shrubs and from raised hopper feeders.

Sparrows typically scratch at leaves to reveal hidden prey such as ants, beetles, and flies, but they also feed in shrubs on a variety of fruit, including dogwood, elderberry, juniper, and Spicebush. They also eat the buds of oak, maple, and apple.

They usually build their nests from grass and line it with animal hair.

Both white-striped *and tan-striped adults show the diagnostic white throat and yellow patch in front of the eye.*

White-crowned Sparrow

THESE PERKY SPARROWS exist throughout North America, nesting far north into the northern coniferous forests and tundra regions. While most are migratory, there are also some non-migratory populations. In the non-migratory populations, the pair may mate for life and become resident throughout the year.

The black-and-white *crown feathers of the handsome White-crowned Sparrows indicate temperament and subspecies.*

Winter homes

Migratory White-crowned Sparrows form winter flocks of 50 or more, establishing a large group territory. Within these groups, each sparrow may have its own foraging area within the larger territory. These winter assemblages tend to return to the same habitat year after year and rarely mingle with neighboring flocks.

Within the winter flocks, there are further levels of organization, based on sex and age. Stripes on the crown are as indicative of dominance as military badges and stripes. Typically, older birds are dominant over the younger birds (identified by brown crown stripes) and males are dominant over females. Males have more contrasting crown patterns than females.

Favorite stopovers

White-crowned Sparrows normally scratch for their food to reveal weed seeds and hiding insects. At feeders, their favorite food is white millet. Once they discover a reliable food source, they are likely to stay for several days, and the same birds may stop at the same place on migration each year. Western White-crowned Sparrows often live in mixed flocks with Golden-crowned Sparrows (*Zonotrichia atricapilla*), which look similar except for their yellow forecrown.

Females build a bulky nest of sticks and grass, lined with rootlets and the hair of deer, cows, and horses.

Zonotrichia leucophrys
Emberizidae

Long neck

Long tail

When raised, crown feathers resemble a slight crest

Puffy crown striped with black and white

Pink bill

Gray breast

Large, slender body

LENGTH 6–7in (15–18cm)
WINGSPAN 9in (23cm)
VOICE Variable song, often consisting of

JFMAMJJASOND

one or more clear plaintive whistles followed by some husky, trilled whistles.
EGGS 1 brood of 3–5 (2–6) pale green or cream eggs with brown spots and blotches.
REARING Female incubates; 11–14 days' incubation; fledging 7–12 days; fed by both parents.

Identify White-crowned Sparrows *by their perky, long-necked posture with a uniform gray underside and throat. Adults have neat black and white striped crowns; immatures have brown-striped crowns.*

IN THE BACKYARD

◼ Provide shrubby fencerows for winter cover and scatter millet and cracked corn under shrubs.

Fox Sparrow

ALL 18 SUBSPECIES of this large, striped sparrow breed in the northern coniferous forests of Canada and Alaska. They migrate south for the winter to warmer latitudes, avoiding accumulated snow cover. Fox Sparrows are named after the red color of the fox, but some subspecies are more brown than red.

Passerella iliaca
Emberizidae

Rufous tail conspicuous in flight

Rusty rump

Rusty or brown on wings and back

Gray around neck

Breast very heavily streaked with rust

LENGTH 6–7in (15–18cm)
WINGSPAN 10in (25cm)
VOICE Brilliant, musical song consists of clear notes and sliding whistles.
EGGS 1 clutch of 2–5 pale bluish green eggs, boldly marked with spots and blotches of red-brown.
REARING Female incubates; 12–14 days' incubation; fledging 9–11 days; fed by male and female.

J F M A M J J A S O N D

Two-leg scratchers
Like towhees, Fox Sparrows scratch with both feet through the fallen leaves in woodland to expose hidden invertebrates and seeds. The energetic manner in which the birds stay in one spot and continue to kick permits them to create a hole in the leaf mulch, thus exposing hidden prey that other ground-feeding birds would overlook.

The Fox Sparrows have a more varied diet than other sparrows, including millipedes, spiders, and ground beetles. Their diet includes quantities of weed seeds, especially knotweeds. They also perch in shrubs to feed on blueberries, elderberries, grapes, and other fruit.

Fox Sparrows use *both feet to scratch the soil and leaves, exposing seeds and invertebrates; adults eat mainly seeds, and young are reared on a complete diet of insects.*

Fox Sparrows that nest early *in the season build their nests higher in trees than later-nesting birds. The higher location of nests may be due to snow accumulation.*

Shy skulkers
Although flocks of 50 or more Fox Sparrows may occur during migration, only a few reside at any one location on the winter range, and these do not defend a winter territory. In the East, they are likely to occur in deciduous forest, while in the West they are more often in coniferous forests. They may also reside in city parks, where they sometimes skulk under shrubby habitats alongside rivers and streams. Fox Sparrows are sociable and often join winter flocks of other sparrows.

IN THE BACKYARD
Provide a brush pile near a feeding station; so long as outdoor cats are not a concern, offer millet and other mixed seed on the ground.

Song Sparrow

FOUND THROUGHOUT NORTH AMERICA, Song Sparrows vary regionally in size and color—taxonomists have subdivided the species into no fewer than 31 subspecies, which grade into one another. Look for Song Sparrows along brush fencerows and old fields where there are scattered shrubs.

Wintering habits

Song Sparrows from northern latitudes often mingle with their nonmigratory relatives when they migrate to southern states and northern Mexico for the winter. Males typically winter further north than females, which permits them to return quickly to claim the best nesting territories. Males that do not migrate normally defend their nesting territory throughout the year; winter Song Sparrow flocks usually consist of juveniles and migrants. Watch for dominance displays at feeders; males are a little larger than females and dominate food supplies.

Varied diet

Song Sparrows obtain food from the ground, feeding mostly on weed seeds. During frigid winter weather, a Song Sparrow needs to eat between about 85 and 4,000 seeds per hour (depending on the size of the seed) to obtain enough calories to survive. During summer, insects such as beetles,

Song Sparrows develop their complete repertoire of songs within a few months of hatching, with local populations having distinct dialects.

IN THE BACKYARD

■ Build a brush pile in a corner of the yard for cover; plant blackberries and elderberries, and provide millet and cracked corn on the ground at feeders.

grasshoppers, cutworms, termites, ants, and flies make up half of the diet along with blackberries, seeds, elderberries, and other fruit.

Female Song Sparrows usually build the first nest of the year among clumps of grass on the ground; later nests are built in low shrubs and conifers.

Song Sparrows typically migrate just far enough south to avoid accumulations of snow. When they encounter snow, they fluff their feathers to keep warm and conserve energy.

Melospiza melodia
Emberizidae

- Stout billed
- Round head
- Heavy breast streaks converge into a large central spot
- Distinct cheek marks
- Long, rounded tail
- Broad, rounded wings

LENGTH 5–6in (13–15cm)
WINGSPAN 8in (20cm)
VOICE Series of notes, starting with bright, repetitive notes, *sweet sweet sweet*. Call note is low, nasal *tchep*.
EGGS Usually 2–3 clutches of 3–5 greenish white eggs, blotched with reddish brown and purple.
REARING Female incubates; 12–14 days' incubation; fledging usually 9–12 days, may be 16; fed by male and female.

JFMAMJJASOND

Dark-eyed Junco

WHEN JUNCOS ARRIVE AT TEMPERATE LATITUDES, you can be sure winter weather will not be far behind: these tiny-billed birds are seed-eating specialists that flee northern winters and deep snows. Watch for juncos under birdfeeders in the garden and you will be well rewarded since they hold the distinction of visiting more feeders across North America than any other species.

Junco hyemalis
Emberizidae

Striking white outer tail feathers

Pinkish bill

Brown, pink, or gray flanks

Small body

LENGTH 5–6in (13–15cm)
WINGSPAN 9in (23cm)
VOICE Loose trill similar to that of Chipping Sparrow. Note is a light *smack*.
EGGS Usually 2 clutches of 4–5 (3–6) pale blue-white eggs spotted with brown, purple, and gray.
REARING Female incubates; 12–13 days incubation; fledging 9–13 days; fed by male and female.

J F M A M J J A S O N D

Ranking in winter flocks

In winter, female juncos generally migrate further south than males. Male juncos risk wintering at colder latitudes since this positions them for claiming the best breeding territories when they return to their northern homes in the spring.

Winter flocks usually include 10–30 individuals that stay together through winter. Banding studies show that individual juncos associate consistently within the flocks. Wintering junco flocks are organized by social rank: oldest males, young males, oldest females, and young females. Dominant birds benefit by staying in the center of the flock, where they are more protected from predators. Juncos maintain their peck order by dominance displays,

Pink-sided Juncos *live in the Rocky Mountain region from Canada to Mexico, and can be identified by their light gray hood and extensive pink sides.*

Identify these western Oregon Juncos *by their black hood, chestnut back and sides. Like other juncos, they have a white belly.*

especially aggressive lunges and tail-flicking, in which the white outer tail feathers are briefly exposed.

It is common for juncos to associate with other birds in winter flocks, especially bushtits, nuthatches, Tree Sparrows, chickadees, and kinglets.

Juncos are sometimes *called "snow birds" because they arrive in southern states in winter and depart for northern latitudes when the snow melts.*

IN THE BACKYARD

■ Provide a brush pile and shrubs for winter cover, and conifers for roosting and protection from severe weather. Let some lawn mature to provide winter seed; offer millet, cracked corn, and hulled sunflower at hopper and ground feeders.

Dark-eyed Junco fledglings *beg food from their parents for several days following fledging. Their streaked breast belies their close relationship to sparrows.*

Most juncos breed in northern coniferous forests and migrate south for the winter, but some mountain populations migrate vertically, breeding among mountaintop conifers of the Appalachians and wintering at lower elevations where there is little snow. Juncos roost in conifers, in old bird nests, and in rock crevices.

Favorite foods

Juncos have tiny bills, ideal for picking up weed seeds, but not large enough to tackle sunflower seeds. At feeders they eat millet, cracked corn, and hulled sunflower.

Even where feeders are well stocked, juncos feed primarily on weed seeds, consuming thousands daily to survive winter temperatures.

Courtship and nesting

In courtship, the junco pair hops with their wings drooped and tail fanned, displaying the white outer tail feathers. From low perches, the male droops his wings, then spreads and droops his tail while singing softly. Females build the nest in a shallow depression, often with overhead protection of foliage or against

Adult juncos eat *mostly seeds and berries; nestlings are fed a complete diet of insects. Initially, parents regurgitate insect meals to their young.*

a vertical surface such as a rock or tree trunk. Females incubate and brood the young; both sexes feed the chicks a high-protein diet of insects. The legs of the young develop quickly, an adaptation that permits them to leave the nest a few days before they can fly. Juncos were once divided into several species, but now these are grouped into the single, widespread Dark-eyed Junco and the Yellow-eyed Junco (*Junco phaeonotus*), found only in southern Arizona. Oregon and Pink-sided Juncos are now considered distinct races of the Dark-eyed Junco.

Bobolink

NAMED FOR THEIR TINKLING, CHEERFUL SONG, Bobolinks usually announce their presence by singing from the air above grassy fields. They have the longest migration of any member of the blackbird family, traveling as far as 5,000 miles from their North American nesting habitat to southern Brazil and northern Argentina.

Rice birds

During the nesting season, beetles, grasshoppers, caterpillars, wasps, and ants make up most of the Bobolink's diet, along with seed from barnyard and panic grasses. They switch to mostly seeds during fall migration.

During the late nineteenth and early twentieth centuries, huge numbers migrated down the Atlantic coast through South Carolina rice fields, where enormous numbers were killed to protect crops. In those years, they were known locally as "rice birds." Now Bobolinks are protected from hunting, but their population is still declining due to habitat loss on the nesting grounds and poisoning from pesticides on their winter range.

Female Bobolinks resemble *large sparrows. They have a striped crown and are buff-colored below. The young are fed on insects.*

Mating and nesting

Each male Bobolink may have several mates. Females build the nest on the ground in a slight depression, such as the rut left by a tractor, using coarse grass and an interior of finer grasses. Often several pairs nest near each other, forming loose colonies that persist in the same field for years.

Males display for *females by singing from perches and from the wing in courtship flights. Each male typically pairs with several females.*

Dolichonyx oryzivorus
Icteridae

Pointed wings

Yellow nape

Solid black below and mostly white above

White rump and scapulars

LENGTH 6–8in (15–20cm)
WINGSPAN 1in (2.5cm)
VOICE Ecstatic song starts with low, reedy notes, rollicking upward while in flight and descending. Flight note is clear *pink*.
EGGS 1 clutch of 5–6 (4–7) pale gray or buff-colored eggs with brown blotches.
REARING Female incubates; 10–13 days' incubation; fledging 10–14 days; fed by male and female.

J F M **A M J J A S O** N D

IN THE BACKYARD

■ Bobolinks require fields that are at least 5 acres (2.2 hectares) in area. Most fields are generally safe for mowing by mid-July, although late-nesting birds might fledge young through the end of July.

Brown-headed Cowbird

ONCE KNOWN AS "BUFFALO BIRDS," Brown-headed Cowbirds used to be found mainly in prairie states, where they followed migratory bison herds, consuming insects disturbed by the vast herds. Cowbirds transferred their insect-eating habits to cattle, and the clearing of forests permitted cowbirds to spread to both coasts.

Cowbird eggs are *larger than those of host species. Even though the speckled egg looks different from the other white warbler eggs, the foster parents accept the cowbird egg.*

Molothus ater

Icteridae

Relatively short tail

Short, sparrow-like bill

Black body with dark brown head

Long, pointed wings

Similar to small blackbird

LENGTH 7in (18cm)
WINGSPAN 12in (30cm)
VOICE Song is bubbly and creaky *glug-glug-*

gleeee. Note is *chuck*.
EGGS Lays eggs (sometimes multiple) in nests of other birds. Cowbirds lay 3–4 clutches, totaling 11–20 white eggs, marked with brown speckles.
REARING Host incubates; 10–13 days' incubation; fledging 10–11 days; fed by host.

J F M A M J J A S O N D

Nest parasites

The migratory association with bison may explain why cowbirds developed their habit of laying eggs in the nests of other birds, as they could not stay in one place long enough to incubate and rear young. Although some species can detect cowbird eggs and either remove or bury them, many species, especially those whose range has only recently overlapped with the cowbirds, become hosts.

Female cowbirds are capable of laying 40 eggs or more. They watch for active nests, then slip in to lay an egg quickly, sometimes removing host eggs. Nestling cowbirds grow quickly, fledging when just 10–11 days old. Cowbird young receive most of the food, usually leading to the death of other nestlings. Cowbirds typically parasitize sparrows and warblers, but are known to lay their eggs in the nests of over 220 species of birds; young have been successfully reared by 140 of these. Species that nest near forest edges are especially vulnerable. The Gray Catbird, Eastern Kingbird, and American Robin may throw out cowbird eggs.

Independent life

Soon after leaving the nest, the fledging cowbirds start feeding on insects and weed seeds in lawns. They flock together in the fall, frequently visiting cattle yards, where they feed on flies and grain.

Only male Brown-headed Cowbirds *have the distinctive brown head and glossy black body; females are uniformly ash gray. Cowbirds often feed on the ground under birdfeeders.*

IN THE BACKYARD

■ To discourage cowbirds at garden feeders, offer mixed seed in tube feeders with trays to capture spilled seed. To reduce the impact of cowbirds on forest birds, manage forests in large blocks that provide more forest interior.

Red-winged Blackbird

ONCE RESTRICTED TO MARSHY HABITATS, Red-winged Blackbirds have adapted to wet meadows, brushy fields, upland pastures, and fencerows across most of North America. The conspicuous patch of red is restricted to the shoulder, but it is often hidden except when the male displays to advertise his nesting territory.

Agelaius phoeniceus
Icteridae

The red shoulders are covered with a yellowish margin

Moderately thick bill

Orange-red shoulder coverts are displayed when singing

Dull, black stocky body

Rounded wings

Fairly short tail

LENGTH 7–9in (18–24cm)
WINGSPAN 1in (25cm)
VOICE Notes include a loud check and high slurred *tee-errr*; song is a gurgling *konk-la-ree* or *o-ka-lay*.
EGGS Often 2 clutches of 3–4 (2–6) pale blue-green eggs, marbled with brown, purple, and black.
REARING Female incubates; 10–12 days' incubation; fledging 11–14 days; fed by male and female.

J F M A M J J A S O N D

Enormous roosts
In the fall and winter, Red-winged Blackbirds flock with cowbirds, grackles, and starlings to form enormous roosts. One roost in the Dismal Swamp, Virginia, had about 15 million birds. Red-wing numbers have increased because of their ability to exploit abundant foods from agricultural fields and feedlots. By some estimates, they are the most abundant land birds in North America.

Race for space
Male Red-winged Blackbirds are among the earliest spring migrants to return to nesting grounds in the northeast and Canada. Males winter further north than females,

The brown-streaked *female resembles a large sparrow and builds the nest without help from the male.*

so they can quickly race back to claim prime habitat as soon as snow melts and exposes bare ground. Females usually return about a week later. Red-winged Blackbirds are present for most of the year in most states.

In early spring, the first males to return promptly establish nesting territories. Once the females arrive, they choose a male and build a nest within his territory. Typically, each male mates with two or three females.

In spring, males *defend nesting territories from high perches, singing and displaying their flashy shoulder epaulets.*

IN THE BACKYARD

Red-winged Blackbirds will visit birdfeeders, especially in the spring, when they are migrating. They readily eat cracked corn and millet.

Common Grackle

GRACKLES ARE ASSERTIVE MEMBERS of the blackbird family, with a long tail and a swaggering roll. At a distance, they appear black, but their iridescent metallic plumage, when seen at close range, is sensational. They are distinguished from most other blackbirds by their yellow eye and long, powerful beak.

Male grackles *court females by ruffling their feathers while spreading their wings and tail.*

Nutcrackers

Before agricultural fields and feedlots became their domain, grackles fed mainly on acorns and beechnuts in deciduous forests. To extract the meaty interior, grackles hold the nut in the base of their beak, applying pressure until they crack the nut. Although most of their diet is grain from agricultural fields, they also eat a wide variety of animal life including fish, frogs, mice, and small snakes, as well as the young and eggs of other birds. Grackles are adaptable and quick learners, able to exploit new foods as opportunity permits. For example, in some areas, grackles specialize in following robins, waiting for the robin to extract a worm from the ground and then rushing in to steal it.

Adaptable nesting

Grackles build a bulky nest of twigs and line it with grass, rags, paper, and feathers, locating the nest in tall conifers in backyards and parks. They also nest in elms and maples, shrubs, and even in the base of Osprey nests. Grackles may nest by themselves or in colonies containing dozens of pairs. Great-tailed Grackle (*Quiscalus mexicanus*) and Boat-tailed Grackle (*Quiscalus major*) both resemble the Common Grackle, but they are nearly crow-sized with huge tails. Great-tailed Grackles occur in the southwestern states, while Boat-tailed Grackles are found in the coastal southeastern states.

Grackles eat a *wide variety of foods and readily visit feeding stations.*

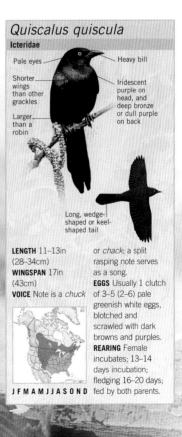

Quiscalus quiscula
Icteridae

Pale eyes

Heavy bill

Shorter wings than other grackles

Iridescent purple on head, and deep bronze or dull purple on back

Larger than a robin

Long, wedge-shaped or keel-shaped tail

LENGTH 11–13in (28–34cm)
WINGSPAN 17in (43cm)
VOICE Note is a *chuck* or *chack*; a split rasping note serves as a song.
EGGS Usually 1 clutch of 3–5 (2–6) pale greenish white eggs, blotched and scrawled with dark browns and purples.
REARING Female incubates; 13–14 days incubation; fledging 16–20 days; fed by both parents.

J F M A M J J A S O N D

Baltimore Oriole

NAMED FOR THE COLORFUL COAT of arms displayed by a 17th-century Lord Baltimore, this flame-colored member of the blackbird family is one of North America's most colorful birds. Baltimore Orioles are widespread throughout eastern and prairie states. Bullock's Oriole (*Icterus bullockii*) is a similar species found in western states.

Icterus galbula

Icteridae

Wings mostly black with orange patch and white wingbar

Orange corners on the tail

Solid black head

Smaller, slimmer body than a robin, larger than a redstart

Flame orange underside

LENGTH 7–8in (18–20cm)

WINGSPAN 11in (29cm)

VOICE Song consists of rich, piping whistled notes. Note is a low, whistled *hew-li*.

EGGS 1 clutch, usually 4–5 (3–6) white, pale blue eggs streaked and blotched brown and black, generally at large end.

REARING Female incubates; 12–14 days' incubation; fledging 12–14 days; fed by male and female.

J F M A M J J A S O N D

Varied diet

Identified by a bold, white wing patch and lack of a completely black head, Bullock's Orioles interbreed with Baltimore Orioles where their ranges overlap. They used to be considered one species—the Northern Oriole.

They eat fruit on shrubs and glean insects from foliage, including ants, aphids, and prickly caterpillars of tussock moths, fall webworms, and brown-tailed moths. They also probe flowers for nectar.

Master builders

Males display in front of females, alternating between stretching to full height and bowing while spreading their tails and opening

Orioles, such as this Baltimore Oriole, *often drink nectar from tree blossoms and will also readily eat juicy fruit, such as sliced orange.*

their wings slightly to display bright colors. Their song is a clear whistle and they give a dry rattle call when alarmed. Females build the hanging, bag-shaped nest, sometimes with help from the male. They use plant fibers, strips of grapevine bark, yarn, and string, and line it with fine grass, plant down, and hair. The nests are typically positioned at the end of a branch, which probably offers them security from climbing predators such as raccoons. The nest may last for years, but it is not reused.

Adult male Baltimore Orioles *have a brilliant orange underpart and a complete black hood. Females are similar, but they lack both the black hood and back of the male.*

IN THE BACKYARD

■ Plant shrubs that bear fruits, such as blackberries, elderberries, blueberries, and serviceberries. Provide 6in (15cm) lengths of string and yarn from a hanging basket in spring.

Orchard Oriole

THE SMALLEST OF NORTH AMERICAN ORIOLES, these trim birds are sometimes mistaken for warblers. Found throughout the eastern and prairie states, Orchard Orioles frequent flowering trees, open woods, scrub, and mesquite. Their varied habitat includes tree-lined streets in prairie cities and live oaks festooned with Spanish moss on southern plantations.

Insect eaters

Orchard Orioles have a greater appetite for insects than Baltimore and Bullock's orioles, consuming aphids, mayflies, beetles, grasshoppers, crickets, and cabbage butterfly caterpillars. Such insects comprise about 90 percent of their diet. Fruits such as raspberries, strawberries, grapes, and mulberries comprise the remainder of the diet.

Males sing from treetops, but also from the air high above nesting trees. The song is a lively warble, with a wide range in pitch. It is reminiscent of the clear whistle of the Baltimore Oriole, but higher than other orioles, with a distinctive down-slurring ending. Females construct the nest, sometimes choosing to nest in close proximity to other Orchard Orioles. They often nest near Eastern Kingbirds, which offer protection from predators.

Females choose a nest site that is usually 10–20ft (3–6m) above the ground in a forked branch. The nest is a beautiful, thin-walled, woven structure made of plant fibers and lined with thick pads of plant down. After the young leave the nest, the parents may divide the brood, each taking responsibility for two or three chicks

Orchard Orioles have *narrow beaks that permit them to probe deep into flowers for nectar.*

This one-year-old male *Orchard Oriole has a distinctive black throat patch. A year later he will have the distinctive chestnut-colored body and black hood of the breeding adult male.*

for the next several weeks. Most Orchard Orioles winter from Mexico to northern South America. In recent decades, they have declined throughout most of their range, except the northern prairie provinces.

Icterus spurious
Icteridae

Wings more pointed than those of Baltimore Oriole

Short bill

Short, square tail

Chestnut body, rump, and underparts

Small and compact

LENGTH 6–7in (15–18cm)
WINGSPAN 9in (24cm)
VOICE A fast-moving outburst with piping whistles and guttural notes; strident slurred *wheeet* occurs at or close to the end.
EGGS 1 clutch of 4–5 (3–7) pale blue-white eggs, blotched brown, purple, and gray at large end.
REARING Female incubates; 12 days' incubation; fledging 11–14 days; fed by male and female.

JFMAMJJASOND

IN THE BACKYARD
■ Plant fruiting shrubs and trees, especially mulberry, blueberries, and brambles.

203

Evening Grosbeak

EVENING GROSBEAKS WINTER IN ROVING FLOCKS throughout much of North America. In some winters, they may show up at birdfeeders in flocks of several dozen, gobble pounds of seed, then fly off in a noisy flurry. Yet these birds have such a roaming behavior that they may be completely absent in subsequent winters.

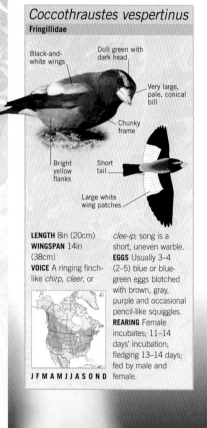

Coccothraustes vespertinus
Fringillidae

Black-and-white wings

Dull green with dark head

Very large, pale, conical bill

Chunky frame

Bright yellow flanks

Short tail

Large white wing patches

LENGTH 8in (20cm)
WINGSPAN 14in (38cm)
VOICE A ringing finch-like *chirp, cleer,* or *clee-ip*; song is a short, uneven warble.
EGGS Usually 3–4 (2–5) blue or blue-green eggs blotched with brown, gray, purple and occasional pencil-like squiggles.
REARING Female incubates; 11–14 days' incubation; fledging 13–14 days; fed by male and female.

J F M A M J J A S O N D

Eastward expansion

Like many northern members of the finch family, Evening Grosbeaks have an irruptive winter distribution linked to the availability of food, such as conifer and maple seeds. Prior to 1900, they were found only in the western US and Canada, but they have since moved eastward, likely due to the combined effects of planting Box Elder (a favorite food) in prairie state windbreaks, and outbreaks of spruce budworm in the Northeast.

Seed and salt appetite

A single grosbeak can consume about 100 seeds in five minutes and a flock might consume a 50lb (23kg) bag

Evening Grosbeaks usually visit feeders in flocks to eat their favorite feeder food—sunflower seeds.

within three weeks. During the breeding season, however, Evening Grosbeaks' diet includes about 20 percent insects, mostly beetles and forest caterpillars, such as spruce budworms. Capable of eating 1,000 budworm larvae each day, Grosbeaks are one of the principal natural controls for this devastating pest of northern coniferous forests. They also favor buds and seeds of maples, and maple sap. Grosbeaks are unusual in their preference for wild cherry pits, which they crush in their powerful bill. In winter, they often feed on road salt, making themselves vulnerable to traffic collisions.

Male Evening Grosbeaks *resemble oversized goldfinches, but they are easily distinguished by their huge bill and near robin size.*

IN THE BACKYARD

■ Plant Box Elder *(Acer negundo)* and put out sunflower seeds on table feeders. Provide salt by mixing table salt with fireplace ash and water, then pour the solution over a log, where it will crystallize.

Pine Grosbeak

LARGE AND FLUFFY, these gentle finches of the far north live in Canada most of the year, venturing south of the border during years when conifer and fruit crops fail. Pine Grosbeaks resemble oversized Purple Finches, but their large bill and tame behavior quickly distinguish them from small finches.

Summer foods
During the nesting season, Pine Grosbeaks frequent open spruce forests of Canada and the Rocky Mountains, where they extract seeds from cones and eat the buds and fruit of maple, birch, poplar, and willow. They also feed on the spore cases of mosses and weed seeds, supplementing their largely vegetarian diet with grasshoppers, flies, and beetles.

Winter survival
In winter, Pine Grosbeaks often eat the dried fruit of Red Cedar, Mountain Ash, and Ornamental Crabapples. At this season, flocks of 5–30 may visit feeders to take sunflower seeds; such flocks likely consist of several family groups. Perhaps because of their infrequent association with humans, they are remarkably tame. It is not unusual for Pine Grosbeaks to continue munching on dried crabapples within a few feet of admiring birders. They are extremely hardy and are often seen feeding in frigid

Female Pine Grosbeaks lack the male's (shown here) rosy color of breast and head. Both sexes frequent Ornamental Crabapples when they venture south during winter.

temperatures as low as −31°F (−35°C). Sometimes they bathe in soft snow. Before retiring for the long and frigid winter night, they usually stuff their crop with a supply of seed.

Nesting
Pine Grosbeaks build a bulky nest of twigs and roots, and line it with rabbit fur, grass, and lichens, usually locating the nest 15–25ft (4.5–7.5m) above ground in a shrub or tree. During the nesting season, the parents develop a special pair of pouches in the floor of the mouth in which to transport food to their young.

Pine Grosbeaks breed in Canadian coniferous forests and sometimes visit northern states in winter. These naïve northern visitors show little fear of humans.

Pinocola enucleator
Fringillidae

Wing size and shape similar to robin

Dull rose-red rump

Long tail

Large and fluffy body

Dark wings with two white bars

LENGTH 8–10in (20–25cm)
WINGSPAN 14in (36cm)
VOICE Call is a whistled *tee-tew-tew*

EGGS 1 clutch of 4 (2–5) pale, gray-green eggs, spotted and blotched with purple and brown.
REARING Female incubates; 13–15 days' incubation; fledging 13–20 days; fed by male and female.

similar to that of the Greater Yellowlegs; also a musical *chee-vli.*

J F M A M J J A S O N D

IN THE BACKYARD

■ Plant Ornamental Crabapples with winter-persistent fruit; at feeders provide black-oil or striped sunflower seeds.

Purple Finch

MORE RASPBERRY-COLORED THAN PURPLE, these colorful finches breed throughout the coniferous forests of Canada and New England and range down the Pacific Coast. They have declined throughout much of their eastern range, possibly due to habitat loss and competition with introduced House Sparrows and House Finches.

Carpodacus purpureus
Fringillidae

Short, notched tail

Head has more of a peak than House Finch

Medium-length wings

Stout bill

Stockier body than related finches

Raspberry color on head, body and tail

LENGTH 5–6in (13–15cm)
WINGSPAN 10in (25cm)
VOICE The song is a fast, lively warble; the note is a dull metallic *tick*.
EGGS Usually 4–5 (3–6) pale greenish blue eggs, scrawled in lines with brown and black, heaviest at large end.
REARING Female incubates; 13 days' incubation; fledging 14 days; fed by male and female.

J F M A M J J A S O N D

Favorite wild foods
Purple Finches feed on the seeds of weeds, elm, White Ash, Red Maple, and sycamore, as well as fruit of junipers and Winterberry Holly. They also eat the buds of maple, birch, and apple. Their summer diet includes insects such as beetles and green caterpillars.

Dazzling performer
When the male courts the female, he hops near his prospective mate, dangling his wings and puffing his breast. Hovering 6–12in (15–30cm) above his prospective mate, he sings softly, vibrating his wings into a blur and cocking his tail. Sometimes he holds nesting material in his beak while singing. The brown-striped female lacks all hints of the male's colorful tones and could be confused with a sparrow, except for her heavy bill.

The female Purple Finch *differs from the House Finch by the bold white stripe over the eye and by dark brown breast streaks.*

Nesting
Both members of the pair build the nest. In the eastern portion of their range, they usually build in a conifer, but western Purple Finches will locate the nest in conifers, deciduous trees, or shrubs, usually positioning the nest 6–40ft (2–12m) above the ground. The cozy nest is built of fine twigs, moss, and dried snakeskin, often with a lining of horsehair and wool.

Male Purple Finches *are usually raspberry-colored on front and back, and lack streaks on the belly. These distinctions help to separate him from the House Finch.*

IN THE BACKYARD
■ Plant dogwoods, junipers, spruce, maples, sumacs, Blackgum, Tuliptrees, birch, and sweetgum. Provide black-oil sunflower seed in tube feeders and table feeders.

House Finch

ORIGINALLY RESTRICTED to western cities, ranches, scrublands, and canyons, an eastern House Finch population began in 1940, when Long Island pet-store owners released illegal stocks to avoid prosecution. This population increased rapidly and spread westward, meeting the western population 50 years later.

Eastern adaptations

Eastern House Finches have adapted to their new range by evolving larger bills (this may be an adaptation for cracking sunflower seeds) and becoming short-distance migrants. Like many other northern birds, males stay closer to the nesting range than females, a fact that accounts for a large proportion of colorful males in winter flocks in northern states. Females are identified by their dull brown color and lack of head stripes.

Favorite foods

Although House Finches have a great appetite for sunflower seeds, their principal food is weed seeds, which may comprise more than 80 percent of their diet. They are especially fond of seed from

The male House Finch has streaked underparts and a brown back. He also has a rounded head, which helps to separate him from the Purple Finch, which has a slight peak to the head shape.

thistle, dandelion, and other weeds, which they obtain from old fields and vacant lots. In the late summer, cherries and mulberries are favorites. The color of individual males results from feeding on a diverse diet (not just sunflower seeds). When given choice, females usually select colorful males over duller rivals, as colorful birds are usually older and make better mates than young, inexperienced males.

Female House Finches *lack the white stripe over the eye, which is diagnostic for the male Purple Finch. Males have a streaked underside, which distinguishes them from Purple Finches.*

House Finches often nest in ivy growing on buildings or behind gutters and porch lights. Females build the nest from grass and plant stems, often incorporating hair, string, cotton, and wool.

Carpodacus mexicanus
Fringillidae

Longer tail than related finches

Bright red face and breast

Shorter and more rounded wings

Brownish back with streaked flanks

LENGTH 5–5½in (13–14cm)
WINGSPAN 9in (23cm)
VOICE Bright song is loose and disjointed, frequently ending in harsh nasal *where* or *che-urrr*. Notes finch-like, but more musical.
EGGS One clutch of 4–5 (2–6) pale gray-green eggs, blotched with browns, purples, and black.
REARING Female incubates; 12–14 days' incubation; fledging 11–19 days; fed by both parents.

J F M A M J J A S O N D

IN THE BACKYARD

Provide fresh water in birdbaths, and sunflower seeds. Watch for swollen eyes, a symptom of avian conjunctivitis. Water is important as House Finches can consume 40 percent of their body weight in water on a hot day. Provide food in open, well-drained table feeders to reduce competition with other species at tube feeders.

Common Redpoll

TINY WANDERERS FROM THE FAR NORTH, Common Redpolls appear at backyard birdfeeders in southern Canada and northern states every two or three years when food supplies become scarce in the far north. In such years, it is not unusual to see flocks of 100 or more individuals.

Winter-hardy

Redpolls probably hold the record for "most winter-hardy bird" as they can actively feed in extreme, subfreezing temperatures.

Many northern birds lay down a fat supply to help them through tough weather, but redpolls have other survival methods. For example, they often keep themselves warm at night by roosting together in dense conifer patches.

They also have a special pouch in their throat in which they store seeds at night. Redpolls typically

Redpoll populations "erupt" every few years, sending these northern finches southward where they delight backyard birders. Nyger and black-oil sunflower seeds are their favorite feeder foods.

fill their pouches in late afternoon and save the meal until darkness falls. Confident that they have a well-deserved seed stash, they can continue their meal as the temperature plummets to as low as $-81°F$ ($-63°C$).

Favorite foods

Redpolls are acrobatic, active birds that often hang upside down as they extract their favorite food—the tiny seeds of birch and alder. They also eat willow buds, and seeds of weeds and grasses. In winter, they frequent semi-open habitats such as forest edges and brushy fields, sometimes mingling with flocks of siskins and goldfinches.

Like many birds of the far north, redpolls are usually very tame when visiting backyard birdfeeders.

Common Redpolls nest in the northern fir forests of Canada. The nest, made of fine twigs, is lined with grass, moss, and feathers.

Carduelis flammea
Fringillidae

Wing bars
Streaked flanks
Bright red cap
Tiny yellow bill
Longer tailed than goldfinches and Pine Siskins
Dark lore and throat
Pinkish breast
Gray with brown streaks on flanks

LENGTH 5in (13cm)
WINGSPAN 9in (23cm)
VOICE Song is a trill

J F M A M J J A S O N D

followed by the rattling *chet-chet-chet-chet*.
EGGS Usually 4–5 (4–7) green or blue eggs, spotted with blue and dark violet.
REARING Female incubates; 10–11 days' incubation; fledging 12 days; fed by female with help from male.

IN THE BACKYARD

■ Plant birch and alder trees; provide nyger seed at feeders. Redpolls also eat willow buds.

Red Crossbill

NAMED FOR THE CROSSED TIPS OF THEIR BEAK, Red Crossbills are conifer specialists found throughout the Canadian boreal forest, with ranges extending into the Appalachian and western mountain ranges. When conifer seed crops fail, winter irruptions occur, bringing these northern residents southward.

Female Red Crossbills *have an olive plumage and dark wings. They use their crossed bills to maneuver through tree branches.*

Loxia curvirostra
Fringillidae

Long, blackish, pointed wings

Short, blackish, notched tail

Crossed mandibles

Dull red, brighter on the rump

LENGTH 5–6in (13–16cm)
WINGSPAN 11in (28cm)
VOICE Song has warbled passages, chips, and trills, *jip-jip-jip-jeeaa-jeeaa*; note is a hard *jip-jip* or *jip-jip-jip*.
EGGS 1 clutch of 3–4 (2–5) pale blue-white eggs dotted with brown and purple.
REARING Female incubates; 12–18 days' incubation; fledging 15–20 days; fed by both male and female.

J F M A M J J A S O N D

Specialized diet

At least nine races of Red Crossbill are known to exist, each with its own calls and range. These various Red Crossbill types favor specific species of conifer and may eventually become separated into distinct species.

The irruptions that characterize crossbill movements often result in each race moving from one forest to the next, tracking good cone crops of its preferred species. Large-billed birds usually prefer conifers with larger cones. They also eat seeds of birches, willows, poplar, and maple, as well as weed seeds and spruce buds, and supplement their diet with insects. Red Crossbills also consume salt and pick mortar from bricks as a source of calcium.

Crossbills are relatively tame birds that permit a close approach. Watch their feeding behavior as they crawl through tree branches, using their bill and feet, reminiscent of small parrots. When extracting seeds, crossbills insert their mandibles (the two halves of their bill) into a cone and force the scales open while they extract the seed with their tongue.

When the male courts the female, he circles overhead, singing and vibrating his wings. Females select the nest site and build the nest, usually locating it well out on a conifer branch 5–80ft (1.5–24m) above the ground.

At least nine discrete populations *or types of Red Crossbill exist in North America, occupying different regions and habitats. Further research may determine that these are distinct species.*

IN THE BACKYARD

To provide calcium, obtain finely crushed oyster or clam shells (available from poultry food suppliers) and mix 5–10lb (2–4.5kg) with each 100lb (45kg) of mixed birdseed. Alternatively, provide the crushed shell in separate trays.

White-winged Crossbill

WHITE-WINGED CROSSBILLS have longer tails and smaller heads than Red Crossbills. Males are pinker than Red Crossbills, and both sexes display bold white wing bars. White-winged Crossbills have bills that are smaller than nearly all races of Red Crossbill. They are generally uncommon, and always fly in flocks.

Small cone specialists

White-winged Crossbills feed mainly on spruce seeds, which they extract by forcing open the scales of the cones and extracting seeds with their tongue. They also eat seeds from hemlock and larch in the same way, as well as weed seeds, berries, and insects, and have cravings for salt. This habit leads to the destruction of many of the birds that gather for road salt along highways in the winter and then fly into traffic.

As an adaptation to surviving long, frigid winter nights, crossbills store seed in a special double-lobed pocket located about midway down the neck. Crossbills begin storing

food in the pouch as darkness falls and during approaching severe weather. The reserves help crossbills survive long nights and extreme weather.

Nesting

The nesting territories of White-winged Crossbills change from one year to the next as they are dependent

A female White-winged Crossbill uses her bill to spread scales, and her tongue to extract seeds from conifer cones.

on crops of conifer seeds for ample food, and they nest in colonies. When males court females, they slowly beat their wings while circling above the female. The pair may sit close to each other and the male often feeds his prospective mate.

Identify adult male *White-winged Crossbills by their rosy red body and bold white wing bars. The male also has a beautiful, canary-like song that fills the spruce forest during nesting.*

Loxia leucoptera
Fringillidae

Black wings crossed with two broad, white wingbars

Long, pointed wings

Crossed mandibles

Black tail, longer than that of the Red Crossbill

Dull rose-pink neck

LENGTH 6–6in (15–17cm)
WINGSPAN 10in (26cm)
VOICE Note is a liquid *peet* and a dry *chif-chif*, song is a succession of trills on different pitches.
EGGS 1 clutch of 4 (2–5) pale blue or light green eggs, scrawled with black and browns.
REARING Female incubates; 12–14 days' incubation; days to fledging unknown; both parents feed.

J F M A M J J A S O N D

IN THE BACKYARD

■ Plant clumps of pines, cedars, junipers, spruce, and larch to provide cones for winter food.

Pine Siskin

NOVICE BIRDERS sometimes confuse Pine Siskins with striped sparrows, but in fact siskins behave more like goldfinches than sparrows. Watch for their extremely pointed beaks and bold wingbars. Their undulating flight is typical of finches, and their rising, buzzy call is distinctive.

Male and female Pine Siskins are similar in appearance, except the male has strong yellow bars on his wings.

Favorite foods

Siskins often feed upside down, extracting seeds from the cones of alder, birch, spruce, Sweetgum, and other trees. Siskins also eat buds of elm, seeds of thistle and other weeds, nectar from Eucalyptus, caterpillars, aphids, and other insects. In winter, they are attracted to the calcium chloride spread on highways to melt ice and snow, and they sometimes peck at salt blocks. Like many northern finches, they find little calcium in their northern foods.

Winter wanderers

Pine Siskins are "winter finches" for feeder watchers in most of the United States, but they are regulars throughout the year wherever spruce-fir forests occur in New England, Canada, Alaska, and western mountains. When food supplies are abundant, siskins stay in their coniferous habitat throughout the year. When seed crops fail, they abandon their usual range and move southward to find more abundant food. In winter they are usually very tame. They readily come to birdfeeders in flocks numbering anything from a few birds to 30 or more.

Courtship and nesting

Males feed their mate during courtship and incubation. The nest is bulky, built of moss, twigs, grass, and lichens, lined with fine grass, moss, and occasionally fur. During the nesting season, both parents develop a pair of throat pouches that serve to store food for delivering to their young.

Pine Siskins use their sharp bills to extract seeds from the small cones of conifers such as spruce, hemlock, and larch.

Carduelis pinus
Fringillidae

Yellow wing stripe in male

Short, notched tail

Yellow at the base of the tail is not always visible

Pointed wings

Thin, sharply pointed bill

Heavily streaked underside

Small, dark rump

LENGTH 4–5in (11–13cm)
WINGSPAN 9in (23cm)

J F M A M J J A S O N D

VOICE Call is a loud *clee-ip* or *chlee-ip*, also a light *tit-i-tit*.
EGGS Usually 3–4 (2–6) pale greenish-blue eggs with brown or black flecks around large end.
REARING Female incubates; 13 days' incubation; fledging 14–15 days; fed by male and female.

IN THE BACKYARD

■ Plant birch, spruce, and sweetgum; at feeders provide nyger seed, hulled sunflower seeds, and ground oyster shell.

American Goldfinch

IT IS HARD TO IGNORE the perky lemon-yellow American Goldfinch during spring and summer, but it can easily be overlooked or misidentified in winter when it molts into its olive colors. Goldfinches are often resident throughout the year, but they vacate extreme northern latitudes to avoid the most severe weather.

The male American Goldfinch has a yellow plumage with black wings and cap during the nesting season. In winter, he molts into an olive plumage and loses his black cap.

Seed specialists

Seeds from birch, alders, and conifers make up the bulk of the goldfinches' diet, but they also eat wildflower seeds, especially members of the sunflower family such as thistle, asters, goldenrod, and burdock. Gardeners who resist dead-heading their flowers will find that goldfinches readily consume the seeds of coneflowers, coreopsis, cosmos, and lettuce. Their reliance on composite seeds helps to explain why goldfinches defer nesting until late summer, when their favorite foods are most abundant.

Winter adaptations

American Goldfinches that remain in northern climates have a variety of adaptations to help them survive.

For example, they fill their crops late in the day for a supply of seed to digest at night, and they choose the most protected shelters for roosting, often deep in a patch of conifers or in tunnels under snow. Their greenish winter plumage has better insulating qualities than their summer plumage.

Nesting

Females select a nest site in dense shrubs in late summer and build a nest of woven plant fibers with a lining of thistle down. Females incubate the eggs, sitting on them for 95 percent of the time. During courtship and incubation, the female relies on the male to feed her, sometimes begging like a nestling when he arrives with food.

Thistle seeds are a favorite food of American Goldfinches, so much so that they may defer nesting until thistle seeds are ripe. They also use thistle seed as a nest lining.

Carduelis tristis
Fringillidae

Deeply undulating flight

Black forehead

Pinkish bill

Black tail

Black wings and tail

Bright yellow body

LENGTH 5in (13cm)
WINGSPAN 9in (23cm)
VOICE Song is clear and sustained and canary-like; during flight, it often repeats *ti-dee-di-di* or *potato-chip*.
EGGS Usually 5 (4–6) pale bluish white eggs without markings.
REARING Female incubates; 10–12 days' incubation; fledging 11–17 days; fed by male and female.

J F M A M J J A S O N D

IN THE BACKYARD

■ Plant birch, elm, maple, and alder; in the garden, plant sunflower, cosmos, and coneflowers. Provide nyger and black-oil sunflower seeds in hanging feeders.

Lesser Goldfinch

SMALL FLOCKS OF LESSER GOLDFINCHES are common in brushy areas, open woods, wooded streams, and backyard gardens of southwestern states. In dry regions, they are usually found near streams and other water sources. Adult males found in southern Texas have black backs, while adult males elsewhere have green backs.

Thistle specialists

The smallest of the finch family, the active and acrobatic Lesser Goldfinch feeds largely on the seeds of thistle, pigweed, wild sunflowers, and weeds. They may also eat the buds of trees such as cottonwoods, and some berries. In California, one study found that thistle seed made up 54 percent of their diet. Occasionally they also eat aphids and caterpillars or feed them to their young. Lesser Goldfinches are especially attracted to salt deposits and water sources such as birdbaths, dripping faucets, and water seeps.

Males court the females with courtship flights and canary-like songs. Females build a tidy nest of woven plant fibers and grass, lined with plant down and cotton. The nest is perched on a horizontal branch of a streamside cottonwood, willow, or sycamore between 5ft (1.5m) and 30ft (9m) above the ground. Females do all the incubation and males often feed the female at the nest. The pair may stay together throughout the winter, but soon after the young leave the nest, they flock with others and remain in flocks throughout the remainder of the year.

Lesser Goldfinches usually *live in small flocks and are readily attracted to feeders that offer nyger seed.*

Carduelis psaltria
Fringillidae

Short, rounded wings

White patch on the wings

Black cap

Dark underwing

Short tail with large, white patches

Bright yellow underside

Black or greenish back

Tiny and stocky body

LENGTH 3–4 in (9–11 cm)
WINGSPAN 8in (20cm)
VOICE Song is more phrased than that of the American Goldfinch; sweet, plaintive note *tee-yee tee-yee* rise and fall.
EGGS Usually 2 or 3 clutches of 4–5 pale blue unmarked eggs.
REARING Apparently female incubates; 12 days' incubation; fledging information unknown; fed by male and female.

J F M A M J J A S O N D

Flower buds and seeds of deciduous trees, berries, and grasses are also popular foods for Lesser Goldfinches.

IN THE BACKYARD

■ Mix equal parts of salt and wood ash and pour the slurry over a log to provide a salt source; provide clean water in birdbaths, as well as nyger, black-oil sunflower, and hulled sunflower seeds.

House Sparrow

A NATIVE OF EUROPE AND NORTHERN AFRICA, House Sparrows were first introduced into Brooklyn, New York, in about 1851. Within 60 years, they had spread to the West Coast and rapidly became one of the most abundant birds in North America. The secret of their success is close association with humans, who inadvertently provide housing and food; they seldom occur in habitats remote from humans.

Passer domesticus
Passeridae

Short tail

Stout black beak

Chestnut nape

Black throat and bib

Short wings

LENGTH 6in (15cm)
WINGSPAN 9in (23in)
VOICE Song is a monotonous series of nearly identical chirps; call is a husky *fillip*.
EGGS Usually 2 or 3 clutches of 5 (4–6) white or greenish white eggs with brown and gray dots and spots.
REARING Female

incubates; 10–13 days' incubation; fledging 14–17 days; fed by male and female.

J F M A M J J A S O N D

Dust-bathing helps the House Sparrow maintain the condition of its plumage and remove parasites such as feather lice. This usually follows water-bathing and involves the same motions. House Sparrows typically dust-bathe in loose soil, or dust on a garden path, or in a flowerbed.

Once pairs form, they may remain together for life. Males have a black bib that becomes more conspicuous as abrasion wears away the surface of the feathers.

Conflicts with native birds

House Sparrows thrive in cities, suburbs, and agricultural areas, where they glean sidewalk crumbs and spilled grain. As their name suggests, they typically nest in human housing, squeezing into air vents and other cracks and crevices in houses and barns, where they build a bulky nest of grass, paper, feathers, plastic, and other debris. Sometimes several pairs will nest near each other, forming small colonies. In rural

Females are generally tan *in color with a light stripe through the eye. They might be confused with other sparrows, but native sparrows have much smaller beaks and usually other conspicuous markings such as stripes on the head or breast.*

areas they compete aggressively with native cavity-nesting species, especially Bluebirds, Tree Swallows, and Purple Martins, often claiming natural cavities and nest boxes before migrants return from wintering areas. Sometimes they usurp nest boxes from established native species, destroying eggs and nestlings. In addition to pirating nest boxes, these adaptable birds occupy artificial cavities, especially cracks and crevices in buildings.

Variation

Since their dispersal across North America, House Sparrows have adapted to local conditions. For example, House Sparrows nesting in the desert regions of the Southwest are smaller and lighter in color than those nesting further north. Males are typically larger than females and dominant. For this reason, females often feed separately from males.

Adaptable diet

Like most highly successful species, House Sparrows are quick to adapt to local foods. They take dead insects from the grilles of parked cars and search bark for insects. They forage mostly on the ground and are attracted to grain spilled from birdfeeders. Although still abundant, the Eastern population has declined since 1900 as cars replaced horses on city streets and spilled grain became less available. More efficient farming practices and competition with House Finches may also have contributed to their decline.

A bulky nest of grass and feathers *is usually crammed into a building crevice. Both adults feed a largely insect-based diet to the young.*

Houses Sparrows gather *in large flocks for feeding and roosting. The flocks often contain birds from several neighboring colonies.*

Bird classification

THE SCIENTIFIC SYSTEM FOR NAMING PLANTS and animals was devised in the 18th century by the Swedish naturalist Carolus Linnaeus. The names given to birds reflect their evolutionary relationships. For this reason, bird names are more than a convenient way to lead one to a correct identification. They allow us all to understand and predict similarities and differences between species.

Birds, and all other living things, have a two-word Latin name—always printed in italics. The first word gives the genus (a grouping of species); the second word identifies a particular species. For example, *Melospiza* is the genus for a large group of sparrows. The Song Sparrow is *Melospiza melodia,* and the very similar Lincoln's Sparrow is *Melospiza lincolnii.* Sharing the same genus name indicates that the two species are closely related. The scientific name of the similar-looking Fox Sparrow is *Passerella iliaca.* The genus name reveals that although Fox Sparrows resemble Song Sparrows, they are actually more distantly related than are Lincoln's Sparrows. Based on similarity, genera (the plural of genus) are grouped into families, and the families into orders. For example, Song, Lincoln's, and Fox

Sparrows all belong to the family *Emberizidae* along with towhees and juncos. However, the superficially similar House Sparrow (an introduced species from Europe) belongs to the family *Passeridae,* the true sparrows of the Old World. Families are grouped together into orders, the largest of which is the Passeriformes or perching birds. About half of all North American birds belong to this single order.

The common and scientific names of American birds are decided by the American Ornithologists' Union, which provides standardized names based on the latest knowledge of bird behavior and relationships. Increasingly, genetic are used to make determinations based on analysis of DNA.

The Purple Finch is *related to other finches, but it is a distinct species and does not hybridize.*

ORDERS AND FAMILIES

This table sets out the relationships between the species described in this book. The information reveals some unexpected facts. For example, despite their common names, the Rose-breasted Grosbeak and Evening Grosbeak are not closely related, as evidenced by their separate families. Likewise, although they look identical, Western and Eastern Screech-owls are now considered distinct species.

ORDER	FAMILY	COMMON AND SCIENTIFIC NAMES
Galliformes	Odontophoride	Northern Bobwhite (*Colinus virginianus*)
		California Quail (*Callipepla californica*)
		Gambel's Quail (*Callipepla gambelii*)
	Phasianidae	Ring-necked Pheasant (*Phasianus colchicus*)
Accipitriformes	Accipitridae	Sharp-shinned Hawk (*Accipiter striatus*)
		Cooper's Hawk (*Accipiter cooperii*)
Columbiformes	Columbidae	Mourning Dove (*Zenaida macroura*)
		Rock Pigeon (*Columba livia*)
Strigiformes	Strigidae	Eastern Screech-owl (*Megascops asio*)
		Western Screech-owl (*Megascops kennicottii*)
Apodiformes	Apodidae	Chimney Swift (*Chaetura pelagica*)
	Trochilidae	Anna's Hummingbird (*Calypte anna*)
		Ruby-throated Hummingbird (*Archilochus colubris*)
		Rufous Hummingbird (*Selasphorus rufus*)

Cooper's Hawk

Rufous Hummingbird

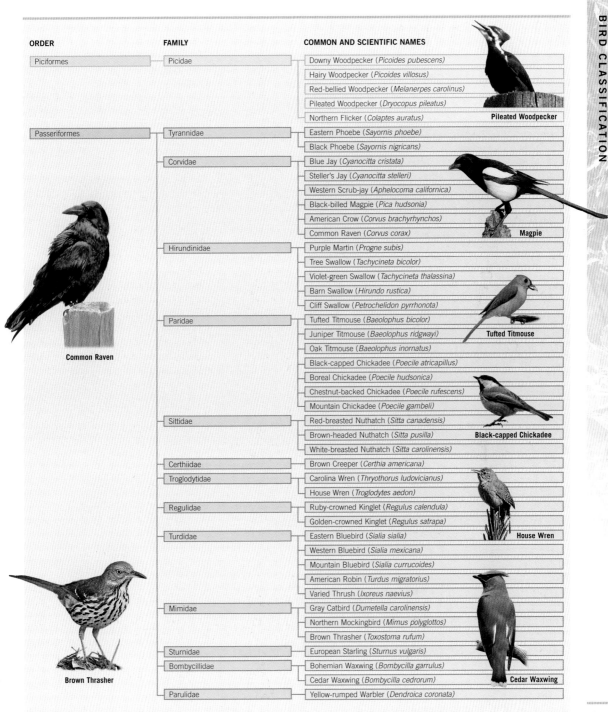

ORDER	FAMILY	COMMON AND SCIENTIFIC NAMES
Piciformes	Picidae	Downy Woodpecker (*Picoides pubescens*)
		Hairy Woodpecker (*Picoides villosus*)
		Red-bellied Woodpecker (*Melanerpes carolinus*)
		Pileated Woodpecker (*Dryocopus pileatus*)
		Northern Flicker (*Colaptes auratus*)
Passeriformes	Tyrannidae	Eastern Phoebe (*Sayornis phoebe*)
		Black Phoebe (*Sayornis nigricans*)
	Corvidae	Blue Jay (*Cyanocitta cristata*)
		Steller's Jay (*Cyanocitta stelleri*)
		Western Scrub-jay (*Aphelocoma californica*)
		Black-billed Magpie (*Pica hudsonia*)
		American Crow (*Corvus brachyrhynchos*)
		Common Raven (*Corvus corax*)
	Hirundinidae	Purple Martin (*Progne subis*)
		Tree Swallow (*Tachycineta bicolor*)
		Violet-green Swallow (*Tachycineta thalassina*)
		Barn Swallow (*Hirundo rustica*)
		Cliff Swallow (*Petrochelidon pyrrhonota*)
	Paridae	Tufted Titmouse (*Baeolophus bicolor*)
		Juniper Titmouse (*Baeolophus ridgwayi*)
		Oak Titmouse (*Baeolophus inornatus*)
		Black-capped Chickadee (*Poecile atricapillus*)
		Boreal Chickadee (*Poecile hudsonica*)
		Chestnut-backed Chickadee (*Poecile rufescens*)
		Mountain Chickadee (*Poecile gambeli*)
	Sittidae	Red-breasted Nuthatch (*Sitta canadensis*)
		Brown-headed Nuthatch (*Sitta pusilla*)
		White-breasted Nuthatch (*Sitta carolinensis*)
	Certhiidae	Brown Creeper (*Certhia americana*)
	Troglodytidae	Carolina Wren (*Thryothorus ludovicianus*)
		House Wren (*Troglodytes aedon*)
	Regulidae	Ruby-crowned Kinglet (*Regulus calendula*)
		Golden-crowned Kinglet (*Regulus satrapa*)
	Turdidae	Eastern Bluebird (*Sialia sialia*)
		Western Bluebird (*Sialia mexicana*)
		Mountain Bluebird (*Sialia currucoides*)
		American Robin (*Turdus migratorius*)
		Varied Thrush (*Ixoreus naevius*)
	Mimidae	Gray Catbird (*Dumetella carolinensis*)
		Northern Mockingbird (*Mimus polyglottos*)
		Brown Thrasher (*Toxostoma rufum*)
	Sturnidae	European Starling (*Sturnus vulgaris*)
	Bombycillidae	Bohemian Waxwing (*Bombycilla garrulus*)
		Cedar Waxwing (*Bombycilla cedrorum*)
	Parulidae	Yellow-rumped Warbler (*Dendroica coronata*)

Pileated Woodpecker

Magpie

Tufted Titmouse

Black-capped Chickadee

House Wren

Cedar Waxwing

Common Raven

Brown Thrasher

ORDER	FAMILY	COMMON AND SCIENTIFIC NAMES
Passeriformes (*continued*)	Thraupidae	Scarlet Tanager (*Piranga olivacea*)
		Western Tanager (*Piranga ludoviciana*)
	Cardinalidae	Northern Cardinal (*Cardinalis cardinalis*)
		Black-headed Grosbeak (*Pheucticus melanocephalus*)
		Rose-breasted Grosbeak (*Pheucticus ludovicianus*)
		Indigo Bunting (*Passerina cyanea*)
		Blue Grosbeak (*Guiraca caerula*)
		Painted Bunting (*Passerina ciris*)
	Emberizidae	Spotted Towhee (*Pipilo maculatus*)
		Eastern Towhee (*Pipilo erythrophthalmus*)
		California Towhee (*Pipilo crissalis*)
		Canyon Towhee (*Pipilo fuscus*)
		American Tree Sparrow (*Spizella arborea*)
		Field Sparrow (*Spizella pusilla*)
		Chipping Sparrow (*Spizella passerina*)
		White-throated Sparrow (*Zonotrichia albicollis*)
		White-crowned Sparrow (*Zonotrichia leucophrys*)
		Golden-crowned Sparrow (*Zonotrichia atricapilla*)
		Song Sparrow (*Melospiza melodia*)
		Fox Sparrow (*Passerella iliaca*)
		Dark-eyed Junco (*Junco hyemalis*)
	Icteridae	Bobolink (*Dolichonyx oryzivorus*)
		Brown-headed Cowbird (*Molothus ater*)
		Red-winged Blackbird (*Agelaius phoeniceus*)
		Common Grackle (*Quiscalus quiscula*)
		Great-tailed Grackle (*Quiscalus mexicanus*)
		Baltimore Oriole (*Icterus galbula*)
		Bullock's Oriole (*Icterus bullockii*)
		Orchard Oriole (*Icterus spurious*)
	Fringillidae	Evening Grosbeak (*Coccothraustes vespertinus*)
		Pine Grosbeak (*Pinicola enucleator*)
		Purple Finch (*Carpodacus purpureus*)
		House Finch (*Carpodacus mexicanus*)
		Common Redpoll (*Carduelis flammea*)
		Red Crossbill (*Loxia curvirostra*)
		White-winged Crossbill (*Loxia leucoptera*)
		Pine Siskin (*Carduelis pinus*)
		American Goldfinch (*Carduelis tristis*)
		Lesser Goldfinch (*Carduelis psaltria*)
	Passeridae	House Sparrow (*Passer domesticus*)

California Towhee

Bobolink

Black-headed Grosbeak

Field Sparrow

Evening Grosbeak

White-winged Crossbill

About Audubon

The National Audubon Society (NAS), founded in 1905, is a not-for-profit organization that has state offices, nearly 500 chapters, and close to 500,000 members. Audubon's mission is to conserve and restore natural ecosystems, focusing on birds, other wildlife, and their habitats for the benefit of humanity and the earth's biological diversity.

Our national network of community-based nature centers and chapters, scientific and educational programs, and advocacy on behalf of areas sustaining important bird populations engage millions of people of all ages and backgrounds in positive conservation experiences. Outside of its network of chapters, Audubon works on areas of national and international conservation policy, working closely with legislators and scientists to identify Audubon's bird and habitat conservation priorities, and to develop the innovative programs and state-of-the-art tools needed to engage everyone in bird and habitat conservation. The National Audubon Society has many programs designed to help birds in a wide range of habitats.

Audubon is the United States Partner for the worldwide BirdLife International partnership. As part of this relationship, Audubon is responsible for the Important Bird Area program (IBAs) for the United States, a primary focus of our bird conservation activities. Once sites are identified, monitoring of key species and management of lands to improve their value to the birds and other wildlife falls to our citizen scientists as citizen stewards of the land. IBAs, as jewels in the crown, sit in a matrix of other lands: suburban lots and agricultural lands.

Analysis of information sent to us by citizen scientists reveals trends in bird species that may indicate particular species require scrutiny and possible conservation action. We place these species on the Audubon WatchList, an important tool for prioritizing conservation work that will help those species most in need.

Several habitat specific programs are helping bird populations that are especially stressed by habitat loss and other factors. Birds and Agriculture encourages wildlife-friendly farming practices. Seabird Restoration Program has developed techniques for restoring Atlantic Puffins and several species of terns, and these approaches are now used in 14 countries by 57 agencies and organizations, benefiting at least 41 seabird species. Coastal Bird Conservation Program identifies, monitors, and seeks to protect the most important habitats for beach-nesting species such as plovers and terns.

Our Audubon At Home program provides tools, resources, and inspiration to people who want to lessen their impact on the world's resources. The home environment is a good place to begin thinking and asking questions that will lead to healthier habitats near our homes. Questions to consider: is it possible to reduce or eliminate pesticide use; how can water be conserved and the quality of runoff protected; are there invasive plants that can be removed and replaced with suitable native plants? Creating a safe and welcoming place also includes actions such as providing food for birds through natural plantings and supplemental feeding, keeping cats indoors, and offering a source of fresh water.

The development of "sprawl," low-density human occupation that replaces farmland and natural habitat, is a leading factor contributing to population declines of many species. These new communities are dominated by turf grass, which has little or no value to birds, yet lawn covers more than 25 million acres of the United States. Each year, around three and a half million acres of farmland and other rural lands are converted to "suburbia." Collectively, these habitat losses highlight the importance of wildlife-friendly backyards and gardens, as sanctuaries and as refueling refuges for migrating birds.

Feeding birds at backyard feeders is a popular activity. In the United States, a recent survey by the US Fish and Wildlife Service indicated that over 55 million people feed birds and wildlife, and nearly 15 million maintain natural areas for wildlife. Birdfeeding brings great pleasure to people, but it also helps birds to survive, particularly during severe weather.

How we manage our gardens can have considerable benefits for birds and other wildlife. Start by replicating the natural plant communities of your region by adding a water feature and nesting places such as nest boxes and shrubs. And encourage your neighbors to do the same, as birds usually require breeding territories that are larger than a surburban backyard.

For further information about Audubon, including how to become a member, please write to:

Audubon
225 Varick Street, 7th floor
New York, NY 10014
Tel: (212) 979-3000
www.audubon.org

Index

Page numbers in **bold** refer to entries in the bird and plant profile sections; numbers in *italics* refer to illustrations.